What else you can do with a library degree

**CAREER OPTIONS
FOR THE 90s
AND BEYOND**

EDITED BY

BETTY-CAROL SELLEN

Neal-Schuman Publishers, Inc.

New York London

Neal-Schuman Publishers
100 Varick Street
New York, NY 10013

Library of Congress Cataloging-in-Publication Data
What else you can do with a library degree : career options for the
90s and beyond / edited by Betty-Carol Sellen.
     p. cm.
     Includes index.
     ISBN 1-55570-264-3
     1. Library science—Vocational guidance—United States. 2. Career
changes—United States. I. Sellen, Betty-Carol.
Z682.35.V62W47   1997
020'.23—DC21   97-18679
                                                                              CIP

Contents

PART III: INDEPENDENT LIBRARIANS: ON THEIR OWN

PART IV: INDEPENDENT LIBRARIANS WITH COMPANIES OF THEIR OWN

PART V: ASSOCIATION WORK AND WORK IN THE ACADEMIC WORLD

Acknowledgments

First I wish to thank the people who did the essential work of helping to find the contributors of articles for this book. These include Margaret Myers, formerly of the American Library Association headquarters staff and now with the Peace Corps in Botswana; the deans and directors of library schools who went through their files to find people to recommend; the "alternative career organization" leaders who announced my request for contributors in their respective publications; and last but not least, my publisher Patricia Glass Schuman. Also thanks to Marti Burt who helped me with computer problems (my problems with the computer that is) and fed our cats more times than her share.

Preface

In 1980 the first edition of this book, *What Else You Can Do with a Library Degree*, was published in response to a puzzling situation. Everywhere people spoke about the "age of information," while librarians, the most skilled of the information professionals, were having a hard time finding jobs—finding the first job just after library school or the opportunity to move up or onward in their careers because of an apparently shrinking job market. In studying the situation, it soon became apparent that some librarians had indeed expanded their career opportunities by using their skills as librarians in nontraditional settings. Some of these people were working for other institutions, some had created their own businesses, some were freelance librarians, a few were working for companies that sell to libraries. The contributors to this first edition were very creative in finding nontraditional job and career opportunities and in using more "generic" definitions rather than library-related ones to explain their skills to employers or clients.

In 1995 the time had come to take another look at the profession of librarianship to see what were the current possibilities regarding career alternatives for librarians. The result is this book, *What Else You Can Do with a Library Degree—Career Options for the '90s and Beyond*. This time there were fewer problems in locating contributors for the book. By 1995, library schools did not need an explanation for what was meant by "alternative careers," there had been publications about the topic, and there were at least three organizations for librarians working outside of libraries.

A few observations resulting from personal experience rather than scientific study are put forth here: there seem to be more librarians working in nonlibrary settings than there were 15 years ago; it appears that a significantly larger number of library vendors find it profitable to hire librarians to sell to other librarians; and more librarians are providing services to libraries from outside the library, on a contract basis. There are other observations to be made about things that have remained the same or are "more so," especially in the explanations for seeking alternative careers: more opportunity for independence and/or creativity, disdain for bureaucracy, desire to earn more, lack of job opportunities in libraries. Some things remain the same as contributors note over and over the need to be flexible, the need to be creative in one's approach to the job market and to the work, and the requirement to be active in creating networks.

The contributors to *What Else You Can Do with a Library Degree* provide an excellent resource for any librarian wishing to consider alternative career possibilities or for librarians who wish to learn of the broader horizons for the field of librarianship. Each contributor, in every case a graduate of a library school, has provided detailed information about his or her own career path, the requirements for the work he or she is now doing, advice for those who would like to do similar work, and recommendations for how to get started. The combined result is a veritable handbook for pursuing an alternative career.

The contributions have been organized into seven parts, each bringing together work that is in some way related. In Part I, Rao Aluri and Andrew and Rhoda Garoogian have started their own publishing companies; Paula Presley works for an academic publisher; and Kate Waters works for a commercial publisher, both editing and writing for children. All of these librarians tell about their work in libraries and about what they do now. Ruth Gordon, has, after retirement as a school librarian, a whole new career as a writer, editor, and reviewer in the field of publishing for young children. Lynne Erickson and Kathryn Leide, contributors to the first edition of this book, continue to produce multimedia resources for programs for the elderly. Murray Martin had experience in writing for the profession during his long career and continues as an editor, author, and consultant after retirement from working in libraries. Raymond Bial is a working librarian at present who is also a published author of nonfiction books for children and adults. He describes how his skills as a librarian have contributed to the quality and success of his work as a writer. Contributors Genevieve Krueger in southern California and Josette Lyders in Vermont describe their work as booksellers. Each of these librarians works from her home. Krueger specializes in searching for children's books; Lyders and her husband, also a librarian, specialize in antiquarian books.

Part II comprises contributions from librarians who work for companies that provide goods and services to libraries. All believe that, being librarians themselves, they can enhance their respective companies' communication and sales to librarians. Most describe the various positions they have had in libraries and in the "vendor community" and describe what they like about what they do and the qualities needed in sales work. Contributions are from Judy Matz of the UMI sales force, Stephen Kochoff and his librarian colleagues at Readmore, Lauren Lee at Brodart, Mary Jo Godwin at Oryx Press, Barbara Herzog at H. W. Wilson, Ann Talley at EBSCO Information Services, Monica Ertel at Apple Computer, Phil Bradley of SilverPlatter, Fae Hamilton at RLG and Linda Robinson of OCLC. Not all hold positions in sales and marketing; some offer support services to librarians who use their products, others are trainers. Sheila Hess, who wrote the final chapter in this part of the book is, after many experiences in traditional and nontraditional work (including an information company of her own), the manager of the library division of a company that provides staff on a temporary or contract basis.

Part III, "Independent Librarians: On Their Own," groups people together not by the similarities of their actual work, but because they are independent information professionals, working on their own and not in a corporate setting—not theirs or that of anyone else. Contributors include Caroline Feller Bauer, a consultant in children's reading and children's books; Nolan Lushington, a library building consultant; and John Cohn, a consultant who still has a full-time job in a library and describes how to do both while avoiding any conflict of interest. Rhea Joyce Rubin is a consultant to libraries. Sue Rosenzweig is an independent consultant and grants writer in a variety of settings. Camille Motta, formerly the librarian at the Urban Institute in Washington, D.C., is developing a new career as a consultant working on "expert systems verification and validation" and also supporting herself as an information broker while earning a Ph.D. in a field called "Information and Decision Systems." Ann Robertson is an information management consultant to businesses and Susanne Bjørner does a wide variety of library-related work, most often in small, usually one-person, libraries. Reva Basch, Katherine Bertolucci, Denise Fourie, Darlene Waterstreet, Alice Sizer Warner, and Mary K. Feldman report on their independent information-related work. Deborah Brennan is a grants writer and project director. David Jank has had a great variety of library and library-related work experiences. He is now doing independent market research and analysis. Each article in Part III includes information on work experience, the "pros" and "cons" of working independently, and advice for those who might wish to do the same. The last article in this section has a different slant. After 17 years as a speech/language pathologist, Sally Pore decided to fulfill a long-held dream; she applied to and was accepted into a graduate library school and successfully completed her work. She was encouraged by an advisor to become a reference librarian in an academic library. After applying, without success, for 98 openings, she believes that because of her cerebral palsy she may never realize her vision of "Sally the Librarian," at least not in a traditional library setting. Pore has worked harder than most to find what else she could do with her library degree and in this article describes the results.

In Part IV are contributions from librarians who work independently but who differ from those in the previous section in that they have employees. Carol Berger founded C. Berger and Company after working many years in a library. Hers is a library personnel and information management consulting firm. Deborah Sawyer realized soon after entering library school that a traditional career was not for her. She now has two companies, one in Canada and one in the United States, that provide "in-depth custom research to support corporate decision-making." Anne Lipow started her own business, after 30 satisfying years as a librarian, which has two parts: Library Solutions Institute, which offers training programs worldwide, and Library Solutions Press, which publishes the training programs in book form. Gloria Dinerman describes the work of her company, the Library Co-Op, how she started it, and then went to library school. Joni Cassidy founded a company that provides cataloging and other technical services to law and corporate libraries, and Lorraine Knight writes about her company that provides technical and automation services to school libraries. Daniel Boivin describes steps along his career path that led to a company of his own. In the last article in this section, Louis Rosenfeld relates the importance of library skills for his company, a World Wide Web design firm.

In Part V, Catherine Bourdon and Ilse Moon discuss the work of association management in their articles; Barbara Welsh writes about her work as a library school placement officer; and Judy Field describes how, after many years of work in a variety of jobs and positions, she became a teacher of library science courses. In the last two articles in this section of the book, Charlotte Carl-Mitchell and Ann Webb, and then Dick Luxner describe the work of prospect research/fund-raising in the academic world.

"Librarians Employed in the Corporate World" is the subject of the articles in Part VI. These authors work in non-library-related corporate settings. In the first article in this section, Elizabeth Bellas, Katherine DeBruler, and Mary Forster write about cataloging an archive of images. Kenneth Cory describes the field of electronic image management. Anne McDonald describes her work as a risk management researcher in "a worldwide service organization" and Claudia Chidester tells about using her library skills as the director of research for a venture capital company.

In Part VII, the final section of this book, are articles by librarians who have used their skills in some unique settings and situations. Karen Alderson describes her work as a licensed private investigator, seeking missing persons. Art dealer Jim Linderman tells how his skills as a librarian give him an advantage over other dealers in his particular field of art—contemporary American folk and outsider art. Carol Jacobs relates the work of an archivist for a symphony orchestra. Dee Baily, a former music librarian, describes the beginnings and development of her own company, Creative Computer Workshop, which offers in-shop computer rental of workstations for the computer graphics market and classes in computer graphics. Betty Welker describes the requirements of her work as a natural language translator and how being a librarian helps. In the final article Roslyn Beitler describes her work as program manager for children's and family activities in the continuing education programs at the Smithsonian Institution.

A careful reading of these articles will provide a wealth of information and possibilities for any librarian considering a career change or for those interested in learning about the amazing variety of places and situations where librarians have applied their education, experience, and special skills.

PART I

Publishers, Writers, Booksellers, Reviewers

1.

Story of a Publishing Venture

by Rao Aluri

I started Parkway Publishers as a sole-proprietorship in November 1992 in Boone, North Carolina, when our family relocated to Boone from Tucson for my wife's new job as the University Librarian at Appalachian State University. When we decided to move from Tucson, the town we loved and where our son was born, we knew that we were moving without a job or a prospect of a job for me. It did not bother us because the move gave us an opportunity to realize a long-held dream—to start a publishing company.

Reasons for my interest in a publishing venture included a strong belief in intellectual freedom and an opportunity to work with young authors.

The first reason is what propelled me to immigrate to the United States from India. I strongly believe in intellectual independence—the freedom to think on my own and arrive at my own conclusions, and the freedom to express my opinions without fear or favor. Moving from librarianship to library school faculty to publishing is a natural progression toward the search for this intellectual freedom. One of my objectives is to afford opportunities to young scholars to express unorthodox opinions.

The second reason grew directly from my experience as a librarian. I wrote my first professional article when I was a reference librarian at the University of Nebraska at Omaha in 1975 and I have continued to write ever since. I was helped in my writing endeavors by a number of colleagues who took time to read and critique my articles and books and to encourage me. I am grateful to all those colleagues including such people as Maureen Pastine, my department head at the University of Nebraska at Omaha, who never hesitated to scribble all over my manuscripts, question everything I wrote, and made a zillion suggestions for improving my articles; my wife, Mary Reichel, who patiently read my drafts and, on numerous occasions, suggested that I get back to the drawing table; thoughtful editors such as Richard Dougherty, who always had an encouraging word and suggestions for improvement; and the editors of Libraries Unlimited, whose work improved my manuscripts. These experiences made me realize the importance of editorial assistance—an assistance that is candid, challenging, supportive, and encouraging. One way to pay back the help I received for two decades is to turn around and help the young and upcoming authors.

What Do I Do?

I published one book in 1993, three books in 1994, and one book in 1995. Additional manuscripts were in the editing stages during the summer of 1995. The books I publish are an eclectic mix and they include a biosystematic monograph on cucumbers, a book on discourse analysis, a book on Justice Brennan, a history of the Spokane Hutterite community, and a book on ideas for integrating geography concepts across the K-5 curriculum. Most of these works are oriented to the academic community since my target market is college and university libraries and college faculty.

When one starts a publishing business, the first question one faces is how to attract manuscripts. I received my first manuscript through a chance conversation with a family friend; when our friend learned that I was planning to start a publishing venture, she recommended the manuscript of one of her associates. I attracted additional manuscripts by placing an advertisement in the *Chronicle of Higher Education*—this advertisement alone brought a number of inquiries and manuscripts, more than I could handle. Another way of getting manuscripts was through word of mouth—through friends and associates recommending authors to contact me. I have received a number of inquiries, for example, from the faculty of Appalachian State University through this method.

When I receive a manuscript, I read it first to see if I am interested in the topic and to determine if there is a market for the book. Usually, authors attempt, in their prefaces, to provide a context for their manuscripts in terms of the existing literature. This information gives me some clues regarding the marketability of a manuscript. Next, I may peruse standard bibliographic tools and indexing and abstracting services to see what else is available on the topic. Occasionally, I ask authors to provide a market analysis for their manuscripts. Once I am comfortable with the topic, the scholarship displayed by the author, and the probable market, I seek the opinion of an outside evaluator.

When I communicate the evaluator's comments and my decision, some authors come back with further information that may prove useful. One author, for instance, while agreeing with the evaluator about the seemingly limited market for his book, pointed out an untapped and potentially larger market. There have been other times when I did not agree with the evaluator. The author's input, consultation with an outside evaluator, and my own analysis of the market for the manuscript result in a final decision about accepting the manuscript for publication.

Once a manuscript is accepted for publication, I send one copy to the Library of Congress for Cataloging-in-Publication data and another to a professional editor. The editor corrects for grammar and usage, standardizes formats, and raises numerous editorial questions—for example, "explain it," or "there is a leap of logic here." One of my authors, after comparing his manuscript with the edited one, sent me a one-sentence note that said, "Thank God for the editors!" The editing process is hard work both for the editor and the author—but spending more time at this stage is worth it for the author and the publisher.

The next stage, once the author and the editor are comfortable with the final product, is getting the manuscript ready for the printer—this includes formatting the manuscript, indexing the contents, designing the cover, selecting appropriate paper stock, and choosing a color for the cover. The printer is sent diskettes, art work, and other necessary instructions.

When the book is in the printing stage, I develop a marketing plan for it. My primary target at this stage is the faculty who teach in the subject area. I identify the sources of relevant mailing lists which I can rent for sending out brochures. With the help of the authors and editors, I create publicity brochures, compile a list of journals that should receive review copies, and compile a list of individuals and organizations that are likely to be interested in the book. Just around the time when the book is ready to come out of the printers, we send out the mailings.

Gauging the potential success of a book is somewhat of a gamble—especially for a new publisher such as myself. But with experience, I am gaining insights into what is likely to sell.

My Background

Coming to publishing from librarianship is quite natural. Most of the skills that are acquired in librarianship are transferable to the publishing field. My library background prepared me for the publishing business in terms of my own writing, experience in newsletter production, management of a corporate library, and marketing.

After working at the University of Nebraska, I entered the doctoral program at the State University of New York at Buffalo, and went on to join the faculty of the Division of Librarianship at Emory University in Atlanta, Georgia. During this period, I compiled, along with my colleague Philip Yannarella, a list of scientific and technical journals available from the U.S. government, and coauthored a book with Judith Robinson on the scientific and technical information resources available from the U.S. government. While at Buffalo, I took a detour for one year and worked on my dissertation topic at OCLC. The topic of the dissertation was subject access to large online databases. Later, I coauthored a book on this subject, *Subject Analysis in Online Catalogs*, which was published by Libraries Unlimited.

I had a taste of publishing from the production side when I was the manager of library services and employee communications at Burr-Brown Corporation in Tucson, Arizona. From the library, we published corporate newsletters that were distributed to all domestic and international employees of the corporation. We used (and the library is still using) a desktop publishing set-up (using a Macintosh computer, and PageMaker) to put together these newsletters.

Managing a corporate technical library also introduced me to the concepts of business and marketing plans. One of the library's responsibilities was to assist marketing engineers in identifying competitors and their products, market sizes, and expected market growths in terms of dollars and units of products. As a part of our employee communication responsibilities, we updated every week such data as shipment and order growths which gave the employees an indication of the company's health. Burr-Brown Corporation further helped me by sending me to the Arizona Executive Program, a University of Arizona School of Business program designed to train the executives of Arizona corporations.

My work as a reference librarian, reference book selector, and a book reviewer taught me the importance of book reviewing media. Consequently, it has been a relatively simple matter for me to identify potentially useful review journals and to send them review copies. There are, of course, difficulties. As a librarian, I never realized the difficulty faced by small publishers in getting their books reviewed. Major review media such as *Choice* and *Library Journal* are not easy to get into and they do not even acknowledge the receipt of review copies. My experience as a reference librarian and library manager put me in touch with various vendors and book distributors. Again, doing business with these organizations as a publisher is somewhat different from doing business as a librarian—I believe that they pay better attention to libraries than to small publishers. Growing experience, however, provides insight into doing business with them. In any case, my experience in librarianship is invaluable in starting and running my publishing business.

Advice to Newcomers

Like librarianship, the publishing world is undergoing rapid changes. Technology is altering the landscape. Some people even predict the demise of book publishing and the dominance of electronic publishing. New graduates of librarianship, however, should see such rapid changes as opportunities for advancement—not as obstacles. Librarians possess significant computer and information processing skills that will position them very well in terms of keeping abreast of and exploiting the emerging publishing technologies. For the foreseeable future, there is still the need for editorial skills, assisting authors in improving their presentations, and packaging information for both attractiveness and efficient retrieval.

New library school graduates are well equipped to enter the publishing business—they often know how to use desktop publishing software; they know how to manipulate graphics; they are knowledgeable about printing and scanning technologies; they are knowledgeable about electronic networks, online databases, and the Internet; and they are attuned to user needs and capabilities. These capabilities will go a long way in building a fruitful career in the rapidly changing publishing field. To them I say, Welcome Aboard!

2.

Publishing Reference Books

by Andrew and Rhoda Garoogian

Nowadays retirement does not mean what it used to mean. Not too long ago you were honored with a dinner, were given a gold watch, moved to a warmer climate, and just sat on the porch with your feet up on the rail.

When Andy came home one evening from Brooklyn College and announced, "perhaps I should retire now because the College is offering an incentive and I think the time has come for a change," we sat down and reviewed our options. Neither one of us wanted to sit on that porch for the rest of our lives. Nor did we want to be carried out feet first from our respective workplaces. We also felt if we did retire now, we were still young enough to channel our energies into productive activities. In other words we would be in control of our lives rather than passively waiting for things to happen to us in our later years.

Andy had been a librarian for 30 years, having begun his career at the Brooklyn Public Library in New York and moving on to Brooklyn College where he had used his reference skills and ultimately became a full professor. Rhoda had entered the field a little later and joined the administration and faculty of Pratt Institute's Graduate School of Library and Information Science where she advanced to the deanship.

After most rewarding careers the time had come to consider what else we could do now that retirement beckoned. It was a frightening yet exciting time. We considered opening that bookstore we had once dreamed about. Perhaps we could open a bagel store? Perhaps get involved in freelance consulting? One thing we did know was that we wanted to be independent and have the ultimate responsibility for any decisions made. Too, we had both enjoyed the library field and had done well. Why not build on past experience and at the same time stretch ourselves by trying something a little new. Why not become publishers of reference books?

The publishing field has traditionally been viewed as very closely tied to librarianship. The fields share a love for knowledge/information and its organization and dissemination. There is one major difference—the profit motive. In our field we responded to our clients' information needs without concern for cost. If we were to open a publishing company we would be required to focus on the ability to supply information essentially to those who could pay for it. Could we deal with this?

After much thought we concluded that in starting a small publishing company we could nourish that spark of entrepreneurship that we had entertained through the years. And we would stand a better chance of surviving if we went into a business for which we had related experience.

Our next step was to decide on the types of materials we would like to publish. In researching places to which we might retire, we discovered a need for statistical resources that provide in-depth information on all aspects of the cities that seemed most promising to live in. We, by the way, elected to move to a warmer climate in Boca Raton, Florida, in 1991.

The area is rich in library resources, one of our primary considerations. Out of the information-gathering process grew our America's Top-Rated Cities series, the mainstay of our small firm now called Universal Reference Publications. We should mention that our son, who is quite knowledgeable about desktop publishing, joined us in this endeavor.

We wish we could state that we started with a grand plan in which we listed our skills and how they could be used. We just began researching, printing, and then marketing. Not every decision was necessarily fruitful, but our prior experience served us well in many ways.

Our research/reference skills (locating, collecting, interpreting, and evaluating data) were put into use immediately. Organizing and compiling the books has been the easiest element of our activities. The actual production aspects required computer knowledge and were thus assumed by our son.

The area of marketing and sales proved a bit more difficult. We soon discovered we had the basic skills of taking a product from the manufacturing state through distribution to the marketplace. The best marketing plans address matching buyers' needs with sellers' products. This is what librarians do best—determining users' needs and then responding to these with information in the most useful form. We determined that our primary clientele would be libraries, which made it somewhat easier to consider the options we had open to us. The difficulty came when we realized that, although we were quite familiar with the field, we had to convince former colleagues of the quality, validity, and need for our products. As librarians we were always at the receiving end of the information chain; we had accepted the final product unless a user pointed out factual errors or printing errors. Now we had a new role to play at the beginning of the chain. Our concern for an excellent product shaped our efforts to produce reference handbooks that were as accurate as possible.

We also remembered how much marketing material had formerly reached our desks every day. It was incumbent upon us to capture attention. One characteristic of librarians was in our favor, we thought. For the most part they are avid—and sometimes compulsive—readers. They would, therefore, read any ad or brochure or publicity piece we sent to them. Not true! Direct mail pieces had to be repeated as many as four or five times.

Now, too, we had to "dirty" our hands with "selling" our product. We believed we could empathize with our potential customers. We had been there. We also had to feel comfortable selling ourselves. This was not as easy for us—it probably is not easy for many others in the field who have traditionally had difficulty "tooting their own horns." This reticence had to be overcome. Frankly, we are still working on it.

Our research and writing skills stood us in good stead in producing press releases, brochures, and ads and in creating displays. As librarians we could also represent the company at exhibits and conferences. The key here is having an awareness of what is going on in the field and knowing what competitors are doing and what are the trends.

We haven't mentioned the administration activities involved in operating a business—such as keeping the books, and paying the taxes. For these we did hire an accountant. We also must be concerned with preparing the reference books for shipment to customers, which means careful packing and delivery through our local delivery organizations.

We are still struggling with the problems inherent in starting a new business, especially one in which we are at once the creators, marketers, and sales personnel. It would still be more pleasant merely to do the research and prepare the manuscript. Now we not only have to be concerned on a personal level with our critics (who may not have the same belief in our books as we do), but we also have to worry about what impact the reviews may have on sales. We are now entrepreneurs. The bottom line is being able to support the activities of the company and perhaps see a profit. It is still difficult for us to decide on the equitable pricing of our books without worrying about the meager budgets of libraries. We must be on the job many more hours. We no longer enjoy the social contact we had when employed by a larger organization. We no longer get paid a salary on a regular basis and we must accept the full blame for any errors.

Nonetheless, we enjoy the freedom to plan our own work and to organize our time. When things go right we experience an enormous sense of fulfillment. We are no longer under the control of a boss or supervisor. We make the rules.

And, finally, we are not at a, pardon the expression, "dead-end" at this time of our lives. Perhaps we are now even more productive.

To those of you who may wish to follow the entrepreneurial publisher road before or after retirement, may we offer some suggestions?

1. Stay in or relocate to a city that has a good university library or is near a large public library. This is particularly important if you intend to do the research and writing yourself.
2. Get to know your local printer, binder, and mailing service.
3. Be prepared not to see huge profits at the beginning—and perhaps even longer.
4. Don't be ashamed to ask for advice from former library colleagues. They are marvelous sounding boards and can offer many a good suggestion.
5. Continue to read library periodicals. It is imperative to be aware of new and continuing trends in the field. Even more important, you'll be aware of what your competitors are up to.
6. Be prepared to attend library conferences and meetings and to be able to represent and "sell" your product.

We are grateful to have been part of an exciting and meaningful profession. Oh, what a field is librarianship! It has allowed us to leave its boundaries and yet to use many of the same skills to make a career change in our "retirement" years.

3.

The Library Degree and Academic Publishing

By Paula Lumpkin Presley

The first edition of this book, *What Else You Can Do with a Library Degree*, was a resource for anxious new recipients of the M.L.I.S. who consulted it for alternative ways to earn a living until a "real" library position became open. The versatility of the library/information science degree was obvious to anyone who skimmed even a few chapters. The first edition was also an excellent resource for career planning—it was a significant factor in my decision to seek the M.L.I.S. to advance my career in academic publishing.

In 1981, I had to leave a position as a legal secretary, in Detroit, to move to Kirksville, Missouri. What seemed like a disaster turned out to be a good move. I soon discovered that Northeast Missouri State University, now Truman State University, is in Kirksville, and that I could complete my undergraduate degree. While earning a B.A. degree in history, I did typesetting for Sixteenth Century Journal (SCJ) Publishers. Then, while pursuing the M.A. degree in history, I became copyeditor of their *Sixteenth Century Journal* and its related monograph series, *Sixteenth Century Essays and Studies*. About the time I completed the M.A., my university became interested in establishing a university press. We learned of a consortium of small university presses in which we could participate. Personnel for the new press consisted of two University employees and talented student assistance. The director, a history professor who still receives only 50 percent released time to direct the press and to act as managing and book review editor for SCJ Publishers, was and still is responsible for acquiring manuscripts, implementating the peer review process, managing the budget—and even stuffing envelopes. I am the only full-time employee of the press; at first, I was the designer-copy-production editor/indexer/ general gofer.[1]

In the 1980s we had the use of hardware and software in the campus publications department to produce camera-ready copy for books and journals. We could also get their advice on typographic design. Our administration and board of governors were committed to high-quality academic publishing, and they shared our goal of working slowly to become a highly regarded university press. The press joined an academic publishing consortium that is still responsible for much of our marketing and order fulfillment.

As our press grew, I felt a need for more education related to academic publishing.[2] There were a number of excellent programs that offered training in all aspects of the publishing business; I was especially interested in a certain university program that offered the M.A. in a discipline along with a certificate in academic publishing, upon completion of the M.A. requirements and an internship with a publisher (usually a scholarly journal publisher). I wrote for more information, and was told that my education and experience (and samples of my work) demonstrated that I was beyond the scope of the program.

The press director and I then examined the goals of the press and my own career goals. I fleetingly considered seeking a Ph.D. in history, but my heart was in publishing and not in teaching. Simultaneously, we recognized a connection between academic publishing and academic librarianship. I applied for admission to the University of Iowa School of Library and Information Science. I couldn't have made a better choice. Not only did the library/information science program provide a basis for my career in publishing, but it gave me an outlook and skills that are transferable to many careers.

In the meantime, the administration of my university changed. There was less and less inclination to continue to subsidize research and scholarly publishing. It was in this climate that I received my M.L.I.S.; it was in this climate that I hoped to advance in a career in scholarly publishing. Instead, the course work and practical experience gained in library school helped me hang on during rough seas and keep our press afloat. We had to purchase our own hardware and software on a limited budget, and I was appointed as the person to decide what to purchase.

Librarians are trained to get the most out of limited funds, and I believe I made wise choices for our press that have enhanced our capabilities over the long run. We did weather the storm and learned many valuable lessons during the process. Our current administration and board of governors are enthusiastic about the press; we can get on with our original goal of producing high-quality books and journals, and pursue a new goal of providing information on the World Wide Web and in other electronic media.

Applying a Library/Information Science Program to Academic Publishing

The interdependent spheres of publishing, libraries, and information retrieval have changed significantly since I received the M.L.I.S. I had courses in information retrieval and advanced information technology, using the technology then available. Now, courses are offered that were only imagined by futurists a few years ago. Even so, the underlying philosophies of M.L.I.S. course work are applicable to my work with both print and electronic publishing. For example, I was impressed with the so-called Five Laws of Ranganathan: (1) books are for use, (2) every reader his (or her) book, (3) every book its reader, (4) save the time of the reader, (5) a library is a growing organization.[3] Even though the focus was collection development, these are good principles by which to evaluate our work with print or electronic publishing. In both spheres, I am involved in or oversee the creation of aids for manipulation, navigation, and preservation of several kinds of information.

Information Creation

Our press does not create the texts we publish, but we do create information based on those texts: tables of contents, lists of figures and tables, abstracts, indexes, hypertext links, jacket blurbs, advertising copy. Before I begin to copyedit a manuscript I analyze its content and organization and ask how this work can be made most useful to its intended audience. I try to convey this principle to our designer when we plan the layout of the book, taking into account its readability and accessibility as well as its overall appearance. While I work with the text I keep in mind the gateways into the text that we will create. My library/information science training gives me sensitivity to the way these items need to appear and the knowledge base for creating such gateways. So that I can keep abreast of standards development and application in the information science fields my employer encourages my membership in the American Society of Indexers (ASI), the American Society of Information Science (ASIS), and the American Library Association (ALA); the use of online discussion groups or lists is also encouraged.

Information Manipulation

Knowledge of how information providers use our publications to create secondary reference works influences the way I edit footnotes and internal citations. It was in library school that I learned about uses for authority files; thus, we use standard biographical sources in much the same way for a book as for a series.

Information Navigation

We think of navigation mainly in relation to electronic texts, but users navigate through print works as well. If there are clear navigational aids to smooth the journey to their destination, they'll get there quicker and with little frustration. Navigational aids include prominent headings, subheadings, sidebars, useful running headers or footers, consistent size and placement of page and section numbers, easily identifiable typeface distinctions in indexes, and so forth. For electronic publications, graphic navigational aids (icons and highlighted text) are used to get from place to place. It is essential that the meaning and use of each icon or text element be consistent and that the links we create take the user to the correct location.

Information Preservation

Preservation of printed material received much attention in the mid-twentieth century, when books were crumbling on library shelves. Librarians, among others, were concerned about the larger implications of the loss of a significant body of printed knowledge. Preservationists (mostly librarians) used microform as one method to keep our intellectual and literary heritage for future generations. In library school I learned to appreciate these grave concerns, and they influence my choices in the publishing world.

There is growing concern about the fragility of electronic material. My M.L.I.S. training gives me an understanding of the broader implications of preservation (or nonpreservation) practices. My professional training and affiliations allow me to evaluate suggestions and become intelligently involved in the development of standards. Instead of feeling overwhelmed in a world where "publishing" is no longer confined to the printed word, I can proceed with both caution and confidence.

What Does the Future Hold?

"The printed word" was the primary medium for scholarly and other kinds of communication for about 500 years, ever since the European development of the printing press in the 1450s. Historians, sociologists, anthropologists, ethnographers, and others have analyzed and evaluated the impact of the printing press on society and its institutions. Now, "the printed word" is but one of many modes of scholarly communication. We are finding new ways to refer to information and the communication of ideas—about "the preserved word."

The concept of preserving scholarly communication is in flux. A not-so-small group of scholars perceive a world in which research findings and scholarly discourse are presented in electronic formats, leaving it flexible and open for revision for a period of time. Librarians and archivists ask how one can preserve or refer to something that is never fixed. Standards are being developed for the world of electronic communication, and these will no doubt affect the way university presses prosper or fail. In the academic world, especially, it is important for library and information science departments to work hand in hand with university presses to produce and preserve scholarly discourse. The goals for such ventures can found in the philosophies of library and information science.

Notes

1. Since then we have enlarged our staff with a professional designer who is also an excellent copy and production editor, and there are plans to increase the presence of the press.
2. For example, I wanted desperately to index one of our books about a subject I knew well; however, the press director believed we needed a professional indexer. We were disappointed with an inadequate index by an indexer who had no subject knowledge. The press director then allowed me to index many of our books. I happened to read about the American Society of Indexers in an indexing handbook, and I joined this great organization. Right away, I noticed the preponderance of M.L.I.S. degree holders among professional indexers.
3. See S. R. Ranganathan, *Library Book Selection* (New Delhi: India Library Association, 1952).

4.

Always a Librarian

by Kate Waters

In 1975 the Simmons College Graduate School of Library and Information Science was an exciting and stimulating place to study. The information age was upon us; librarians were leading the way in database retrieval of information; and the traditions of search and service were continuing to be reinforced by a dynamic teaching staff.

I entered Simmons intending to become a medical librarian. As a physician's daughter, I grew up familiar with hospitals and clinics and waiting rooms—waiting for Dad. My part-time jobs in high school and full-time jobs after college were in hospitals. During one potentially harrowing semester, I enrolled in a children's literature course taught by Maggie Kimmel, now at the University of Pittsburgh. I was an instant convert to the joys of sharing books with children.

A true child of the sixties, I held out for a job at the Boston Public Library instead of joining the staff of a more well-endowed suburban library. Two months after graduation, I started my real library education at a small branch library in Dorchester. For the next 11 years, I was a children's librarian, then a young adult librarian, and finally the young adult literature specialist at the Boston Public Library.

Boston has a small community of people involved with children and books. During those years, publishers, public librarians, school librarians, teachers, reviewers, and bookstore people kept in close touch. Many of us met once a month to talk about new books and emerging themes in literature for young people. We organized conferences and workshops for the communities. A benefit of being part of such a close group was that we could also try our hands at each others' businesses. I wrote book reviews for several children's literature periodicals, held forth in the newspaper occasionally, visited classrooms to do booktalks, participated in focus groups at local publishing houses, and learned the business of selling books. This was truly a setting in which one could become steeped in one's field.

In 1986 I decided to make a change. I had become a tad removed from the young people I wanted to serve and the desire to flap my wings in another town was becoming enticing. The essential questions, of course, were where would I go and did I want to remain with librarianship. New York had seemed like an embracing place each time I visited, so my search began there.

At this point I had to learn employment strategies that were new to me. I hired a headhunter to manage my introductions. She made me think for the first time about what it is we librarians actually do. Her posture was that we have unique, transferable skills—many of us have a subject speciality; all of us can retrieve, manage, and disseminate information; and, if we have practiced, we have our finger on the pulse of the reading public. The New York Public Libary was suffering from massive financial cutbacks, and the prospects there looked grim. I was encouraged to investigate book publishing. It was interesting to find that the people who interviewed me had shed the image of the bespectacled, hair-in-a-bun librarian. They saw that our contact with the reading public—the world they need to sell books and magazines to—was an asset.

I accepted a job at Scholastic, Inc., in the children's magazine division. They were looking for someone to refashion their elementary magazines to reflect the move toward whole-language teaching. This meant including much more literature, more story, in the magazines and organizing them around a theme. The literature and the teaching philosophy I knew. The world of magazine publishing was entirely new. At my first group meeting, it seemed like my staff was speaking a foreign language!

Like many large companies, Scholastic encourages people to move among divisions. I am now a senior editor in the book group, acquiring and editing nonfiction books for children. From my years as a librarian, I brought with me time spent in schools, knowledge of the curriculum, and a sense of what draws kids to which books.

Librarians also know what materials are out there and what aren't. I think of the many times a child asked me for "a book about...." and I couldn't help because there wasn't one. In 1988 I decided to try to fill some of those gaps and began writing nonfiction for young people. I believe that some of my book proposals were accepted because I am a librarian—because I am perceived as knowing what books are needed and at what levels.

Although they may seem so natural to us, the skills we learn as part of our graduate programs, and, I believe, the natural talents that lead us to consider librarianship a pleasing profession, are not shared by many people. The impulse to "look it up" and the ease with which we navigate information sources are marketable skills. We are perceived as longing for accuracy—a fine quality for nonfiction publishing. We are perceived as being highly organized. The experience we have dealing with the public, whether in person or online, is an asset. While the abundance of information available electronically to children and adults boggles many minds, we are seen as the people who can organize it and access it. This is a prime time for the transfer of our skills outside the domain of the library.

5.

Media for the Elderly

by Lynne Martin Erickson and Kathryn Leide

We aren't writing this to tell you how to succeed in business without really trying; we wish we knew. We are writing this to tell you how we started our nonprofit corporation (something like a business) without really trying.

At the American Society on Aging conference in 1995, Rosie White Messer said, "I'm a storyteller. I'm a storyteller because I believe in the power of story. When we tell our stories, magic happens. We don't feel so alone. We find we are not so different from one another. Connections are made. I believe that stories can change the world." We believe that, too.

Storyteller Mary Carter Smith says that stories from all over the world demonstrate that "no one is better than another because of ethnic origin, that all of us are beautiful, all of us have frailties, and that people are more alike than they are different." These are important messages for every community, messages that can change the world. We believe that librarians can play an important role in providing opportunities to gather these stories to strengthen our communities. But how? To answer that question, we'll start with a story of our own.

Our History

We were both library school students at the University of Wisconsin–Madison in 1975. The course was LS 712, "The Public Library"; the professor was the late Muriel Fuller. We were assigned to design a library service for one group in the community. We chose to take a library program out of the library to a senior center and a nursing home.

We used our backgrounds in school librarianship and English education to plan a multisensory program that would encourage people to share their memories. It was October, so we focused on fall and Halloween. We wanted to help people remember years past and to encourage them to share their stories. We took fall slides, large-print fall poetry, ghost stories, old rubber masks, and fresh applesauce. And we brought back some great stories—about fall activities and some very ambitious Halloween pranks.

We got lots of requests to take our program to other places. It occurred to us that we couldn't go to all those places at once, but that our program *Resources* could—if they were available at the library. Dr. Margaret Monroe helped us to put together a grant proposal to produce and package multimedia, multisensory program materials for use with groups of older adults. On July 1, 1976, the Wisconsin Division for Library Services granted Library Services and Construction Act (LSCA) funds to the library school for our project.

That first year we produced three program kits (Remembering County Fairs, Train Rides, and 1924), made copies for each of Wisconsin's ten public library systems, and presented a workshop for librarians and activity directors in each of the systems to train them to circulate and use the kits.

We were asked to present a report of our project to an American Library Association preconference in Detroit in 1977—"Library Services in Support of Independent Living for Older Americans." We were totally unprepared for the response of the librarians from other states: "How can we get copies of these kits?" We sprang into action.

We formed our own nonprofit corporation, Bi-Folkal Productions, Inc. Why "Bi-Folkal"? Central to the work and to our name is the *folk* tradition of handing down stories. Bi-Folkal Productions has two focuses: remembering and sharing stories (just as "bifocal" glasses have two focuses.) Bi-Folkal's purpose was to duplicate and distribute the kits which had been produced under the grant. We made arrangements for copyright with the Office of Education. And we sent out our first kits in August 1977.

We produced another three kits with a second year of funding. In our final year of LSCA funding, we developed and presented pairs of workshops for librarians and activity directors in ten cities. The sessions were designed to use the new kits as models to put together Bi-Folkal–type kits focusing on local topics. Our grant funding ended July 1, 1979.

The ideas we talked about then are still the same today—remembering, sharing stories, multisensory memory triggers, and involvement. Those ideas are packed into every one of our reminiscence, or storytelling, kits.

A Bi-Folkal Kit

Our kits focus on different broad topics, but each title begins with the word "Remembering." We'll tell you about the one called "Remembering Work Life." At the center of each kit is a media presentation. "Many Hands" is in slide/tape and video format. It begins with how we are called to work, looks at how work has changed, and considers the reasons why we work. It asks for our own work histories—from the time we first thought about what we wanted to be and that first job, right on past retirement. Twenty-five booklets titled "Lines of Work" include sing-along music, poetry, and other discussion starters, all in large print. A cassette tape offers a piano and small-group back-up for a sing-along session on one side, and stories on the other. Skit scripts of conversations about work in four different settings provide program opportunities that are dramatically different. A timeline lists events and inventions affecting the workaday world since 1880, with space for adding individual work histories.

"Nothings awakens a reminiscence like an odor," according to Victor Hugo. The "Work Life" kit includes stickers with scents of pine (outside work or cleaning with Pine-Sol), baby powder (work that may or may not provide financial compensation), soap (cleaning or cleaning up after work), and lemonade (for that first entrepreneurial activity in the old neighborhood).

Shapes and textures to touch people's memories include antique business cards, a wooden bobbin, a carpenter's pencil, a coin purse, a swatch of denim, and a key—the sign of responsibility at work.

The rest of the kit opportunities are to be found in the program manual. In addition to tips on how to use each kit piece, and lots of other ideas, there is an extensive resource list to lead programmers and participants to other library materials. It's all packed in the blue and yellow kit bag, ready to check out of the library to go to Grandma's birthday party, the senior center, a nutrition site, a scout meeting, or the folks' golden anniversary celebration. Anywhere that the experienced and the curious get together, a Bi-Folkal kit can go, to bring back old memories . . . and to create new ones.

The Ideas Behind Bi-Folkal

Our kits are multisensory; we try to approach each topic using sight, sound, touch, taste, and smell. All five senses trigger memory and transmit information. In any group, but especially with older adults who may have sight or hearing losses, the more senses you involve, the more people you involve. And that involvement is the reason for these programs—the goal here is not for people to come and watch, but to participate.

These reminiscence programs meet many needs: the need of the family to know and embrace its history, the need of older adults to put their lives in perspective, and the need of the community to understand and honor the accomplishments of earlier generations.

Dr. Ronald Manheimer, Director of the Center for Creative Retirement, has reviewed our kit "Remembering the Depression":

This kit fosters a sense of importance for the plight of the individual in the Depression, it encourages the viewer to be a living historian, and it does not compromise on quality or depth by trying for a simplistic presentation. I have shown the program to the young and the old and combinations thereof. It always meets with enthusiasm and a visible deepening of historical understanding.

The slide/tape in that kit nears its conclusion with these lines:

And Franklin D. Roosevelt would be back again in 1940. By then the worst was over. But not before the Depression made a hero out of every sufferer who made it through. Your history needs to be shared. At the least, younger people will feel proud to be your children. At the most, your insights can form a survival handbook for tomorrow.

When someone dies, the great loss is not that person's unlived years, but the loss to the world of that person's unique point of view. An African proverb says, "When an old person dies, a library burns."

The teacher who started the Foxfire project in Rabun Gap, Georgia wrote, in his introduction to the first Foxfire book of oral histories, "Daily our grandparents are moving out of our lives, taking with them the kind of information contained in this book. They are taking it not because they want to, but because they think we don't care." We do care. We all need to care. Bi-Folkal kits can help us learn how people made it through the Depression, understand how automobiles changed our lives, hear the part that music has played—and can continue to play. We need to know about school days—and the Chautauqua idea that learning is only begun in school and continues throughout all of life. We can hear the poetry of rural life at another time in remembering farm days. "Remembering Birthdays" is our statement on aging. It asks people to celebrate their years of work and play, sadness and joy, laughter and tears. We all need to get to writing our survival handbooks for tomorrow.

What We've Accomplished

We began Bi-Folkal with a mission, lots of energy, youthful enthusiasm, and good library research skills. Period. You don't see business experience, marketing plans, management instincts, or sufficient capital on that list.

In the 20 years since then we have produced 20 program kits and lots of individual programming resources. We have published catalogs and distributed our materials throughout the country. We have done lots of workshops to talk about reminiscence and multisensory memory triggers, intergenerational memory-sharing, and how to preserve the memories that are shared. We have done exhibits and made presentations at conventions of librarians and activity directors, and for the aging network.

We have taken workshops and classes on marketing, business planning, and grant-proposal writing. We have purchased computers and set up an inventory and invoicing program, and we have worked with word processing, spreadsheet, and computer graphics software.

We've had good years and not-so-good years, great months and awful ones. We've had some time to think about the advantages and disadvantages of working for ourselves.

The lack of "job security" (guarantee of being paid on payday) can be difficult. We essentially work for ourselves; we are responsible to ourselves and to each other. Consequently we push ourselves harder than we might if we were working in a traditional structure. We accept impossible deadlines for ourselves, and we often meet them.

But we do what we do because we think it's important. We've had support all along the way. Our families and friends encourage us and have been known to pitch in for a major kit-packing or order-filling crisis.

The Future

We fervently hope that kit packing and order filling will be the biggest crises we face in the next few years. We are pretty sure that they won't be. The future for LSCA-funded purchases of Bi-Folkal kits is less than bright. In addition to convincing libraries that special materials and services for older adults are important, we need to convince them that they are important enough to purchase with their regular budgets. We envision a time when expenditures for older adults are similar to those for children's materials, services, and programs. Getting libraries across the country to share our vision will require renewed energy and enthusiasm.

Twenty years ago we took the thread of an idea and tugged on it. We didn't know what would happen. What happened is a collection of materials designed to help the people in each community spin their own yarns, to create together a unique tapestry. When the perspectives of the present are woven on a warp of the stories of the past, a sturdy fabric is formed, a fabric that will be needed for the future. You couldn't really call us dreamweavers, because we never dreamed exactly what Bi-Folkal would become. All we ever wanted to do was change the world.

6.

On Behalf of Children

by Ruth I. Gordon

Once I heard the following story—and I know it to be true. A colleague in library school was working at the California State Prison at San Quentin. An inmate told him that everyone who taught courses there jealously guarded his own field and excluded others. What this prisoner admired about librarians was that the entire world of knowledge was their field, bounded only by subject arrangements. I feel this way about librarianship.

Every day I try to accomplish a task that is difficult for me: I try to write at least a paragraph or two as I work on book proposals, books, and articles. It is always easier to edit someone else's work because it isn't "my child." As for editing my own material—that's why publishers provide editors. Writing letters to authors can be wrenching for editors, especially when the authors need to make major changes and clean up their prose.

When I retired as a school librarian a few years ago, I became a freelance editor and writer of books: anthologies and stories for children. I am also a professional book reviewer. As an editor I will only consider books if I am comfortable with the subject. I've lost editing dollars because I refuse to pretend I know a subject when I do not. I am told this practice is unusual in publishing; some of the material I read, especially in history, history of science, the classical humanities, biography, has obviously been written by people who did not know the subject and edited by people who knew even less. Alas, this also applies to reviewers who don't seem to know enough to realize error when it bumps them in the face. As a result, librarians who buy from these reviews often have a stock of inaccurate books on their shelves. Yevgeny Yevtushenko put it this way in "Lies": "Forgive no error / you recognize, / it will repeat itself, / a hundredfold...."

The best education I received was in my home. All of us were readers and our parents encouraged study beyond homework. The family ate together and the table talk was far-ranging. I remember my father giving my brother an anatomy lesson while he carved a chicken. I was not a willing participant and forswore chicken for a short time; however, even now I know the structure of the bird, its veins, musculature, viscera, nomenclature. It is not a matter of great interest, but it is interesting.

Aside from the home, attending school in New York was an advantage because our high school, a public one, was quite extraordinary; studying for Regents exams provided a strong foundation for college, university, and anything else I wanted to learn. I graduated from Tufts University with a degree in English and classical humanities and prepared to become a teacher. I have never regretted the several years I spent in the classroom both in California and Italy; I enjoyed teaching young people. An advanced degree from Brown helped broaden my appreciation of history and its constant repetition of events. I have two library degrees, both from University of California at Berkeley. The Ph.D. is in the history of books, printing, and publishing, a vibrant, dynamic subject which guarantees that I also regard the book as an aesthetic object. As a librarian working with people—in preschool through postgraduate professional education—knowledge of the book as art makes a difference for me, especially when dealing with illustrated books.

I also learned something unpleasantly important in the library school: women were second-class citizens. So, the "chip on my shoulder" that resulted from the anti-Semitism of some of my elementary school teachers and the extreme quota system in place when I applied to college created a fighting edge in me. Ladylike, genteel actions had not accomplished a great deal. Libraryland gives the appearance of having changed, but in fact too many major library systems have men at the top and women assistants who do much of the work. Only after library school did I learn the words Frances Clark Sayers had applied to librarians in service to children: "We are a belligerent profession." Yes, yes indeed—and we still must be.

Graduate schools in the serving professions—and I think of librarianship not as a science but as an art involved with helping people—impose technique on a personality. The technique does not change the person, but it does alter the way one observes the world and, more important, it provides contacts with others. Thus, when I don't know how to respond to a query, whether my own or one from someone else, I do know whom to contact. Nowadays contact is even easier with e-mail and the other tools of communication.

Had it not been for librarianship and my active membership in such organizations as the Association of Children's Librarians of Northern California (ACL)[1] and the Association for Library Service to Children (ALSC) of the American Library Association, I am not sure that I would have had the opportunity to have books and articles published and to start freelance editing.

Above all, I credit ACL for teaching review techniques. This organization, now over six decades old, was founded by concerned school and public children's librarians cooperating during the depths of the Great Depression. Among its purposes is the continuing training of newer librarians in book evaluation, library activities for young people, and the exchange of ideas about the profession, especially in our region. We produce *BayViews*, a monthly review periodical which is considered by some in publishing to provide the most stringent evaluation, especially of nonfiction titles.

Because of the people I met in publishing for young children, opportunity came to my door. Personal contact, not an agent, provided the opening I did not know I was seeking. A few years before I retired—and I retired well before 60—I was asked to provide flap copy for a fine anthology of poetry. I wrote the editor that I didn't think my name would mean much despite my having chaired a Newbery Award Committee and ALSC's Notable Children's Books Committee. Those must have been the reasons I was asked to write some puffery. Instead, I told the editor that were I to compose an anthology on that subject, I would include other authors. "OK. Write one," was the response. I did; I worked with superb editors and supportive publishers, had warm relations with the marketing department, and the book received strong reviews. Meanwhile, I was asked if I thought I could edit a nonfiction book and I said I'd try. That book, too, received positive reviews and my relations with the authors and editors at the publishing house were cordial and warm.

An editor tries to establish an intimate relationship with the author. Unfortunately, major publishers have fired some of the best editors in the business for reasons that can only be determined by "bottom line" ledger mentality. In some of those gargantuan houses, editing is now being done by committee. Thus, newer editors are prevented from developing their own editing personalities and style, and the relationship between editor and author is sabotaged. It is a trend many of us hope will end—the sooner the better. Because of these changes in publishing, many full-time editors have been let go and they now freelance for the houses for which they worked. This obviously has cut into my contracts, although some of the small presses and alternative publishers still need freelancers. Payment for freelance work is by the hour and it helps pay the mortgage. As a matter of fact, I recently learned that the work paid me enough to qualify for a Social Security pension and receive Medicare when I reach 65. Work may or may not be a pleasure; but earning money for doing something enjoyable is certainly a pleasure.

Editing and reviewing call for the sum total of everything I have learned personally and academically. That is why a wide background is important. I am weak in art history and many of the hard sciences, yet, when I must review a book in subjects about which I possess only a shadowy notion, I set out to learn the subject. The outlines and history of a field and important dates and persons in its development provide ideas about what the author of the book being reviewed is trying to do and how successfully he or she has accomplished it.

Recently, I read a piece of historical fiction in which the protagonist said that when the U.S. Civil War ended he would like to become a lawyer and attend Howard University. That didn't sit right. Because I maintain a good research library in my home office, it was easy enough to check dates. The author of the novel was wrong as was the copyeditor (if there was one), because Howard was established much later. In another recent book, a lightweight and amusing sports novel, someone is referred to as the keeper of a perfect scorecard. Unfortunately, she scored called strikes incorrectly and the dust jacket art was wrong, too. Copyediting? Editing? Did the author check? All the years I spent watching baseball came into play over those details.

In both fiction and nonfiction, nagging careless misstatements, even seemingly minor ones can call the entire book into question. As an editor, it's my job to make the book as error free as possible even when I know the publisher has a competent copyeditor. One of the many advantages of editing and reviewing is that my mind is kept alert and alive. It is the rare day when I don't learn something new or correct old ideas. The world's knowledge is changing and it is important that I change with it. Having frequent conversations with my friends and colleagues; attending meetings; watching "nonfiction" television; and reading books, newspapers (two dailies, several weeklies), and periodicals in several fields all help to expand the knowledge acquired over several birthdays.

Throughout my life I have been thankful for libraries and many of the people who work in them. Not only do I receive great pleasure from the books I borrow to read, but the library staff who help me find sources to ascertain the correctness or incorrectness of information make my work easier. The materials, databases, and indexes that are stored on library computers, and the people who know where to search are invaluable.[2]

Just a few thoughts about freelancing, particularly after retirement. Remember that every minute you waste is your minute, not an institution's. Be sure to have a good tax preparer to handle your business affairs, one who understands royalties, the freelance tax code, and the rules of depreciation for the home office, periodicals, equipment, business travel, and the like. Try to stay as active as you were when you went to the office every day. But remember to take time to contemplate and try not to be a workhorse. The freedom afforded by working for yourself can be daunting, but on the whole it is enjoyable. Make the choices, and if they're the wrong ones, change. If they are the right ones, the personal satisfaction is enormous.

Notes

1. The Association of Children's Librarians of Northern California, P.O. Box 12471, Berkeley, CA 94712.
2. It bothers me when I write letters to library directors and to heads of public service departments to praise the people who have helped me, and later learn that the librarians have not been told. Aside from the fact that my letters should be acknowledged, the fact that praise is not passed on to librarians on the front lines is miserable personnel practice. When this happens I think I am ashamed of my profession, particularly lately when the schools of librarianship are changing their titles to school of management and information science. Perhaps the words "librarian" and "library" are now pejoratives in the minds of deans and university officials.

7.

Writing and Publishing for the Library Market

by Murray S. Martin

Entering the independent workforce is a challenging experience. Most librarians work for their whole lives within an institutional setting, but often undertake activities on the side. For many years I undertook a variety of tasks that could best be defined as independent consignments—writing, consulting, and teaching—even while continuing my regular work.

Perhaps my international background has led me to do what I am currently doing, namely writing for and seeking authors for library publishers. Born and educated in New Zealand, I learned early that you have to reach out across the world if you want to master your craft. For 13 years I worked for the then National Library Service (NLS) of New Zealand. The NLS operated what was probably a unique nationwide network of library support, lending materials to schools, small public libraries, independent groups, and individuals who lived in isolated places. My service ended with a stint as order librarian in the National Bibliographic Centre, with responsibility for ordering library materials for the NLS and all government departments. This entailed working with trade commissioners, dealers, and vendors throughout the world. It impressed on me the difficulties all remote libraries must cope with—three to four months for surface mail, and lack of ready communication with others—and the need to seek information from all sources, even the most distant. The latter need is barely recognized in this country, mostly because there is so much available locally, but also because of a tendency to discount other countries' publications. As part of my job, I reviewed fiction, nonfiction, and children's books for the several buying guides issued by the NLS and the New Zealand Library Association, which gave me early experience in writing and satisfied at least some of the latent desire to write, derived from my degree in English literature.

By 1963, I needed to explore firsthand some of those other places. New Zealanders are inveterate travelers. By good fortune, the university librarian at the University of Saskatchewan had been born in New Zealand. At the time my application arrived, Andrew Osborn was consulting there and gave a hearty recommendation to any New Zealand-trained librarian. In Saskatchewan I worked first as branch librarian and then as serials librarian, thus being introduced to North American ways. Over the years I had corresponded with Carl Jackson, at that time director of libraries at Pennsylvania State University, about vendors and supply problems; a letter asking him about applying to a United States library school elicited the response that I did not need any further training and was I interested in a position at Penn State. Immigration hassles delayed my departure for nine months but, finally, on New Year's Day 1967 I arrived in State College and began work the next day as acquisitions librarian. During a 13-year stint at Penn State, I became successively assistant director for technical services, assistant director for collection development, and associate dean, with responsibility for planning, personnel, systems, and budgets.

Although I had written some articles and many book reviews, my first venture into "real" publishing was at the invitation of Herb Johnson, heading the newly established JAI Press. He said, "You are always talking about budgets, why don't you write about them?" The result was my first full-length book, *Budgetary Control in Academic Libraries* (JAI Press, 1978). It seems that, since then, I have never ceased to write. There is always an article or a book in progress.

Moving to Tufts University as university librarian in 1981, I exchanged a large library for a modest one, and a relatively isolated library setting for a city where there were more librarians than in the whole of New Zealand. Once more I assisted in the establishment of a library automation system, an invaluable experience. At this point in my career, I became even more convinced that cooperative collection development was needed. When I attended the first national resource-sharing conference in Pittsburgh in 1973, interest was, to say the least, lukewarm. Active participation in the Boston Library Consortium and the Universal Serial and Book Exchange convinced me even more of the need for cooperation. Since then cooperation has become an integral part of planning for all libraries.

When the time came for retirement in 1990, it seemed natural to expand what I had been doing part-time. Over the years I had consulted now and again on collection development and technical services and my list of publications had grown substantially. I had just completed major fund-raising and set up plans for continuing the renovation and expansion of the library. For the next couple of years I worked with Aaron and Elaine Cohen on library planning and gained deeper knowledge about the practical implications of policy decisions.

One of the results of retirement was the decision to move to a quieter community with easier travel access. Since my major contacts were in the Northeast and yet I continued to travel widely, northern Connecticut provided an appropriate location. Not only were there excellent air and road connections, there was also access to good library support at the University of Connecticut and Yale University. I was able also to maintain my contact with Simmons College in Boston, where I had been a guest lecturer for some years.

At first, trying to handle an entire office (even for only one person) was a problem. I had to relearn basic chores, such as looking after the mail and the filing. It also meant buying proper equipment and constructing a new support network. Joining the American Library Association's Independent Librarians Exchange Round Table (ILERT) helped greatly in the transition. That transition can be difficult, but friends help. The value of that support cannot be overpraised.

From my home office I write news columns for two library periodicals, and serve on the editorial boards of others. Second, I have become managing editor of the JAI Press series Foundations of Library and Information Science. That means soliciting manuscripts, working with authors or editors, and also writing more chapters, articles, and books. Proposals have led to yet other books, this time for ALA Editions. On occasion, I teach collection management at Simmons College and continue to undertake consulting missions with colleges and universities.

To keep up to date, it is essential to continue attending conferences and seminars, which are also good places for adding to the stable of authors. In addition, I now have the time to attend literary conferences—mostly relating to Commonwealth literature—which has led to a further string of articles. Incidentally, I find that the kinds of analyses implicit in literary criticism are also relevant for the examination of libraries and librarianship. In a kind of combination of the two, I am presently working on a book with a professor in a Nigerian library school and helping him get a new journal off to a good start. While Nigeria may seem unrelated to my own experience, in fact, modern Nigerian librarianship owes its start to another New Zealander, John Harris.

It may not sound like a full-time occupation, but writing is very time-consuming, even with the help of a computer, and requires a lot of reading to keep up with the latest developments. News columns must, after all, be relevant and up-to-date. Networking is also vital. I am fortunate to have collected a wide range of contacts over the years.

I owe a lot to Betty Turock, who gave me the chance to become a library columnist, and to Sheila Intner who has shepherded me through two book proposals for ALA Editions, and given me other opportunities. Many of the librarians I have worked with over the years, notably Milton Wolf, have responded readily to requests for books or articles. These people are cited simply to underline the importance of maintaining an active network. It is an essential part of marketing, something that a regular employee does not have to be concerned with, unless seeking a new position.

Writing itself does not produce a substantial income—besides, royalties are delayed by at least one year. It works best when combined with other sources of income. In my own case there is a basic retirement income, but writing can be combined with seminars, workshops, part-time work, or consulting. The basic rule is to begin with what you know best—in my case, budget planning and (odd couple) literature. Continue to attend meetings, set up poster sessions, give papers. These form a kind of public relations campaign and ensure name recognition. Besides, a jury of your peers—the audience—is very important in determining whether your ideas are worthwhile or not.

Nevertheless, it is good to try something new. Editing or proofreading forces the learning of new skills and emphasizes the interconnections between language and machine, the exact needs for bibliographies and footnotes, and familiarity with the many style manuals, very different from what seems so simple in reading the results. If you have had no financial experience or have never run an office, there are many organizations that provide useful short courses or seminars. Before you get too deeply into problems with the IRS it would be a good idea to attend some of these, particularly if you envisage expanding your scope and taking on other employees. I was fortunate to have a second degree in accounting. If I had not, such training would have been a priority need.

The working environment also changes. Although I am still more comfortable with pencil and paper in preparing first drafts, I have come to recognize that the computer is essential. The Internet provides a totally new way of gaining access to news and information. Although it still relies on the old skills of grammar and spelling, electronic communication (and telefacsimile) greatly simplifies the construction of a resource network and speeds up communication. There are, of course, costs, and it is very helpful to be able to join an existing node, for example, through a local library consortium.

There will aways be a need for independent librarians who can use their skills as consultants to help others, whether fellow librarians or business organizations. The need is to develop a niche that suits you and then to market yourself. The latter has always been difficult for me, but the help of one's peers can make up for much. One of the blessings of independence is that you are not confined by the strictures of a job description nor by institutional decisions. On the other hand you are now responsible for everything you do, and the organization of time is essential. Writing demands that time be set aside on a regular basis, which can clash with the often unpredictable timing of consulting calls. Remember, too, that the deadlines are now being set by your customers. Plan ahead and leave some elasticity in your timetable. I once had to fill in for a colleague in giving a seminar in a somewhat unfamiliar field and had to do a lot of catching up in a short time. It was worthwhile, but put some other ideas on hold for a few weeks.

Without a library degree, it would be impossible to undertake my present tasks, but other skills are also needed. So be prepared to keep on learning.

8.

Research, Writing, and Photography: Three Ingredients for Success as an Author

by Raymond Bial

Earning a library degree was neither the first nor the last significant act of my life. Since childhood I had wished to become an author. I was never certain of exactly the kind of author; I simply loved to write stories and brief essays—to conjure bright images and to scribble them onto sheets of lined paper.

Always the pragmatic type, however, I'd initially planned to become a lawyer, then later a history professor. Yet I'd always struggled to remain a generalist with the broadest possible interests in history, literature, and art. So, after completing my undergraduate work, I knocked around for several years. My love of writing deepened and I also cultivated a profound interest in photography, along with a continuing interest in social and cultural history and a penchant for organizational management.

Following the rubric of "art for art's sake" I made many wonderful photographs and refined my writing skills, but shied away from any kind of commercial work. Eventually, thinking that I could freely pursue photography and writing on my own terms, yet still have a means of earning a respectable living, I entered library school and received my master's degree in the summer of 1979—again without specializing in either public or academic libraries, but taking a number of invaluable courses. In fact, pursuing the degree has proven to be one of the pivotal events of my life. The course work lent structure and direction to my work and helped me to sharpen my research skills greatly.

Shortly thereafter, I became a professional librarian and a library director several years later. However, I often tell colleagues that even if I had never entered the library profession my degree would have been extremely important to me. On a personal level, I met my wife Linda in library school, and three children later, we're settled in a middle-class life in a mid-sized town in the Midwest. On a professional level, soon after acquiring the master's degree, the three main ingredients of my work as a nonfiction author—research, writing, and photography—coalesced in the form of a book about a small farm town, *Ivesdale: A Photoessay*. Funded by a small grant from the Illinois Humanities Council and sponsored by several local libraries and historical museums, the project gave me an opportunity not only to apply my talents as a photographer and writer, but also to take advantage of my course work in reference services and administration. Indeed, these research skills became the proverbial third leg of the three-legged stool on which my work as an author of nonfiction books had to be based.

This project led immediately to others, all of which blended research, writing, and photography, and culminated in well-regarded books. Among the titles were *Upon a Quiet Landscape: The Photographs of Frank Sadorus*, *First Frost* (with Kathryn Kerr), *Common Ground: Photographs of Rural and Small Town Life*, and *In All My Years*, a collection of portraits of elderly black people. Not long afterward I published two books with the University of Illinois Press—*Stopping By: Portraits from Small Towns*, and *The Carnegie Library in Illinois*. All of these books were warmly received, garnering many wonderful reviews. But they didn't generate much in the way of income for me or their publishers. A blend of documentary and fine art photography, my work was informed by a highly personal tone that didn't have wide appeal beyond regional and/or scholarly markets.

I did generate some income, which I devoted to my small photography business, but I wasn't much interested in commercial work until 1987. With a second baby on the way and in need of a bigger house—and with Linda planning to leave her full-time job to stay home with the children—my photography and writing abruptly became implicated with our household finances. The challenge was how to support a growing family on a librarian's salary, so I started taking small photography assignments. We managed to get by, but I asked my agent if any larger commercial publishers might be interested in considering photo-essays for children. She asked for a list of ideas, and the first editor who saw them liked not just one, but two of them. Contracts followed (including respectable advances) and my first two children's books, *Corn Belt Harvest* and *County Fair*, were under way. About a year or so later, they were published and each received many excellent reviews. In undertaking these books, my training and experience as a librarian was even more critically important. Accurate, thorough research is essential in all writing, especially nonfiction. I typically begin research with an online survey of the literature, after which I identify the most important books in the field. I also continue to learn more about photography by reading books located in the library or borrowed from other institutions.

The success of *Corn Belt Harvest* and *County Fair* led to a contract for *Amish Home*, which not only received great reviews but was named an ALA Notable Book for Children. I signed up for two more books in this series: *Frontier Home* and *Shaker Home*. Both of these books required the same kind of in-depth research that had been necessary for *Amish Home*, as did my most recent book, *The Underground Railroad*. As the subject matter broadened, I also had to locate and travel to sites for photography shoots. For instance, how does one find stations along the Underground Railroad, many of which are located in out-of-the-way places such as the tiny village of Ripley, Ohio? Until recently, few books had been published about places related to African American history, but a good reference librarian can find the necessary information and thereby arrange a successful trip.

In recent years, my computer skills acquired as a librarian have been increasingly valuable in both research and communication. E-mail is a wonderful means of keeping in touch with editors, librarians, and authors—including contacts in Russia where I would like someday to photograph for a children's book. I've had the first reviews of two of my books published electronically on various newsgroups. I also read newsgroups for information on subjects ranging from evaluating children's books to purchasing used camera equipment.

I love my job in the library and probably won't give it up any time soon. However, my work as an author has been a key factor in the realization of my professional goals and objectives. With 25 books completed and several others in the works, I'm not only persisting, but flourishing as a generalist. Through each new book I have not only an opportunity for creative expression, but also a chance to learn more about a subject of keen interest to me. I also feel that each of my books deals with a critical issue and makes a significant contribution to American social and cultural life. Without my graduate degree in library and information science I doubt whether I would have achieved more than a small portion of the success that I've enjoyed as an author of photoessays for children and adults. I also wonder to what extent the quality of the books would have been diminished if it had not been for my expertise in research and reference.

9.

Out-of-Print Book Finder

by Genevieve A. Krueger

"Some people have a library in their home—
we have our home in a library." —Jim Krueger

This describes where I live. Jim and I raised our six children surrounded by books—thousands of them. I search for out-of-print books, on any subject, and have been doing this for the past 18 years. At this point, roughly counted, there are approximately 15,000 books in our home. Some are in every room, including the kitchen (cookbooks of course) and the bathrooms (health and medical books, magazines). Many of them are for sale, many are not. Many are special collections for each child and grandchild, plus my own collections of Christmas books, Pinocchios, Hans Christian Andersen, Volland Press, and school books from 1880 to the present.

Having a mother who loved books, and being a librarian by profession I was always on the lookout for books; when traveling with my husband we usually stopped at bookstores, and thrift stores. One year we tried to collect the first 100 numbers printed by Pocket Books, just for the fun of it. We didn't quite find them all but each purchase and then the research on books, illustrators, and publishers gradually added knowledge of the general book world. A friend gave me a copy of *AB Bookman's Weekly* and a big door opened. I studied the publication and compared descriptions of editions, bought some

reference books, attended a book collecting class and a class in restoration of materials, and made a card file of my inventory. That was
the beginning. Then one day at Dutton's Book Store in North Hollywood the owner, Dave Dutton, asked me if I would like to do book
search for them, as they didn't have time for it themselves. Voilà! I
subscribed to *AB Bookman*, and began advertising. I was hooked—
caught up with the wonderful people who wanted books, the wonderful people who supplied them, and the fascinating stories in the books
themselves. A whole new world opened up for me.

Now I would be looking at books, not as a librarian but as a bookseller. And there are definite differences. The way you look at books as
a bookseller includes the condition of the book and its use. Library
books have to be marked with ownership labels; the fewer marks on a
book the better from a collector's point of view. Libraries appeal to readership; booksellers appeal more to the desire to own a book or give it as
a gift. Both guide their patrons and help them choose the most suitable
from the many books available. Discovery and delight in something
beautiful and old is more often the reward of a bookseller. Satisfaction
and thanks, as well as the basic goal—putting the right book in the
hands of the right person—go with both aspects of the profession.

When I chose my business name I used my own name—Gen
Krueger Books, Out-of-Print Bookfinder. An artist friend designed my
business cards and stationery with a Rip Van Winkle logo and I've
been using the same design ever since. "Bookfinder" is a more positive
title than "book searcher" and every bit of positive thinking helps. At
this point I can locate between 50 and 60 percent of the requests I
receive—and I receive approximately 200 or more new requests a
month. My "books wanted" file in the computer (I use DBASE III) contains over 3,500 requests—for six months of this year. I keep requests
active for one year, and then make a backup request file. Many times
the books appear one or two years later, and often the person still
wants the book.

I work from my home. The phone and the mailbox are constantly
busy. I advertise my wants every two weeks in *Bookseller* magazine,
out of Ann Arbor, Michigan. I formerly used *AB Bookman*, a fine publication but too expensive for my advertising habits. Responses from
the readers of *Bookseller* keep me on the phone and the computer,
and writing orders and mailing them for the two weeks between ads.
With each order I send out want lists of the most recent requests so
this keeps things moving too. And, of course, I have my favorite local
bookstores to check several times a week, and those farther away on a
fairly regular schedule.

The Internet has a system working now, but I have not had time to
look into it yet. It is the wave of the future, and we will all be listening
to its pulse. For now, the traditional mail network is a very good one;
it is relatively inexpensive and includes many who may not be on the
Internet. Profit on searches is small and there is not time for too
much growth, so I am happy with the present system.

It took almost seven years for my business to show a profit on Schedule C for the IRS. This past year, partially because of national publicity in the *Los Angeles Times*,[1] my sales increased 33 percent and I had to hire a part-time helper to wrap packages for mailing. Not big business yet—just more volume and more books changing hands and finding new homes.

Another facet of the book business is putting out catalogs or lists of items to sell from your inventory. So far I have only put out three or four catalogs or lists. Many booksellers put out monthly or quarterly sale catalogs, and this is an aspect of the business that can be done at home as time permits. This activity helps clear off the shelves, so you can buy more books and fill them up again. Catalogs are like dessert, a pleasure to mull over and digest, and I always look forward to receiving them.

Several times I have thought about operating a bookstore but the benefits of home employment outweigh those of a store. My schedule can be open, for anything I want to do—I can travel, go out to lunch, scout around for books, and visit grandchildren with greater freedom when self-employed. And being my own boss means a great deal. I found to my surprise that I worked better on my own than with others and could set limits (or not set them) as the occasion demanded. The pressure is there, but it is so different from an outside workplace. The only real problem is that sometimes it doesn't "look" like I'm working (for example, when I am checking out references or digging for information). Liv Ullman mentions in her book *Changing*, that she has to shut herself away from everyone when she is writing, because it doesn't look like she is doing anything and interruptions abound.

Another surprise is how often I refer people to other services, such as specialty bookstores, and, most especially, libraries. Many people are not aware of library services and how to avail themselves of them. I use my reference knowledge almost every day and consult librarians about questions myself, but most often I direct my callers to available help.

About ten years ago I realized that I loved children's books more than anything else and I have specialized in them ever since. When someone calls and asks for "Pickles the Firehouse Cat," I know that Pickles is a character in the Jenny Linksy books by Esther Averill and I look for Jenny books instead. When a call came this week for "Paul the Penguin," I found Paul (who was really a puffin) in the house of *Lucky Mrs. Ticklefeather,* by Dorothy Kuhnhardt. The fun of being able to do this comes from years and years of studying, reading, and almost writing children's books. And when someone asked for a fairy tale book with seven crows—with seven crowns on their heads—on the cover, and I found it on a shelf in Seattle, the wonderful serendipity that comes with this job came to the fore. Because children's books almost universally recall happy memories, finding them again brings back the happy feelings connected with holding and reading the book—even the location under the tree where it was read, and the smell of the apple blossoms. Part of my "reason for being" is to provide today's children with similar memories made of books and stories—so they can share them with their children, and their children's children.

Almost all requests are satisfying to complete, but some are particularly fulfilling. One time an older woman in a convalescent home told me she was named after a book called Lucille and wondered if I could find a copy so she could pass it on to her niece. I found a lovely flower-bedecked copy and she was so happy. Another time a young woman asked me for Romney Gay's *Tale of Corally Crothers*. She had just lost both her parents and felt the book was her only tie to her family and childhood. The woman could recite the whole book from memory, and as she had moved around a lot as a child and could take few possessions with her it meant a great deal to her. When I found the book she cried, she was so touched. That kind of response is what makes this business so special. I feel that I am doing more than selling books—something more valuable and worthwhile. It happens so often it is like being in the right place at the right time.

I have a folder full of thank-yous that I treasure—it's what helps me plow through some of the details of the business that have to be handled. I have received flowers, cards, videos and cassettes, and a silver spoon (from a Mary Poppins collector), but mostly wonderful letters that make me feel a part of someone else's life. "Don't worry, the shrieks you heard last night were from my husband," a woman from Orange County wrote. "You wouldn't think a grown man would be jumping up and down for joy but he was! *Pinto's Journey*, a favorite children's book, is a hit! Thanks so much." And how about these— "Thank you just ever so much for allowing 'Elsie' [Dinsmore] to come back into my life." "Thank you so much for finding a piece of our childhood! Now it's a piece of our son's!" "Thank you so much for *Beautiful Joe* and making my Dad's dream come true." "Finding this book is better than a glass of Dom Perignon in Paris at sunset gazing at the Eiffel Tower!"

Los Angeles has a movie/TV climate that requires books often, and quickly—as props for shows, as reference for scripts, and as copies for showing producers. This is an interesting part of the business and sometimes I am a part—a small part—of a developing movie or television show. My books have appeared in Steven Spielberg's *Amazing Stories*, *The Story Lady* with Jessica Tandy, *Lorenzo's Oil* (where they needed pre-1972 storybooks for the young boy), *Forrest Gump* (my 1940s copy of *Curious George* appears in the opening scene in Tom Hanks's briefcase and in the closing scene under his son's arm as he boards the school bus), *The Indian in the Cupboard*, and *Casper*. I also helped with some older Dr. Seuss books for an excellent TV documentary on the venerable rhyming Doctor.

A recent interview with a *Los Angeles Times* reporter was triggered by the finding of a book for another reporter. Since that article, written by Jeannette Regalado, appeared I have received hundreds of letters and phone calls from all over the country responding to the yearning for books. The article was picked up by a wire service and was printed in over 350 newspapers—a tribute to books, and the love for them in today's movie/TV/computer world, and very affirming to writers, librarians, booksellers, teachers, and readers everywhere!

The College of St. Catherine in St. Paul, Minnesota, prepared me well for my life and work. It is a Catholic women's college that emphasizes using your potential lovingly, professionally, and spiritually to make a contribution to the world you live in. I received my Bachelor of Science degree in library science there in 1951 and I also majored in English. Marriage and family came first with me and I spent the next 15 years at home with my three boys and three girls. When they were all teenagers I went to work part-time at St. Robert's School in Burbank as a teacher's aide. Knowledge of books and working with my own children prepared me for this job and I learned from my teachers and the children. At the same time I worked two days a week proofreading at a local newspaper—ink is in my blood as well as print. Early on I volunteered at our church library and spent many years there. I also volunteered at my children's school as librarian for 8 years, ordering, organizing, conducting book fairs, and staffing the library. This work kept me in touch with new books, making booklists, cataloging, and working with children. I know times are changing and whatever your early choices are they eventually fit together. And of course, I was always reading, reading, reading.

Whether you are a retired librarian, a new librarian with children at home, or a middle-aged librarian who wants to change directions, being a bookseller/searcher is a niche that needs filling in your own unique way. I highly recommend and enthusiastically encourage you to try it!

Note

1. Jeannette Regalado. "Literary Sleuth: Novel Strategies Help Hired Gun Track Down Hard-to-Find Books," *Los Angeles Times*, 11 July 1994,

10.

An Antiquarian Bookseller

by Josette Anne Lyders

I bring an eclectic education to my new work as a bookseller. My undergraduate concentrations of study were French, Spanish, and government, and I have a master of arts degree in liberal studies from Dartmouth. In the area of library science, I have a master of science degree as well as a doctor of arts degree from Simmons College. Such breadth of study has fortified me well for adventure into the labyrinthian world of antiquarian books.

I have worked in public, academic, medical, and school libraries, and I am also a library educator. I have been active in library associations for nearly 30 years. My varied experiences in libraries are pertinent to bookselling in some pleasantly surprising ways.

The most direct connection to bookselling for me came about through attendance at library conferences, where, fortuitously, I met my husband, Richard Lyders, a librarian and an avid book collector.

As time passed, we began to recognize the transferability of our "know-how" in librarianship to another book field. Years of accumulated knowledge about information, books, and library clientele would be invaluable in the antiquarian book world. We saw bookselling as a branching out of work we already loved. Additionally, the prospect of independence in a business that we could sustain for the remainder of our lives was most appealing.

Entering the Antiquarian Booksellers World

It began in subtle ways for us. We started weekend visits to book-stores around Houston. We went first to the smart and sometimes flashy bookstores—in Houston there are some 70 of them and they are very large and attractive. Gradually we found the used book deal-ers, of which Houston also has a surprising number. We found "A Book Buyer's Shop," "All Books Used & Rare," "Booked Up," "Half-Price Books," "Ruppert Books," and more. Our Sunday afternoon vis-its to Detering Book Gallery on Bissonnet Avenue were particularly special—for the welcoming ambience and the proprietor's expertise.

How I Became Involved In Bookselling

I edited *Texas Library Journal* for eight years. I also handled the journal's advertising and developed a fascination for Texas publish-ers—Corona, Eakin Press, Hendrick-Long, Taylor, Texas A&M Univer-sity Press, UT Press, and many others. I became excited over items in their backlists, particularly in Texas history, which I began collecting.

Because of Richard's library work we had invitations yearly from vendors in town to the Houston Book and Author Dinners, and then to the Texas Book and Paper Shows. We enjoyed both more than I have space to describe.

Our most valuable visits over time were to the exhibits presented at the American Library Association annual conferences and midwinter meetings, and at the Texas Library Association annual conferences. We also took the splendid opportunity to become familiar with book-stores in all the conference cities.

Realizing that I was developing a substantial collection of Texana at the same time that Richard was developing a fine collection of first-edition American short stories, we began to dream of something new. One day, after returning from yet another trip to the Scandinavian furniture store for more bookcases to hold our burgeoning collections, we conferred seriously about the possibility of opening a book busi-ness for our "retirement." With a little searching, we found *A Manual on Bookselling* (Harmony Books, 1987). Its two chapters on antiquar-ian books convinced us. Jacob Chernovsky's chapter (Chernovsky has been editor and publisher of *AB Bookman's Weekly* for 21 years) gave an overview of the changes in the antiquarian book trade since the 1930s, and an optimistic vision for the future. The chapter by Michael Powell (owner of Powell's Bookstore in Chicago, which we had often visited) pointed out that used book dealers have a lot of fun. Their bookstores operate longer than others, and "used-book men seem to live forever, in itself not a bad fringe benefit" (page 271).

Early retirement for Richard was a great attraction after being a li-brary director for nearly 20 years in the high-powered Texas Medical

Center. I was not ready for retirement, but my work as an editor, consultant, and part-time educator left room for partnership in a new venture. Neither of us wanted to quit the world of books and learning in which we had thrived for decades. We knew that the entrepreneurial challenge of bookselling would allow us to indulge our interests in literature and run our own business for as long as we liked.

In 1994, we began the giant move from Texas to Vermont. We were both drawn to the rural north, and I had strong feelings for Vermont from my years there in the 1970s. With consideration of our impending book business, we had developed criteria for the new home we would buy: a very large, old, farmhouse with a big barn in a lovely setting with views of valleys and mountains. (Probably everyone who dreams of a home in Vermont for *any* reason has these same criteria).

While having lunch at the Thrush Tavern in Montpelier one sunny day during the hunt for our new home, we tried out names for a book business and settled on Lyders Fine Books. The "Fine" in the name is a term used in the antiquarian book business to denote a book that is in almost new condition. (We had decided years before that we would focus our collecting, and hence our bookselling inventory, exclusively on first editions in beautiful condition.) That very afternoon, we went to the Vermont Department of Taxes to get a registration application for our new business.

With great good fortune, we did find just the right house, in "fine" condition, in the hill town of Peacham. The enormous, unfinished "attic" area on the second floor in the back extension of the house looked like perfect space for a business. We had it finished, complete with cathedral ceiling, indirect lighting, wall-to-wall carpeting, and a bank of windows for a panoramic view of the valley and the distant White Mountains of New Hampshire. It is an attractive place in which to work and to invite book buyers.

What Is an Antiquarian Bookseller?

According to the opening of Philippa Bernard's extensive handbook on the trade, "Dealers in antiquarian books are a varied community, in which the great metropolitan firms, the country bookshops, the book-fair exhibitors, and the catalogue specialists all play their part; and their customers are no less diverse."[1]

Such dealers handle used books, publishers' remainders, rare books, incunabula, out-of-print books, and first editions preserved with great care for those who will eventually be their collectors. Many dealers specialize in a particular category or subject. Some have shops open to the public, while others operate by appointment, through printed catalogs distributed by mail, through antiquarian journals, and by way of search services that today include the electronic marketplace offering computerized book matches.

Antiquarian book dealers may take part in professional associations that provide guiding principles, information, and forums for activity and development of the trade. Membership in these state, national, and international associations is not open as in library associations; it involves application and approval procedures. The general pattern began with the Antiquarian Booksellers Association, founded in England in 1906. It continues with the Antiquarian Booksellers Association of America, founded in 1949.

What I Do in My Business Now

We have divided our work, with each of us contributing particular strengths: Richard does selection, automated collection management, and handling, and I do catalog design and editing, marketing, and business records maintenance. We both enjoy reading to become more familiar with books, authors, and the vagaries of publishers' first editions.

Catalogs We prepare a catalog of some 250 to 400 listings four times a year. We choose the books to be listed from our shelves, download each book's entry from our computer program Bookmaster III, which contains our entire inventory, and format the listings on WordPerfect 6.0 for Windows, designing camera-ready pages to take to the printer. Annotating and then editing the listings for accuracy and content are necessary and interesting tasks in completing the catalog.

Business Management As in any business, we maintain files and keep careful records of every activity: advertising, purchases and sales, expenses for utilities, automation, services, and travel. Developing, maintaining, and using the mailing list is a time-consuming task, even though I keep this on the computer. This is one task that will not grow easier with time. Richard handles the packaging and mailing of books as orders come in.

Book Buying Trips We plan such trips by using dealer association membership lists and state maps to find "clusters" of shops that we can visit economically in day trips or on concentrated tours. We also attend auctions, and go out to inspect private collections on request.

Book Fairs We were accepted to membership in the Vermont Antiquarian Booksellers Association which sponsors two fairs a year. We worked our first fair in Burlington, an enjoyable experience from planning the booth display to actually being there, meeting the public, and conferring with other dealers. Surprisingly, sales are not the most important goal of working a book fair; the contacts for the future, tips on business "how-to," and the opportunity for visibility really are the significant reasons for participation.

Reading That the luxury of sinking into a chair to read can be considered work is probably the greatest pleasure of the antiquarian book business. There is not only the enjoyment of the literature itself, but also the increasing awareness of important relationships among authors, editors, publishers, printers, and dealers. One finds out about

mentors and followers, schools of thought, and prizes for distinction
or merit. There are rarities to discover and categories of collectibles to
learn. The reading we do leads to satisfying participation in a fascinating world.

How the Education and Skills of Librarianship Contribute

Study and practice in librarianship cover a spectrum of topics, from
the obvious bibliographic knowledge to the less-appreciated "people
skills." The same are needed in antiquarian bookselling.

Bibliographic knowledge Access to the literature of the humanities,
the sciences, and the social sciences, as well as to the general reference sources in print and automated versions is of quintessential importance to the bookseller as it is to the librarian. It is not enough to
have the books—one must be able to tap a large variety of resources
to learn about such things as types of literature, background of authors, publishing history, sale prices, and answers to a myriad of
questions that may surface regarding textual content. One pleasant
surprise about the importance of my first 20 years of library experience to bookselling was the value of "reading shelves" and developing
collections in public and school libraries. I can identify scores of authors and titles from that time that are highly collectible today! Finding these old books is like greeting long-lost friends.

Organizational skills Every inventory needs organization, whether it
be as small as the few thousand volumes of the specialty dealer or as
large as the many thousands in the general stock of a used book
store. The cataloging and classifying skills learned by librarians, as
well as the ingrained habit of alphabetizing everything, transfer beau-
tifully into the work of bookselling.

Management skills Just as any library needs good management, so
does any bookshop. While the reputation for dusty, inefficient, homey
hideaways remains attached to many antiquarian book stores, business success requires the management staples of planning, organizing, directing, coordinating, reporting, and budgeting. Every library
science student learns these practices; their careful application works
wonders in any business setting.

People skills Respect for the inquiring mind and desire to provide
service are attributes of a good librarian and of a successful bookseller. Both require skills in listening and talking with people, observ-
ing nuances in their questions, and striving to supply the desired information or item. The service ethic demonstrated in librarianship is
not only desirable in bookselling, but also vital to the credibility of the
business. A satisfied customer is one who has received the best efforts of the bookseller as well as the particular volume he or she
prizes.

Room for Growth in Antiquarian Bookselling

I believe that this country's experience with automation has now dispelled the notion of a paperless society and actually increased the appreciation for the book. There is no dearth of publishing, no lack of readers, and no slacking off of customers for books. Collectors of books are dramatically on the rise, as evidenced by upwards of 100 book fairs held annually in the United States. Chernovsky's article in *A Manual on Bookselling* compares the growth with less than a dozen book fairs held each year during the 1970s.

Advice to Others Interested in the Field

It is not easy to make a lot of money in the antiquarian book trade, although for a few it is possible, and for everyone the pursuit brings its own rewards. A prerequisite to entering the field is a fascination with finding, preserving, and making available worthy literature. Some preliminary activities to help the prospective book dealer test the waters are suggested below.

- Read several books about the trade, and study periodicals in the field.
- Visit as many used book stores as possible all around the country. The American Library Association conferences in widely scattered cities provide ample opportunity between meetings to go to local bookstores as well as to visit publishers (and even antiquarian dealers) at the conference exhibits.
- Spend time following your own subject interests in the literature, and collect what you care for. Such personal pursuits will teach you a lot about supply and demand, rarity and commonness, and the ways to learn about value.
- Talk with bookstore owners about their collections and their interests and concerns. Use your best powers of observation to determine patterns of material available for sale.
- Attend book fairs whenever possible—they are amazingly educational and consistently enjoyable. Compare the offerings among the dealers' displays.

Note

1. Philippa Bernard, *Antiquarian Books* (Hants, England: Scholar Press, 1994), vii.

PART II

Products and Services for Libraries

11.

Selling Solutions to Libraries

by Judy Matz

I came to the field of library science for what I hoped to be a career of diverse opportunities. In the early 1970s library science was an open and flexible field that offered the opportunity to explore many specialties. At that time, it was more common to move from public to academic libraries, from academic to special libraries. The *Occupational Outlook Handbook* reported a shortage of professional librarians and projected a broad career path with lots of flexibility. In short, I chose library science for its many choices but without the need to select a specialty within the field.

Upon completing my M.L.S., I immediately went to work in a busy urban reference department at the Wilmington Institute Library in Delaware. It was my first chance to put my theoretical library education into practice. A broad, nonspecialist approach to staffing there allowed me to gain experience in programming, cooperative projects with other agencies, and extending public library services beyond library walls. In 1976 I moved to Cambridge, Massachusetts, to head the children's services program for the public library and its branch system. The wealth of resources and cultural diversity in Cambridge were exhilarating. This dynamic environment allowed me to focus on the concepts of delivering quality service and marketing these service values to library staff and library patrons.

By the late 1970s, the library field had begun to change and my old edition of the *Occupational Outlook Handbook* was sadly out of date. Recession had begun to shrink funding for libraries, and criteria for library jobs had become more stringent. I felt that prospective employers wanted to hire me for exactly what I had already done. I realized too that I had gained little experience in the technical services area or in research-level collection development. Starting over in another specialty or shifting to a research library would require a loss of compensation. Opportunities for change were no longer there.

Looking for a way out of this career box, I determined that my public services training and experience had given me a great gift. I had the ability to recognize a need, to research that need both formally and informally, and to formulate a series of recommendations to create a solution. As this realization sank in, the word "sales" came to mind immediately. Matching that talent with my desire to learn more about libraries started the process of career change. Armed with a one-day seminar on sales careers for women and a copy of *Literary Market Place,* I began to send out letters of inquiry. Not surprisingly, the most favorable responses came from small firms with the ability to take a risk on a fledgling and untried salesperson.

Within a few months I had landed a job as the only sales representative for a small, academic book jobber. My training consisted of establishing a close and warm relationship with the owners of the company and asking lots of questions. My customers became my best trainers—they told me what was important to them. Almost immediately, I began to build a body of information on the acquisitions process, technical services, early efforts in library automation, and the policies and practice of domestic and international publishers. During this time I learned to plan and manage a rigorous travel schedule and to administer a home office. Consistent planning, good organization, and the ability to focus on my top priority amidst many distractions were the same skills that I had learned and practiced in libraries.

Five years later I pursued an ad in *Library Journal* to represent Bell & Howell's micropublishing division in the Northeast. With sales experience and a track record behind me, the interview process was easier and more fun. I was eager to learn more about a broader range of products and services, and anxious to solve more problems. Moving to a large corporation increased the stakes with firm sales goals, performance standards, and, of course, more pressure to achieve. The accompanying rewards for greater risk included increased earning potential. When Bell & Howell purchased UMI in 1987, I was fortunate to make the transition to the UMI sales force.

UMI holds the world's largest commercial repository of research materials, including journals and newspapers, dissertations, out-of-print books, and research collections. This wealth of information offers something for every library in each library market segment with respect to serials management and collection development. With the late 1980s came the CD-ROM database explosion. Learning the content of each database was the easy part. Tackling customer technology issues was challenging, as libraries have evolved from single-user workstations to networks and then to remote access in just a few short years. Working on a landscape of escalating change generated the opportunity to forge a new sense of partnership with customers and to serve as a sales consultant towards resolution of public services and technology issues.

I have been privileged to work in a sophisticated and dynamic sales organization, where each representative is provided incentives by a series of individual product goals. A strong body of informed and highly motivated colleagues makes every interchange a chance to learn and grow and to explore new ideas. A large sales group representing many product lines develops the need for more organization and more geographic focus. Due to this expansion I became a regional sales manager, supervising the account executives who service libraries in eastern North America.

The heart and soul of field sales is the visit to a library customer. As a regional sales manager I wear three hats on the sales call. First, as a salesperson, I am there to listen and to learn the needs of that customer, to discuss program and delivery issues that may improve overall service, and to stay abreast of changing buying trends. Second, as a sales manager, I am there to act as a consultant to the local account representative, to assist him or her in assessing library needs and in developing a series of recommendations to address those needs. Finally, as a company representative, I am there to collect and interpret customer feedback, suggestions, and new ideas which will be considered for implementation.

A regional sales office may be a large corporate suite or a tiny home office. Since mine is the latter, I have quickly adopted new technology as it comes along. Voice mail, fax, a cellular phone, and a laptop computer are vital to staying in touch with salespeople who are always on the road and a busy corporate headquarters staff in the Midwest. Off-site field sales management requires good communication skills, and usage of every available telecommunications tool.

More frequently than not, life gives us what we wish for. So if you want a sales career, your first step is to give yourself a skills and personality inventory to make sure that you match your dream. The typical salesperson is an optimist at heart, a good listener, and one who does not internalize rejection. The field person works alone, without the benefit of an on-site support system. This can be both exhilarating and lonely. New ideas or problems cannot be shared with a colleague at the water cooler, but may have to wait for days for peer feedback. A salesperson is self-directed and usually plans his or her own itinerary and strategy to meet assigned sales goals. A salesperson needs to be adaptable and able to shift priorities easily. A universal truth in business is the bottom line. Companies need profit to prosper and grow, and the sales force generates revenue to this end. Pressure to achieve revenue goals can be uncomfortable. A successful salesperson has the ability to generate energy from within and to create a positive pressure from the inside out, ranking projects based on priority and breaking goals into bite-sized pieces.

Reengineering is another fact of life in modern business. As library vendors strive to meet the challenges of new technology and a changing business climate, they must be prepared to change focus and direction quickly to meet market needs and competitive environments. Frequent and successive reorganizations can be difficult and unsettling, requiring a healthy dose of flexibility and fortitude.

Personal networking is one of the best ways to learn about opportunities in library sales. Vendor representatives who visit your library bring a wealth of information on new products and services. My colleagues in "vendorland" are flattered when asked about their own career decisions and happy to share information and advice with someone planning a career change. Other librarians should be also consulted for their knowledge and experience with their library suppliers. Your own colleagues will have strong opinions on the quality of service and the level of satisfaction they have received from specific companies and from individual company representatives.

In shopping for a prospective employer, there are four paths you may want to explore on the way to a first job in library sales. A small company can be a great place to start. A smaller company affords an opportunity to learn both product and sales skills in a nurturing environment with maximum access to key executives. The entrepreneurial spirit is exciting and motivating. Decisions are made quickly, without multilayer approvals. A small company may be receptive to taking a risk on a new salesperson.

On the other hand, a larger firm with a developed hierarchy is more likely to offer the advantage of a sales trainee program. The trainee may be sent to the field to work under the tutelage of a senior salesperson. This one-on-one learning experience is an opportunity to learn from a proven performer, acquire consultative selling skills, and benefit from collaboration on business plans and strategy.

Database providers, automation vendors, and bibliographic utilities frequently advertise training positions for graduate M.L.S. candidates. Obviously searching skills and the ability to provide bibliographic instruction are key job requisites. A training position provides an arena to use library skills, while learning to plan on-site visits, manage time and travel, and develop presentation style, without revenue responsibility. Such a position offers good visibility and high profile; the successful trainer will attract the attention of a sales manager looking for internal candidates.

Large library vendors maintain an inside sales group or telephone sales group to launch new products and stay in touch with customers on a regular basis. A telephone salesperson may work independently or in tandem with a field salesperson, but most certainly bears a sales goal. Telemarketing offers the chance to learn products and services and to master the selling process as a member of a team. Success in this area is frequently a springboard to an outside sales opening.

Understanding how a library works and how decisions are made within a library system are key advantages to moving into a library sales position. No decision to acquire a new product or service is simple or unilateral. Library training and experience allow you to approach every member of a buying equation with empathy and a common language. This equation includes library staff who will work on the front lines with patrons, supervisors of general service areas, directors who oversee the entire library operation, and perhaps chief financial officers or library boards. Each of these librarians may have different key issues and varying priorities regarding the acquisition of a new product or service. Library experience will help you provide the right information to the right person within the process. Experience will help you understand how implementation will occur and how your product will work via the existing automation infrastructure.

A career in library sales is challenging and rewarding. It opens up a wide vista of library experiences and exposure to various service solutions—a perspective that you could not see from just one library. You will stay current with new developments in library automation and technology. Good compensation is the reward for a risk well taken, but a deterrent to return to traditional library work. Last but not least, and best of all, you will have the greatest customers in the world—librarians!

12.

A Conversation with the Librarians at Readmore

by Stephen T. Kochoff

Readmore, Inc., with offices in New York City and in New Jersey, is a subscription service with academic, corporate, and medical libraries as its core market segments. Readmore is a division of B. H. Blackwell, the UK-based book and periodicals supplier with offices throughout the world.

Readmore has a good cross section of librarians on its staff, both in a variety of positions—including the President and CEO of Readmore, Dan Tonkery—and with a range of experiences. Together our combination of backgrounds contributes strongly to the functions we perform at Readmore. Some patterns and commonalties emerge from our group profile: we welcome the freedom to move forward without impediments, and to think creatively and sometimes daringly. The vendor community encourages great flexibility, rapid response, and closure, as well as continuously offering stimulating challenges posed by the dynamic nature of the library and publishing environments. Rather than recap our careers, this essay will discuss how the librarians of Readmore moved into the vendor community, what our jobs are, which personal and professional skills are significant in our work, what we gave up when we left traditional librarianship and entered the business world, and how library education prepared us for our careers. Finally, we offer our advice to those considering vendor opportunities.

How Did We Get Here?

For Amira Aaron, working for a vendor depended on serendipity and an enlightened boss. While she began her career in an important academic library, through fate her position there connected her with an administrator and boss " . . . who cut through red tape and was not embroiled in academic procedures. I was involved with the design and implementation of a local integrated library system at a relatively early stage in library automation." When this administrator moved to a subscription vendor, Amira also moved. She later returned to an academic library, and has since returned to a subscription vendor. Amira has found moving between the communities deeply rewarding.

Similar experiences emanate from a conversation with the other librarians at Readmore. Only one had not intended to work in a traditional library setting, and all others have worked in library settings, in a range of positions and a range of libraries, including some of the largest and most prestigious in the United States. Each person has worked in a library, with or without the professional degree, so each has had an opportunity to experience libraries from the inside.

Early on in the professional careers of many of the Readmore librarians, opportunities were presented that were off the beaten, traditional path of beginning librarians, opportunities that broadened our horizons. As a beginning librarian, Amira Aaron was involved in the design and implementation of a local integrated library system. Dan Tonkery, as a neophyte librarian at the National Library of Medicine, played a key role in setting up the Medline network and was active in the development of the online industry. Within two years of graduating with his M.S.L.S., Steve Kochoff was administering a National Endowment for the Humanities grant of nearly $300,000 in what was then only the second public library in the United States to be designated an "NEH Learning Library," an experimental program that has since grown over its almost 20 years to include a wide range of public libraries throughout the country.

Many of the librarians at Readmore had similar, nontraditional experiences when they embarked on the profession of librarianship. One librarian has not worked in a "real" library since college. Another new member to the profession chose the vendor community as her first professional position based on her paraprofessional experience, because she felt that, although a good bit of dialogue was occurring among the various camps of librarians, publishers, and vendors, not much communication was being achieved. "We spoke the same language of serials, but were from two very different cultural backgrounds. Publishers and vendors needed librarian sensitivity courses and librarians needed to walk on the wild side of Wall Street." While most of our pre-vendor experiences were certainly worthwhile opportunities, they gave us a view of the wide scope and variety of the profession and sometimes offered the excitement to experiment with new, untried concepts. Often, a combination of fate and planning led to our vendor careers.

What Are Our Jobs?

As Readmore's Academic Automation Specialist, Amira Aaron is involved in the development and implementation of system interfaces with client systems, some writing and marketing, planning for the Internet and electronic journal services, and development work on the bibliographic aspects of Readmore's in-house system. Rachel Frick and Jenni Wilson are in sales and service capacities, each charged with learning about librarians' specific serials needs, determining and ensuring that Readmore is fulfilling those needs, and meeting with librarians who are not currently Readmore users.

Exploring and developing the future role of the vendor in an electronic knowledge universe captures the essence of Marilyn Geller's position as Internet Product Specialist. In the long term, Marilyn views her primary responsibility as "finding the role of the vendor as the mediator between libraries and publishers in the electronic environment. In the short term, it involves much training of both Readmore's employees and clients. It also involves the creation of new products and services provided over the network, and the translation of old, established products and services to this new environment."

All the other members of the Readmore staff who participated in this article have positions that involve them in "interface" capacities, that is, working closely with publishers and clients, frequently with much client contact. Dan Tonkery is often involved in meeting with librarians to discuss Readmore's services and to learn from them firsthand their needs and their expectations of a serials vendor. Letty Alvarez has much public contact as Readmore's UnCover Product Specialist. Sandy Gurshman and Joanne Jahr interpret for both librarians and publishers the myriad complexities of serials from both publishers' and librarians' perspectives.

What Skills Are Important in the Work We Do?

Embracing technology and its applications influenced all of us who work at Readmore, a company devoted to innovative uses of technology. Dan's background at Illinois began in a program that combined library science, medical librarianship and computing. From this experience Dan clearly saw the tremendous importance and impact of computing. As a vendor Dan has had the resources to experiment

with and implement a variety of novel and exciting technological applications.

A thorough knowledge of the library automation field and related
standards, and of library technical services operations and integrated
library systems are some of Amira's professional skills involved in her
work. Systems analysis skills are also vital, as are an understanding
of the serials/acquisitions business and a solid technical understanding. Good communications skills—listening and writing—flexibility
and openness to new ideas, the ability to move and respond quickly,
decisiveness, and an even temper are all important, required personal
attributes.

In addition to library education, Rachel Frick advises that taking
the time to show common courtesy, truly listening, and lending a
sympathetic ear are always important as are being self-confident,
strong-willed, and very perceptive. Other useful professional skills are
public speaking, management and organizational skills, and knowledge of the vocabulary of librarianship.

Marilyn sees herself as an adventurer. "Any good explorer needs a
combination of boldness and caution. From my perspective, it's also
important to know the basics and to be able to look at 'old' things
from a different perspective. For me, the basics include knowing how
our scholarly communications community works together to create,
gather, and provide information to endusers." Sandy Gurshman notes
that the job requires an ability to deal with people, both customers
and staff, and a library background to work with customers and then
communicate library needs and practices to the Readmore staff. "I
can explain the workings of a library to vendor staff and publishers,
publisher practices to librarians and our staff, and vendor procedures
to both publishers and librarians."

One commented, "It helps that I like to do crossword puzzles and
enjoy reading mysteries and espionage tales because I use both traditional and nontraditional methods of finding these publications—
mostly 'non.'" Another, in a sales capacity, noted, "The skills necessary to carry out these duties include the ability to talk to strangers,
willingness to travel extensively, and developing a thick skin. You
must be able to listen critically and respond accordingly. Follow-up is
a key responsibility in any sales position."

All agreed that the vendor community nurtures and thrives on the
entrepreneurial spirit, by encouraging risk taking in its commitment
to experimentation and through the resulting development of new and
enhanced products and services. Whether developing new methods of
document delivery, exploring the realm of electronic journals, or utilizing the Internet to its fullest potential, the vendor environment
flourishes through constant evolution and reevaluation.

What Are the Trade-Offs in Leaving Traditional Librarianship?

Uniformly, the librarians gave up the bureaucracy found in most larger institutions and gained opportunities for fruitful collaboration with quick results. One observed, "In the vendor community you also get headaches, heavy time commitment, lots of excitement, opportunities for creativity, good salary, concern for the bottom line but fewer budget constraints, being on the forefront of technology, having an impact on more than one library at a time, meeting people from all over the country, travel, staff development."

Another noted, "I think most librarians think money is evil, or at least crude. All of my experience in traditional libraries has been in the academic environment where our users were never referred to as 'customers' or 'clients.' They were 'patrons,' seekers of knowledge for the sake of knowledge. To make the leap from this environment to a commercial enterprise, I had to change my perspective on making money. I have come to believe that we earn money by providing a good service or creating a good product, and that, to continue to provide that service or product, we must earn money."

Sandy observed, "The only down side to working in the for-profit sector is a diminution in a type of collegiality that librarians in public and academic libraries enjoy (librarians in corporate libraries also must forego this advantage). Nonetheless collegiality still exists through organizations that support interaction of vendor members with librarians, publishers, and other vendors. In meetings we are able to pursue common goals—standards, improvement of working relationships, etc. The real benefit is the opportunity to reach so many others in the industry." Another, in comparing and contrasting experiences in both worlds, says, "I'm not sure if I could ever work in a library again." A point to be emphasized based on the responses from all participants in this essay is that we felt that we could play a wider, broader role in the library and information science community by being part of the vendor community.

What Are the Necessary Personal Characteristics?

Employee characteristics include keen minds that are able to store and use large amounts of trivia, an ability to work independently, an understanding and utilization of technology, lack of fear—chutzpah—and the concomitant comfort with risk taking, a commitment to service, creativity, flexibility in the face of rules and roles, and the ability to think with a global vision. "We look for sharp, bright people who can move quickly and work independently on their own initiative. We look for creativity, good personalities, good communication skills, and an understanding of the industry." Other qualities include flexibility and self-confidence, the ability to be self-reliant, to adjust to new directives, to think freely, quickly, independently, in a self-assured manner. All feel that there continue to be many opportunities in the vendor community for experienced librarians with good communication and personal skills.

Challenges for Library Education

How can library education make an impact on this career route? Good courses in systems analysis, business and management, economics, marketing, communications, and strategic planning are important. Library education should prepare people to embrace the idea of constantly learning new technologies, and should teach about the richness and multiplicity of participants in the world of scholarly communications beyond libraries. "There are so many pieces of this community, all contributing to the library in its mission—and they were all left out of my library school courses. When I was attending library school, I never really had the opportunity to consider nontraditional options because I never knew they existed." Library schools should develop more partnerships with vendors, by continuing to invite vendor representatives to lecture on a variety of topics, by developing internships with library vendors, and by altering library school curricula to include courses for those who wish to pursue nontraditional library careers.

Some Other Advice

All the Readmore people interviewed agreed that everyone benefits from having professional librarians in vendor situations. Library clients benefit from talking directly to another librarian who understands how things work in libraries. Vendors benefit from having people with a library education and background—because librarians are better able to focus on what is of real value to clients and to create truly marketable services and products. As librarians we benefit by broadening our understanding of our community.

Another noted that "one problem with working for a vendor is the mistrust and wariness with which you are viewed by a number of librarians—your motives are suspect, all of a sudden. Additionally, the factor of competition prevents the exchange of information which would be very helpful in some circumstances. It is important to have professional colleagues in the same organization you can talk to and bounce ideas off of. Overall, though, it's an exciting, creative place to work . . . however, I want to stress that I am still a librarian and will always be a librarian, no matter where I work and what I do." All

Readmore librarians spoke glowingly and encouragingly about their professional lives in the vendor community.

In summary, careers with library vendors are characterized by the wide latitude to move and experiment, the lack of bureaucracy, the freedom to assume increasing amounts of responsibility, the ability to blaze one's own job and actively define and redefine its responsibilities, and the opportunities to respond to a wide variety of stimuli, differing situations, and constantly engaging challenges. The required expertise involves blending traditional library and information science education with sales, marketing, management, business, and technical skills and strong personal skills. And one respondent noted, "I would suggest investing in a sturdy suitcase and a couple of pairs of very comfortable shoes." Certain truths are indeed universal and enduring!

FIGURE 1
Participants' Profiles
(alphabetical by first name)

Name	Position at Readmore	Years with Vendors	Library Degrees
Amira Aaron	Academic Automation Specialist	over 10	M.L.S., UCLA, 1972; Ph.D. coursework in library automation and management, UCLA
Dan Tonkery	President and CEO	over 10	M.S.L.S. (biomedical communications), U.Ill., 1970
Jenni Wilson	Midwest Marketing Manager/Readmore Academic Services	under 5	M.S.L.S., U.Ill., 1992
Joanne Jahr	Bibliographic Researcher	under 5	M.L.S., Pratt Inst., 1972
Letty Alvarez	UnCover Product Specialist	under 5	M.L.S., SUNY–Albany, 1993
Marilyn Geller	Internet Product Specialist	under 5	M.S.L.S., Simmons College, 1978
Rachel Frick	Regional Service Representative	under 5	M.S.L.S., UNC–Chapel Hill, 1994
Sandy Gurshman	Manager of Publisher Services	over 10	M.L.S., Rutgers, 1981
Steve Kochoff	National Sales Coordinator	over 10	M.S.L.S., U.Ill., 1973; D.L.S., Columbia, 1992

13.

Collection Development with a Library Vendor

by Lauren K. Lee

Like most librarians, I came from a solid, well-rounded, liberal arts background. But when it was time for graduate school, I suddenly felt the need for a practical degree. I wanted to get my master's degree and be able to say "I am a (———)." So, I chose librarianship, having never worked in a library, and was able to say upon graduation, "I am a librarian." I was suddenly qualified for a specific set of positions. The options seemed clear and I embarked on a fairly traditional career.

While at Emory I had become interested in technical services, particularly cataloging, and so intended to head in that direction. However, Atlanta had become home and the first position I found in that area was a public services job for the Cobb County Public Library System, a medium-sized system in suburban Atlanta. I was fortunate to have as my first director Mary Louise Rheay, who encouraged the involvement of young professionals in library committees and in the American Library Association.

Selection captured my fancy immediately and among my pet projects were a massive weeding of the central library collection and a long-range plan for the development of the reference collection.

There were many rewarding things about working with the public; however, I still wanted to try technical services. I was able to work four hours per week in cataloging, but I also started looking for another position. I found it at Georgia Institute of Technology as serials librarian in the acquisitions department. There I was exposed to the acquisitions practices of a larger library, such as approval plans, standing orders, and employing specialty jobbers.

I found, however, that I missed the variety of the public library setting, and when Atlanta-Fulton Public Library had an opening for a materials selection coordinator, I knew the job would be a perfect fit. Before I left six years later, I had become collection management administrator with responsibility for selection processes and policies, the evaluation of collections, and materials budget allocations. I worked with research collections at the central library as well as with small, medium, and large branch collections. And I unofficially served as the liaison between public services selectors and technical services staff.

How did all this lead to my present job with a book wholesaler? In the normal course of business I had been investigating, using, and evaluating various vendor services. The project that shaped my future was building opening-day collections for 13 new or expanded libraries. In order to accomplish this gargantuan task, I knew that I would have to use vendor services to the utmost. In the process, I became fascinated with what vendors can do for libraries. Brodart was one of those vendors, and in May 1990 they created a new position with my name on it—Manager of Collection Development Services.

My primary responsibilities are to plan and implement various collection development services for our customers, but I'm also somewhat involved in sales and marketing efforts related to those services. I now supervise a department of seven, including one children's materials specialist. I work with our customers by telephone, fax, and e-mail, and in person. As a matter of fact, one of the most rewarding parts of my job is being able to travel to libraries all over the country and observe firsthand what they're doing and how they are doing it. I also get to see many of my friends and colleagues at national and regional conferences.

My first task at Brodart was to work on their system for creating retrospective selection lists. This included opening-day collections but soon was expanded to accommodate standard replacement ordering or other needs for collection enhancement. My job is to make this system as flexible and as user-friendly as possible; we do the time-consuming searching and availability checking while the librarians concentrate on making their final selections. This involves keeping up with bibliographies, review journals, and specialty publishers. Frequently I have to create special listings myself when we just can't find a published source that will do the trick. Lately I've worked on literary criticism for high school students, the occult, reading list classics, and substance abuse.

My second major focus has been our new service for ongoing collection development—Title Information Preview Service, or TIPS. We wanted to design a service based on the public library model of selection—the heavy use of review media supplemented by selected publishers, series, and authors. It has been very exciting to be involved in the development of a new service. I worked with our programmers, with customers in test sites, with staff from the review journals, and with our advertising staff. I have seen the product grow from the idea stage, through the development stage, to the delivery of a full-fledged collection development service. What a fascinating and satisfying experience!

Looking back, all my prior job experience helped bring me to this particular path. I had actual selection experience in three very different library settings. I had coordinated activities among a group of selectors. I had ordered and received materials, and had allocated, encumbered, and expended funds. I had worked with many vendors and knew what I appreciated (and didn't appreciate) in their approach to librarians. I was familiar with publishing and reviewing and with the tools available to selectors. And last but not least, my early interest in cataloging paid off. I find it very useful now to understand the relationship of acquisitions records to cataloging records and the role of integrated library systems in today's automated environment. I can talk MARC tags with the best of them.

My "librarian-ness" allows me to communicate with our customers as a peer. In many cases, I have "been there" and can identify with their needs and frustrations. In fact it has been to my great benefit to have worked in several libraries and have "tried on" a number of different roles. I feel that it is easier to move up if you move around. My advice to other librarians is to try different things and then pursue what fits you best. Volunteer for committee assignments, be active in professional organizations, meet and talk to as many colleagues as possible. My vendor persona then pipes in and adds "See vendors as partners, not as wicked capitalists."

I think you can tell that I am quite happy with my job. It has built-in variety in terms of library types and sizes, subject matter, and formats. It allows for creativity. I have found that I really enjoy writing a monthly "advertorial" and working on the concepts for advertising. I can still be a practitioner of the art of collection development, especially on the occasions when a customer entrusts me with the actual responsibility for title selection. I am still a librarian—I just have the privilege for working for more than one library at a time. And because of that opportunity I plan to stick to the "else" that can be done with a library degree.

14.

A Career Path to Marketing

by Mary Jo Godwin

"See that my ashes are 'bound' in good leather and shelve me with the autobiographies," I once joked to my colleagues at the public library where I worked. That's how convinced I was that my last days here on earth would be spent within the walls of that institution. After all, it was the only public library in the town where I was born, and the only place that I had worked after graduating from college. I had moved up the ranks from library assistant to assistant director following the completion of my M.L.S. and I was appointed director of the library three years later. It was a very rewarding 13 years with enough challenges and opportunities to keep me engaged and inspired. The thought of abandoning the soil of my professional as well as personal roots never crossed my mind. This was home and the place where I lived and worked.

This was also the 1980s, however, and my husband's career was taking a different path. For more than two years we had experimented with a "commuter marriage" while he worked during the week in a city approximately 200 miles from our home. But now the commute was going to be between New York City and rural, eastern North Carolina, a distance too far to be practical or productive. I informed the library board of my intent to leave and immediately signed up for the job placement center at the upcoming American Library Association midwinter meeting.

My first inclination was to look for middle management or assistant director positions with one of the many large public library systems in the New York area. Although salaries were comparable to my director's pay in North Carolina, the thought of being a tiny voice among the hundreds in these megalibrary systems was disconcerting after having had the advantage of calling my own shots for nearly ten years.

I sent resumes and made phone calls to the librarian-oriented employment agencies that I found in the classified sections of the *New York Times* and library professional journals. The response was discouraging. There were numerous openings for law librarians, catalogers, bibliographers, and indexers but none for public library administrators.

My husband's job was with the federal government and so I investigated the employment possibilities in a federal government library. I spent weeks completing the SF-171 forms, requesting college transcripts, and documenting continuing education courses in order to get a place on the federal librarian register. Being a generalist whose work experience beyond the public library consisted of a brief internship in an elementary school media center, I held out little hope of being hired for the more specialized positions in government libraries. Several weeks later I received my GS rating but accompanying it was an announcement that the register was closed.

It was at the ALA midwinter meeting placement center that I found my best leads. Through its job postings I secured four interviews—two for department head positions in large public libraries; one for a reference post at a private, small, four-year college library; and one for assistant editor on the staff of the *Wilson Library Bulletin*. The thought of being an editor or working in publishing had never entered my mind until I saw the job listing in the placement center notebook. The requirements called for an M.L.S., knowledge of composition and grammar, and an understanding of the issues important to librarianship. At the time, I had just published my first article and was fulfilling an appointment to the editorial board of my state association journal, *North Carolina Libraries*. This was an all-volunteer group that met quarterly to proofread and lay out articles, plan the editorial calendar, and identify potential advertisers. I loved the collaboration that went into each issue, the debates about grammar and style, and the thrill of seeing the finished product. My previous publishing experience had been as coeditor of my high school yearbook. Not much to offer an information publishing giant like H. W. Wilson, I thought. But here was the chance to spend every day creating a magazine that was important reading for thousands of librarians and to get paid for doing it. I saw this as an opportunity to use my undergraduate degree in English, previous work experiences, and understanding of the profession to enlighten and entertain other librarians, and at the same time expand my very limited view of the issues and challenges important to the library community. That was the job I wanted and went after.

I had encountered *WLB* during my last semester in college. We met during an assignment for an independent study course called the "World of the Library." I had enrolled hoping for an easy A and a boost to my grade point average. I got the A and along the way gained first-hand knowledge of what library reference work was really about. I decided right then that teaching English was *not* how I wanted to spend my days. I was going to be a librarian like those I read about between the beautiful covers of *WLB*.

While I was in library school *WLB* was the first source I regularly consulted for many assignments. I found profiles of role models, practical solutions and ideas that I was anxious to try out in my library, along with timely reviews and news. There were memorable articles that helped to deepen my understanding of principles basic to librarianship such as intellectual freedom, access to information, community outreach, and international librarianship. It was almost incomprehensible that I might actually join the staff of my favorite journal.

The placement center interview with Wilson's vice president of human resources went smoothly and I anxiously returned home to await a phone call from *WLB* editor Milo Nelson. Within a week he called and arranged an interview in New York. I took along examples of my writing, everything from my thesis to the weekly library news column I wrote for the local paper, and some issues of *North Carolina Libraries* that I had helped edit. I have never been able to recall any of the questions Milo asked me during the interview. I guess my answers were appropriate because I got the job and soon began what turned out to be an incredible journey.

The most notable difference in being a librarian and being a librarian/editor was a sense of freedom. Freed from the administrative hassles of day-to-day library operations, I found working at *WLB* to be an oasis for the mind. There were manuscripts to be read and thought about, important events to be covered and synthesized, and interesting people and books to meet and get to know. The never-ending stream of correspondence from librarians throughout the country enabled me to build a network of creative, innovative, and entrepreneurial professionals who kept me well informed about what was happening on the front lines and in the stacks. I gained new insights about matters related to library education, automation, and funding. My editorial chair was an incredible vantage point from which to see ideas take shape that would make a difference in our profession. For the first time in my career I had the luxury of time for professional reading and discussion. It was part of my job to have dinner with the leaders in the profession and listen to what they had to say about my favorite topics—libraries and librarians. I saw the magazine as a sort of clearinghouse and my role as one of filtering and organizing an increasing flow of information—sort of like being a librarian's librarian.

I was relieved to learn after being on the job a few months that my skills and knowledge as a librarian were as important to my success at the magazine as they had been in the administration of the library. The mechanics of publishing were easy enough to learn on the job (and had to be relearned when a desktop publishing system replaced the cut-and-paste assemblage of the magazine). Much of the production routine was similar to the methods I used in the educational media production courses I took in library school. I was able to take advantage of conferences and seminars offered by the magazine publishing industry to learn more about editing, layout and design, and circulation and advertising. Just as technology was transforming the way librarians worked, so was it revolutionizing the possibilities for a magazine like *WLB*.

It was nearly three months after Milo Nelson announced to the *WLB* staff his intent to resign as editor that I seriously considered applying for the job. With encouragement from the other editorial associates, I pursued my ideas for the magazine's future with the Wilson management and they made me an offer. I was delighted to have an opportunity to apply the management skills I had used successfully in the public library to the challenges of running a magazine. Budgets, marketing plans, promotional ideas, and services to readers were some of the responsibilities I added to the editorial functions I was already performing. With the help of *WLB*'s talented staff of librarian/editors and the marvelous resources that a company like Wilson can provide, I launched new columns, expanded the editorial pages, increased ad sales, and ushered the magazine into its 75th year of publication. This had to be the job of my dreams.

It was also the first time I had worked in a management capacity for a privately held company. Nothing in my library science training nor years in county government had prepared me for that experience. It was a different playing field and I had to scramble to figure out how to make my way in the corporate world. I sought guidance from other librarians whom I knew had successfully made the transition, and I read everything that came along about corporate culture. There was a measure of comfort in knowing that our market, the magazine's customers so to speak, was made up of librarians and information professionals, and that our product was a beloved fixture of the professional literature. Nevertheless the day came when my professional principles were put on the line and I knew that I must resign rather than carry out the company president's instructions.

It took several weeks before I could begin to think about what I might do next. Even though I knew more about the management of public libraries than ever before, I questioned whether or not I was still marketable as a public library director after working outside of that arena for eight years. I applied for two public library director jobs but didn't make the first cut. The only opportunity to continue my librarian/editor career was as a freelancer, and I wasn't sure I had the financial resources to survive on my own. Through friends and contacts I had made while at *WLB*, I filled the next eight months with a variety of writing and editing projects. Working out of an office in my guest room, I relished the work that dealt with libraries and found the other projects interesting, but it was hard to focus on the tasks at hand and also concentrate on marketing myself for the next project. I gained a bit more financial security after landing a part-time job with a very small, independent publisher who was about to release her first and only publication—a ready reference and referral guide that only a librarian could truly appreciate. I functioned as the press's office manager, publicist, marketing director, and sales representative. My boss was the author and publisher, and also a well-connected, politically savvy lawyer with a social conscience. The arrangement provided me with a great deal of moral support, a steadier income, some time to freelance, and an opportunity to look for a more permanent position as a librarian/editor.

Once again I found myself at the ALA midwinter placement center, but this time the postings were fewer and most were for entry-level positions. I didn't even fill out a card for an interview. Somewhat discouraged I moved on to the exhibit hall where a chance meeting with a publisher led to an invitation to lunch and an exciting job offer. Phyllis Steckler, president of Oryx Press, asked me to market her titles to federal government libraries. She particularly wanted a librarian, not a seasoned salesperson, to work this segment of the Oryx market. I was stunned. I had never sold anything tangible like reference books and online databases, but I considered myself a pretty good salesperson when it came to selling others on the value of libraries. Could I transfer those skills to this assignment?

I knew Phyllis and Oryx to be leaders in the library and information publishing field. Many of her authors were librarians and her publications were recognized for their accuracy and excellence. She had high standards that I admired. Her offer had much the same appeal and promise that the *WLB* editorship had provided, without the drawbacks of working for a big publisher with an impenetrable glass ceiling. I felt comfortable with her terms and expectations.

I joined Oryx as director of government sales in March 1993. For the next two years I was based in Washington, D.C.; I worked out of my guest room office, calling on government librarians, listening and learning about the unique collections they maintain and the variety of services they provide. I represented the company at meetings of groups such as the Information Industry Association and I even sold some books. Best of all I had ample opportunities to apply my management skills, editorial experience, and knowledge of books and libraries to a wide variety of marketing tasks. Most recently I relocated to the company's headquarters in Phoenix, Arizona, where I work as director of marketing services reporting to the executive vice president, Natalie Lang. My new duties include managing the telephone sales representatives and coordinating exhibits at conferences. It is like having three very distinct jobs, and because Oryx is a small publisher I have the flexibility to be involved in editorial decisions and to consult regularly with practicing librarians about the need for new products and resources. Having had the experience of working alone for a while, I can better appreciate the advantages of having daily contact with a creative group of professionals like those at Oryx. It has proven to be a stimulating environment in which to work. My understanding of strategic marketing has expanded and I continue to learn more about the business side of publishing from experts like Phyllis Steckler and Natalie Lang. Both of these women have worked for major corporations and know how to negotiate deals and compete successfully—skills I want to develop. Among the rewards of my new job are opportunities for personal and professional growth and continued contact with and access to people who have something worthwhile to say about librarianship and the future of libraries in the information age.

Although I did not actually plan any of the twists and turns along my career path, I don't regret any of the experiences. I knew early on that what mattered most to me was being a part of the process of connecting people and ideas and information. My training in library science prepared me for a lifetime of opportunity. It has been an unexpected dividend that I was able to accomplish this goal in settings beyond as well as within the traditional library. Today technology enables us to escape the constraints of space and time and to pursue ideas and information on a global scale. Instead of having the 921s as my final resting place, maybe I will be scanned and stored on a tiny chip where I can virtually continue to be a part of the great information chain.

15.

Working for a Library Vendor

by Barbara Herzog

What else can you do with a library degree? Join the Miami Dolphins football team, for one thing. That's the first position I was offered after beginning my quest for an alternative use of my M.L.S. Although I ultimately turned down this opportunity, it set me on a serendipitous road to a series of satisfying and exciting positions with private companies that are vendors to the library marketplace. I've heard many reasons why librarians dismiss the thought of going to work for a library vendor. The most often articulated one is a sense that it's abandonment of the profession for which we've all worked so hard and with which we identify so strongly—a retreat to "the other side." Another reason, which is less often spoken, but, I believe, at least equally important, is that librarians view the change from the secure and familiar world of libraries to the less familiar, more cut-throat world of business to be a very risky one, and they hesitate to take the chance that such a change represents. I'll admit that my recollections of my first weeks on the job at a private company are vivid with frightening memories—a fear that I would never be able to learn how to do this job, which seemed so different from the library jobs I'd held—as well as shock that people were actually fired for not performing up to expected standards, something which had never occurred in all my years working in libraries. Now, from the perspective of several years working for two different library vendors, in a number of different capacities, I'd like to suggest that this may be an important career alternative for many of you to consider.

Ten Reasons to Consider Working for a Library Vendor

- You'll be able to serve the library community in an entirely new way, by ensuring that the librarians' point of view is brought to the vendor.
- Colleagues in libraries will become more comfortable in their dealings with vendors who are themselves librarians.
- If travel is something you long for, a number of vendor positions provide such opportunities.
- In many cases, working for a vendor provides you with the opportunity to work with all kinds of libraries.
- The pay is often better than in comparable library positions, while the other benefits are equal.
- Working for a vendor can provide exciting challenges and the opportunity to learn new things while building on library-related knowledge and skills.
- Certain types of positions offer greater flexibility of options for organizing your own time and tasks. This can be a useful preparation for those of you who may have an ultimate goal of running your own business.
- If you decide that working for a vendor is not for you, after all, and decide to return to libraries, you'll find that your resume stands out from the rest because of the time you've spent working in another milieu.
- Many fewer people apply for these jobs than for attractive library jobs at corresponding levels.
- Finally, a most compelling reason for exploring options in the private sector is the alternative it provides for librarians who have reached a point in their careers where they've become as good at what they do as they can be; that there's little left to learn and that all of the challenges have been met. At this point, most people assume that it's time to move into management. However, for those of you who, like me, realize that library management is not for you, I urge you to think seriously about pursuing opportunities in the private sector as an alternative.

My Path to Private Companies

I began searching for a career shift after earning my M.B.A., which I did on a part-time basis, taking advantage of the opportunity to attend graduate school tuition-free while working as a reference librarian at a state college. I found my M.B.A. course work to be stimulating, challenging, and fun (more so than my M.L.S.), but when I'd completed the program, I was at a loss as to how to integrate my new body of knowledge with my existing identity—I couldn't visualize myself as anything but "a librarian with an M.B.A."

I considered pursuing opportunities in the business libraries of large academic institutions or in corporate libraries, but these things didn't offer the level of change I wanted, and to be truthful, I really felt burned out on reference librarianship. Pursuing a management position in libraries was not an option; I was quite certain that management, especially of other people, was something I didn't enjoy, nor was I particularly effective. I met with my advisor and explained my impasse. Finding himself equally without a clue about career options for me, he suggested that I read the classified advertisements in the *National Business Employment Weekly*, which compiled the classified section of the *Wall Street Journal*. Excited by this brilliant idea, I sat down immediately and began perusing the ads. There was nothing I could even remotely relate to, until, nearly at the end, I spied a tiny, 3–line ad: "Librarian wanted; apply Miami Dolphins." I mailed off my resume, and waited for the phone to ring. It did, and I was flown to Miami to meet Joe Robbie, the owner of the football team, who dreamed of building his own stadium, housing an archival collection of newspaper clippings bearing tribute to the glory of his team and his name. The perfectly competent file clerk maintaining the files "wouldn't do" once his dream was fulfilled; a professional librarian was surely needed to give this collection the care it was due. While I ultimately decided that the tediousness of the position far outweighed the novelty, it did renew my determination to forge a new career path.

I returned to my search with renewed energy, but decided to confine my searching to more familiar territory, concentrating on the classified advertisement sections of journals in the library field. An ad in *Library Journal* caught my attention. CLSI, a library automation vendor, was seeking a systems analyst to design automated circulation system components; experience with library automation was required. I had never worked in a library with an automated system, and neither my M.L.S. nor my M.B.A. had provided much involvement with computers. I steeled myself to send a resume, and, much to my surprise, was called for an interview. To prepare for the interview, I pored through library journals trying to give myself at least a conversational knowledge of library automation; I paid particular attention to the CLSI advertisements in an attempt to form some sense of what the company was trying to achieve. The day of the interview arrived, and I found myself buoyed by an almost karmic force—usually a quiet, shy person, I talked nonstop, leaving my interviewer little opportunity to delve below the seemingly polished surface. A few weeks later, I was offered the job.

I resigned from my reference position, despite having recently achieved faculty status and the coveted tenured assistant professor level. Panic didn't set in until the end of my first week at CLSI, when I attempted to prepare my first "weekly activity report" and discovered that I had no idea how to navigate the word processing software. As the weeks went by, I found myself learning very quickly about the computerized systems used to keep the office running, as well as about the automated system that the company sold. My responsibility as a systems analyst was to write very detailed documents, called "product specifications" or "specs," describing exactly how a new feature being added to the automated circulation system would work. My experience as a librarian helped define circulation needs for the programmers.

After a few years as a systems analyst or functional applications analyst, which is a term I find more clearly describes the position, I was promoted to product manager for circulation control systems. The product management function is typically described as a "cradle to grave" responsibility for the assigned product. While design of the circulation function remained at the heart of this position, I now added responsibilities at both ends of the process—I assumed more responsibility for interacting with customers and prospects, often in large groups. After completing the design of CLSI's "second-generation" product and bringing it to the point of market readiness, I decided it was time for a new challenge. Serendipity again: a position at H. W. Wilson was brought to my attention by a colleague. Working for H. W. Wilson is about as close to coming home to libraries as is possible within the vendor world, and I jumped at the chance to apply for the position of "Library Relations Representative" for the New England region. Historically, H. W. Wilson had never had a sales force of any kind; but the need for a presence out in the field, to speak for the company as well as to listen more directly to what the library marketplace had to say, developed as the company became more involved with electronic products.

My position entails visiting libraries that are users or prospective users primarily of our CD-ROM products, and/or less frequently of our online services; I spend time making them aware of the features of our products that distinguish them from competitors' products. This often involves the satisfaction of introducing librarians to CD-ROM technology, giving them the confidence they need to introduce the new electronic information products to their patrons and funding bodies.

How Do You Get There from Here?

If what I've said so far has made you think that working for a vendor may be for you, I would recommend several things. First, get a job in a library; one's value to a vendor depends on library experience. Second, participate in new projects being undertaken in your library; people prominent in library automation today are often those who took the risk of getting involved in automation projects early on. Third, diversify your library experience as much as possible; a vendor values experience with all types of library operations and their potential customers. Finally, become and stay informed about the library marketplace; attend conferences and read the library and electronic information industry press.

I'd like to note here that I don't consider the M.B.A. degree to have been instrumental in my success in private industry, although I suspect that it may have made my resume stand out. The important purpose it served in my career path was just in giving me the kick in the pants I needed to take the risk of moving from the library world to the vendor world.

If It Sounds Great, but You Still Can't Relate . . .

After my years of work experience with vendors, it's clear to me that many of the functions performed in libraries are directly translatable to the vendor environment. If you think about the skills you use in performing your job, you'll find all kinds of areas to which you can relate. Library vendors may not require or advertise for an M.L.S. when hiring for most positions, so it will be up to you to make them recognize the benefits of employing librarians; prepare a resume that highlights your skills and talents rather than job titles. As more and more librarians explore and take advantage of the vendor alternative, the benefits of hiring people with the education, experience, and professionalism of librarians will quickly become apparent.

Working for a library vendor may not be for everyone, but I know from experience that it's a viable alternative for many librarians who, like myself, have reached a turning point in their careers, but find traditional career paths to have little appeal. In my work in vendor relations, I have seen librarians' eyes widen with surprise, and their shoulders relax, when they see the M.L.S. after my name on my business card; I have heard many times a sigh of relief followed by, "Ah, you're a librarian; you understand what I'm talking about." I derive tremendous satisfaction from this sense of camaraderie, and am grateful to have found a career that allows me so many new ways to exercise my own skills and interests without abandoning my profession.

16.

I Am Still a Librarian

by Ann Talley

I was once asked by a customer if I "used to be a librarian." After pondering this question for a few seconds I replied "I still am." As a librarian practicing in a nontraditional environment, I often find myself explaining just what I do and how I came to be doing it. First, I work for a subscription agency. Second, I have a slightly nontraditional role even within the company. I am the editor of *The Serials Directory: An International Reference Book*, published by EBSCO Information Services. *The Serials Directory* is an annual reference guide that publishes information concerning serial publications.

As you may or may not know, a subscription agency orders serial information (journals, individual articles, and electronic databases, for example) from publishers and other suppliers on behalf of libraries, individual researchers, and corporations. The service enables libraries to easily obtain the serials they need, and usually makes the actual purchasing of those materials more affordable in the long run.

EBSCO Information Services is the largest such agency in the world. It is not surprising that an agency whose business is to provide customers with the means of learning about or accessing millions of journals and articles from all corners of the globe would also provide the services that help customers find the information they need regarding those serials. *The Serials Directory* is another way in which EBSCO strives to provide the best service it can to those needing serials information. Most of the information EBSCO deals with is sought by librarians whose job it is to acquire periodicals for their libraries or to retrieve specific information desired by a patron. Since EBSCO deals directly, indeed almost exclusively, with librarians, it makes sense that EBSCO would employ librarians to perform important roles in their operations. This is where my story begins.

How Did I Get Here?

To be quite honest, a career as a librarian was actually a second career for me. After having received an undergraduate degree and working on completion of a master's degree in criminal justice, it became readily apparent that I was not going to save the juvenile delinquent population of the world nor was I going to find employment that would even provide me the opportunity. I needed a full-time job of some sort; an advertisement for a library assistant in the Birmingham Public Library catalog department opened new doors for me. Within a year of being hired, I was enrolled in library school at the University of Alabama Graduate School of Library Service. It was finally apparent what I wanted to do "when I grew up." Or so I thought.

I had been one of those students in college who took elective courses in many subject areas, such as computer science, management, business, and economics. Therefore, my skill set seemed perfectly matched for an area where the need to automate was recognized and in process, as was the need for effective managers in this relatively new area. Besides, it didn't hurt that I had worked for the largest public library in the state and would be able to participate actively in many innovative projects from concept to implementation.

Shortly after I completed my M.L.S., the library where I worked began the project of automating circulation, and thus began my first steps in a library career that would soon lead outside the hallowed halls of an actual library. My first *librarian* job was to train library staff members on proper bibliographic entry, as well as to assist in the general operations of the computer system. The knowledge gained from preparing training materials and conducting training sessions for everyone from department heads to clerical personnel, and from serving as a troubleshooter for terminals and a mainframe computer system eventually led to a position as system coordinator for a network of libraries in the state. There, responsible for an integrated system supporting circulation, cataloging, and acquisitions, as well as the administrative functions of the network office, I quickly expanded my basic computer knowledge, developed vendor relationships, and honed the organizational skills learned in library school.

Through the growth and knowledge gained from this position and the relationship established with the system vendor, I began another chapter in my nontraditional career at CLSI (now GEAC Computers) as an installation consultant. While once again going to a library almost daily, the role undertaken once at the library was quite different. Now I was there to assist other librarians in planning and/or implementing their online systems and actually showing them how what they already knew how to do could now be done on a computer. Innumerable times I called upon skills and knowledge learned on the job in a library in order to assist customers in devising methods of getting the automated system to do what they had previously done manually. My library experience proved invaluable as I crisscrossed the country applying knowledge of libraries and their functions to the different automated systems sold by the company to various types and sizes of libraries.

When I conceded the victory to the road, my next nontraditional job was with EBSCO Subscription Services. In charge of quality control for the Title Information Department, my primary responsibilities involved establishing a training program where standards for data entry would be established and adhered to for the sake of consistency. The main goal, of course, was to have all data entry personnel keying information identically, alleviating confusion and promoting efficiency. After a year in quality control, I was placed in the newly vacated position of editor of *The Serials Directory*. Even though I was familiar with the publishing industry as a consumer, I have found that my experience as a librarian is invaluable in working with this publication. Along with the already established, fine editorial staff, I have been able to initiate changes for improvements based on what I know the library community wants and needs. Personally, I have learned more about the pressures and deadlines that go into editing a book and getting it ready for publication. I still perform training; the staff has learned how librarians use publications, what our needs and desires are, and the format we expect to see when using quality reference books.

The Serials Directory is primarily a library tool, and I have been able to use my knowledge to help us streamline and improve our product's package to better meet the needs of librarians and their patrons. Having worked in a library setting with automated systems, I understand the way librarians search for and use information. This has been extremely helpful in my experience in the publishing business in general, and specifically with EBSCO Publishing. For instance, *The Serials Directory* is arranged alphabetically by subject based on the MARC record. Therefore, my understanding of the structure of MARC records and of LC and Dewey subject classifications has helped me immensely in making decisions regarding the reorganization of subject headings in *The Serials Directory*. Also, my experience as a librarian has given me the ability to juggle various projects at once, and my organizational skills have been integral in handling the amount of work required to publish a five-volume, 8,000 page reference work. The experience is not unlike having trucks of books awaiting cataloging, or lines of patrons all waiting to check out at the same workstation or wanting their reference questions answered yesterday.

Librarians, as a part of their duty, are in regular contact with publishers and distributors. Having direct experience has given me insight into how the publishing industry works and how it should work. As I have been in a librarian's shoes for well over a decade, I know exactly what kind of service librarians expect from a publisher, which enables us to publish a book that will meet their needs.

What to Expect in the Future

The next few years are going to be a challenging time in library science. More and more information will *only* be available online or on CD-ROM; computer database experience will be all but mandatory. It is imperative that I, along with every librarian in the future, have an understanding of these various outlets and how to use them. Experience with electronic databases and computer-related publications and serials will only increase a librarian's career opportunities outside the library, and will make a librarian's role of utmost importance in the business world. A library degree does not mean a career of checking materials in and out, collecting overdue fines, and fielding reference questions. Far from it. Our society has moved, and will continue to move, from an industrial-based society to an information-driven society. We will have to know what the information is, how to classify the information accurately, and how to make it accessible to those who need it. The power in years to come will belong to those people who control the information. And, of course, where there is power, there is opportunity.

17.

The Road Ahead: One Librarian's Journey

by Monica Ertel

You gain strength, courage and confidence by
every experience in which you really stop to look fear in
the face. . . . You must do the thing you think you cannot do.

These words by Eleanor Roosevelt have been a guiding force in my career. At times, this credo has made my life a little uncomfortable but always interesting and definitely challenging—two critical and essential components for me in enjoying my work.

Looking for a Road to Follow

Like most people who went into the library science field 20 years ago, I had a liberal arts degree which made it rather difficult to find a job when I graduated from college. I had planned to work in the area of special education and began my advanced degree work in this area, but when I met a former classmate, who had graduated a year ahead of me, selling pots and pans at a major department store because the job market was so grim, I decided to reevaluate my career goals.

During this same time, I was also working part-time as a page at a local public library. A young librarian took me under her wing and began to mentor me gently as I searched for a potential career. Until I began to work in the public library, I had no idea that librarians needed an advanced degree nor did I have a good understanding of the many facets of the field of librarianship. I had always been an avid library user throughout my life but had not thought of this as a career. My mentor began subtly to point me in the direction of library school. I was very resistant at first but under my mentor's guidance, I slowly began to see the fascinating possibilities in this career. And as fate would have it, she was more than right. I can't imagine another career that could be more satisfying.

The Journey Begins

My emphasis in library school was in the area of public libraries, but other than my stint as a page at the local public library, it turns out that I have never worked in one. The job market was tight for everyone in the mid-1970s. When I graduated, public libraries were not hiring, but institutions and corporations were beginning to understand the importance of having an information professional as part of their organization. My first job was as a research assistant at SRI International (Stanford Research Institute), researching and writing data sheets in the area of chemical economics—an area I knew nothing about, but keeping Eleanor Roosevelt's credo in mind, I applied for and got the job anyway. Part of this job was also to take care of a small, very specialized collection of books, journals, and clipping files for the other researchers. My foray into the wonderful world of special libraries had begun.

After leaving SRI, I became the first librarian of a small but very active collection at a company that conducted quite a bit of contract research for the U.S. Government—everything from air-conditioned space suits for the astronauts to solar-powered tomato sorters to deadly laser weapons. Again, this was an area that was totally new to me but I knew that I had the skills to find information—they had served me well in my previous job.

My next job gave me my first experience in building a library from scratch, as well as experience managing people. This time the library was part of Memorex Corporation, a very large computer peripheral and recording tape company, again topics unknown to me. I had also never built a library from the ground up, but by then I had enough confidence to know that I could do this. In addition, I had built up a network of professionals in other local special libraries and knew that I could also depend on my colleagues to help me along the way. (This generous help and unselfish assistance is something that I will never forget and hope always to continue to return; for me it is one of the most rewarding aspects of this career.)

After nearly five years at Memorex, I was encouraged by a former Memorex vice president to look at the possibilities at a very new, very innovative company—Apple Computer. At the time, I really had no desire to leave the comfort of my job at Memorex and I especially had no desire to build a library from scratch again. While it's extremely satisfying, it's also a long, laborious, and stressful process. But the prospect of joining this friendly company—which had as one of its corporate goals "To have fun!"—was too much for me to pass up and I joined Apple in the summer of 1981. It's been a wild ride ever since.

The Journey Continues

I was hired by Apple in 1981 to establish their library. What a joy to join a company that had a good grasp on the importance of information and the role that libraries play in this arena! My previous companies had all been good places to work, but it was a constant struggle to justify why we needed to spend resources on a library and to try to educate people about the things that a library could do for them. This was not the case at Apple. Because the company was so young, many of the employees were fresh out of college and were used to using their university libraries. They also were more familiar with and accepting of new technologies, which at that time consisted of things like DIALOG and ORBIT. My challenge was not to convince people about the utility of a library—it was to try to keep up with their demands and provide service to them using the latest information technologies. I was definitely on a rapid learning curve.

In the early days, Apple was also a company that had very little traditional organizational structure. You made your job what you wanted and the person with the best idea and the best way to implement it was encouraged and often rewarded. I took full advantage of this opportunity which has given me many chances to use my library skills in areas not traditionally thought of as "library-type" jobs.

One of the first things I did when I got to Apple, besides establishing their library, was to organize a users' group for librarians who were using Apple technology in their libraries and information centers. I must admit that my initial motivation for doing this was entirely selfish. While I told my interviewers that I would automate this new Apple Library, in truth, I had never used a personal computer, let alone seen one. But I knew that there were many people doing interesting and creative things with their Apple II computers in public, school, university, and other special libraries, and I also knew that librarians were generous in sharing their expertise. My thought was that I would start a group where I could get information to help me keep this wonderful new job I had just obtained and then, I hoped, give something back to our members. The group started locally and small, but in a few years' time the Apple Library Users Group became one of the largest user groups in the world, with over 20,000 members worldwide. We have continued to publish a quarterly newsletter, publish an annual book titled *Macintoshed Libraries*, and distribute templates with library applications for such programs as HyperCard and AppleWorks. Most recently we hosted a World Wide Web site (http://www.alug.apple.com). I also organize and staff a booth at one or two library conferences a year, giving me and my staff experience in directly marketing our products to customers. I never asked permission to get this venture going—I just recognized the need and created the opportunity.

Several years after I was hired at Apple, I was also asked to take responsibility for Apple's Corporate Documentation Group. This group is responsible for managing the manufacturing documentation (not manuals) for the company and it involves verifying drawings, assigning part numbers, tracking changes to bills of materials, designing automated systems, and training employees to use this system. One of my first challenges in this new job came when I held my first staff meeting. I was immediately questioned by one of my new staff "Why do you think you're qualified for this job?" I was a bit flustered by this direct question but tried to respond by stating that a librarian's skills are an excellent match for this type of job and that, while I had a lot to learn, my years of training as a librarian provided me with the perfect background for this job. This also gave me the opportunity to manage a fairly large group. I thoroughly enjoyed the three years that I spent managing this group.

During one of Apple's many reorganizations several years later, I found myself in a new organization called the Advanced Technology Group. This has turned out to be a wonderful home for the Apple Library and for me. This group is responsible for looking five or more years into the future and working on new technologies for future products. The library found a kinship with this research group and an eager partner to use the skills of librarianship in the information technology research area. One of the byproducts of this was the formation of the Apple Library of Tomorrow (ALOT) program, which I began in 1988 as a way for Apple not only to help the community, but to learn about how people use and adapt to new technologies. No one asked me to institute this program; rather I decided to do this after sitting in meeting after meeting, listening to researchers talk about natural language queries, human interface issues, intelligent agents, multimedia databases, and network research. I realized that these were areas that many libraries were struggling with and that they could provide a great deal of valuable feedback if we looked at libraries as "living laboratories." I also realized that our researchers never even thought of libraries when they thought of these issues. So I put together a proposal, presented it to my boss, and, to my delight, he approved it. To date, we have given nearly 50 grants to a wide range of libraries, from large libraries such as the Library of Congress to small school libraries such as a K–12 library on a Zuni Indian Reservation in New Mexico. Internally, this program has done much to help people realize that libraries represent much more than friendly places with books on the shelves. It has shown my colleagues at Apple that libraries are much, much more.

The Apple Library had recognized the importance of the Internet several years ago and began an aggressive training program for all employees, helping them get up to speed on the "information super-highway." It's been a huge success and has increased awareness that our library staff excels at skills such as technical training, designing Web pages, and consulting on information management. It has also increased awareness of the skills that librarians bring to the Internet research area. Since the Apple Library was one of the first groups within Apple to begin to delve into the World Wide Web, it was here that we began to experiment with an Apple corporate home page. We talked to some other groups that had content they wanted distributed to customers, helped them get the information into HTML format, and Apple's presence on the World Wide Web was initiated. As awareness of the Internet grew, the Apple Library's expertise in this area was recognized and the library became the home of Apple's corporate presence on the Internet (http://www.apple.com).

A Fork in the Road

Most recently, I have been given the biggest challenge of my professional career. Because of the growing importance of the Internet and the concern over the information explosion, there has been increased awareness of the need for people who understand not only the technical issues, but the social and cultural ones as well. The whole area of understanding how to deal with the information explosion is becoming more important, and research into the arena of digital libraries and all they represent is being seen as critical to dealing successfully with the phenomenon of the information superhighway. I am currently the director of the Knowledge Systems Lab at Apple which is chartered with researching a wide range of information technology issues, such as tools for finding relevant information, developing agents to assist in creating intelligent documents, studying the creation of networked communities, and looking at "national information infrastructure" policy issues such as continuing to support the Apple Library.

Finding Your Way Home

Librarians have a great many skills that are readily transferable to many areas. Our ability to organize information, understand people's information needs, deal with all walks of people at all levels of our organization, feel comfortable with ever-changing technologies, make sense out of ambiguous situations, teach people often complicated skills, negotiate with vendors, and most important, get the big picture about how information fits into the overall scheme of things make our skills highly valued and sought after. But we often don't succeed in making people aware that it is librarians who hold these skills. So when an employer is looking for someone with the above skills, the word "librarian" rarely crosses his or her mind. It is important for us to change this perception. And we need to do this by being proactive and seizing opportunities. Sometimes this means asking for new challenges, at other times, it means simply going ahead and implementing our ideas without formal approval. In any case, you hold the future of your career in your hands and it is up to you to move it in a direction that satisfies you. You must also be open to new challenges and not be afraid to travel in unknown territories. While I've been fortunate to work for a company that is fairly enlightened, it still hasn't been easy to make people see the strengths and advantages a library degree brings to the job. Like Eleanor Roosevelt, you sometimes have to do the thing you think you cannot do in order to make yourself as well as other people aware of your true potential.

18.

Training for Technology

by Phil Bradley

I obtained an honors degree in librarianship from the Polytechnic of North London in 1981. This qualification was a general librarianship degree, which had a heavy emphasis on such areas as cataloging, classification, and library management. It had no computing element in it at all.

At the time I obtained the degree, I had no real idea of what kind of library or information center I wanted to work in; I did, however, know that I wanted nothing to do with computing whatsoever. Shortly after obtaining my degree I got a temporary job (later made permanent) with the British Council, which is an organization partly funded by the British Government Foreign and Commonwealth Office, and has as its goal to promote Britain abroad—all the arts, business, education, and so on. I was employed to answer questions relating to aspects of British education in all its forms for the 80 overseas offices of the British Council. I then started to develop a specialty in this area, as well as in the creation and maintenance of small reference centers. As a result of these areas of expertise I quite literally traveled the world, going to different offices and providing advice, and helping to organize and run three of the largest educational exhibitions ever seen in the Far East.

I worked for the British Council for six years before being introduced to CD-ROM technology, and I instantly fell in love with it, realizing the power of the technology, and the way in which it could, and would, influence the development of the provision of information to endusers. Since the British Council was not at that time equipped to exploit the medium fully, I decided to leave and join a company that was engaged in this activity. The day after I left my resume with a library recruitment company, SilverPlatter approached them with a request to find a librarian who wanted to work with this emerging technology. The role that they wanted filled was that of technical support manager. Although I had little experience of computing in general and none at all in the technical aspects, I did have what SilverPlatter required—a qualification in librarianship, and a keenness and willingness to become involved. They felt, rightly so, that it made more sense to employ a librarian who could quickly pick up technical issues and explain them to other librarians in terms they could understand, than to hire a "techie" who would understand the problem, but might not be able to appreciate the needs or requirements of the library community that the company served.

Over the next four years I worked closely with British librarians, and at the forefront of CD-ROM technology, as well as running the technical support function of the European arm of the company. I also began to get more involved in giving talks about the technology and in running training courses. My skills and abilities as a librarian meant that I understood the role and value of the technology in the customers' environments; at the same time I was able to apply the knowledge gained at SilverPlatter to advise them on the best way to install the software and the hardware required to make effective use of CD-ROM.

This particular aspect of my job became more and more time-consuming, to the point that I relinquished the role of technical support manager and became what the company calls the "Global Training Director." I had the responsibility of ensuring that all customers worldwide could obtain whatever training tools they required to assist them in using the full range of SilverPlatter products. Again, I found myself traveling around the world to talk to groups of SilverPlatter users, and to run training courses and seminars. I still spend a lot of my time doing this, but have become increasingly involved in the Internet and its role in electronic publishing.

I now work on a part time basis for SilverPlatter, spending the rest of my time offering general CD-ROM courses and Internet courses to librarians in the United Kingdom, as well as providing a consulting service to companies that are considering becoming involved with the Internet.

None of this work would have been possible without my initial librarianship qualification, and I have been able to use this as a firm basis upon which to build. As a result, I am able to offer an unusual, but valuable range of skills—librarianship, technical knowledge, a deep understanding of the electronic publishing industry, and last but not least, I can talk knowledgeably about countries from Australia to Japan to Turkey!

19.

Bibliographic Data Conversion

by Fae K. Hamilton

My library school education was only a small step toward a career in library automation, specializing in bibliographic data conversion. The skills that have proved most useful to me have been acquired, not in school, but through on-the-job experience.

I became interested in library work through a part-time job as a student assistant in my college library. I shelved books, did pre-acquisition searches in the card catalog, and learned about other library operations in a completely unautomated environment. I majored in psychology and also studied mathematics and linguistics. My enjoyment of library work, combined with my desire to obtain a "marketable" skill without completing a Ph.D. program, resulted in my decision to enroll in library school.

The University of Michigan library school in the early 1970s offered very few automation courses. Practical experience with online cataloging and reference databases, which is routine at library schools today, was not available then. I did take one course in library computer applications, which included some programming. My cataloging courses emphasized practice rather than theory or history, and were good preparation for my first jobs, even though automation was not mentioned.

While at Michigan I continued to hold part-time library jobs, stretching what could have been a one-year program into two years. Working as a cataloging assistant at the university business administration library gave me excellent practical experience to reinforce what I was learning in the classroom. At the time of my graduation the job market was not very good for librarians. I have always felt that my library experience, possibly even more than the degree itself, helped me get my first jobs. The degree was a minimum qualification for the jobs, but the experience gave me the edge over fellow graduates who had not worked in libraries.

After a brief stint as a cataloger at a community college library, I became the assistant head of copy cataloging at Wayne State University Libraries in Detroit in 1974. It was at Wayne State that my experience with automation began. Michigan libraries at that time were getting ready to join OCLC, which was in the early stages of its transition from an exclusively Ohio venture to a national bibliographic utility. I helped do the libraries' OCLC profile, which involved analyzing the existing manual systems and deciding how best to automate them. I learned the MARC format and OCLC cataloging procedures, and was part of a team that trained the whole department. I had always had an aptitude for teaching and was glad to find a use for this skill in my professional life.

During the time I was there, Wayne State was the home of the Michigan Library Consortium, which became the OCLC training and support center for the state. Although I was not directly involved in training at other Michigan libraries, I observed with interest the emerging group of librarians who worked, not for individual libraries, but for library networks. These people had what seemed to be glamorous jobs. They traveled to libraries to help with OCLC profiling, conducted training workshops, traveled to OCLC to be trained themselves, and fielded phone calls about system questions and problems.

My Wayne State experience stood me in good stead when my husband and I moved to the Boston area in 1976. The Massachusetts Institute of Technology libraries were looking for a head of the OCLC section of the cataloging department, and I was offered the job. In this job I furthered my knowledge of OCLC and of cataloging procedures, supervising a group of paraprofessional copy catalogers and also serving as the OCLC resource for the libraries.

When a job as a member services librarian at NELINET came open two years later, I applied for it. NELINET, the New England Library Information Network, is the OCLC broker for New England and also offers other automation services to its members. Remembering my experience with the Michigan Library Consortium, I welcomed the chance to have one of those glamorous network jobs myself.

At NELINET I enjoyed working with a variety of libraries. My own experience was exclusively in academic libraries, but at NELINET I was able to work with public and special libraries as well. I enjoyed the chance to travel throughout New England, and to use my teaching skills. I found that I enjoyed the consulting relationship with libraries and librarians, sharing my knowledge and experience without being a manager, a position I never really enjoyed. I also became part of a wonderful community of network coordinators throughout the country, meeting my counterparts during occasional trips to OCLC. The common wisdom at that time was that librarians who had made the transition from library to network work would never go back to working for a library. Although that has not proved true for all network coordinators, it has been true for me. I have never again had a full-time, permanent job in a library since leaving MIT in 1976.

In my NELINET experience I first encountered a duality that was to stay with me throughout my career. I found that I enjoyed and had aptitude for two different sides of the library automation industry: customer support and development. Customer support people work with libraries as consultants, trainers, and problem solvers. These positions require people skills as well as computer knowledge. While they can be glamorous, they can also be stressful, often involving busy schedules of travel, public speaking, and many phone calls. Development people usually do not work directly with libraries, and their jobs are more technical than people-oriented. These are the people who create new automation systems or improve existing systems. Some are programmers, and others are librarians who use their library knowledge to develop the specifications for the systems.

After two years as a member services librarian at NELINET, I transferred to a more technical job in NELINET's library systems department. I worked with libraries' MARC records on tape, providing libraries with tape files of their OCLC cataloging records. This was the beginning of my experience with data conversion, which was to become my primary interest and specialty.

In 1981 I made another transition, to the world of commercial vendors, by joining CLSI, one of the earliest vendors of library automation systems. My first job there was a technical one, writing functional specifications for new system features as part of CLSI's development department. Later I became a conversion consultant, helping customer libraries load their MARC cataloging records into their CLSI systems, and still later I was promoted to conversion manager. My CLSI experience enabled me to broaden my knowledge of library automation. While my previous experience emphasized cataloging, at CLSI I also worked with other aspects of library operations, including circulation, acquisitions, and the online catalog. My library experience helped me gain credibility with the customers, some of whom were wary of commercial vendors.

While at CLSI I took some evening courses in computer programming. Although I did not do programming in my jobs, taking the courses gave me a better understanding of what computers could do for libraries. I became skilled as an intermediary between programmers and librarians, explaining and interpreting the requirements of each group to the other.

My conversion work at CLSI was absorbing and stressful at the same time. I increased my knowledge of data conversion, working in partnership with several library conversion vendors who did work for CLSI. The job enabled me to do technical work and also maintain a consulting relationship with libraries, and proved to be a good mix for me. But as the conversion function grew, I found that I was trying to do too much work with too little staff, a common problem for library automation vendors. I also found that I did not enjoy being a manager, even of a small staff. Although I very much enjoy working with people, I do not enjoy being responsible for other people's work in a supervisory relationship.

After five years at CLSI I accepted a job with SilverPlatter Information, one of the pioneer providers of CD-ROM products to libraries. At that time, all of SilverPlatter's development work was being done in England, and I was the sixth employee of the U.S. marketing and support office. I enjoyed working in a small office and doing a little bit of everything, from answering the phone and sending out sales literature to writing documentation and providing technical support to customers. It was exciting to work with a new technology, and I loved the occasional business trips to London, one of my favorite cities.

At SilverPlatter I also expanded my data conversion experience. SilverPlatter at that time worked primarily with journal citation databases, receiving the data on tape from the database owners and developing conversion programs to format the data for CD-ROM. I wrote the conversion specifications, or database designs, that the programmers used to develop the conversion programs. Since most of these databases were not in MARC format, I gained experience with converting a wide variety of other formats.

During my time at both CLSI and SilverPlatter, I sometimes thought about going off on my own and doing freelance work in library automation. Since I did not consider myself an entrepreneur, these thoughts probably would have amounted to nothing but daydreams if a freelancing opportunity had not been handed to me, so to speak, on a silver platter. A former CLSI colleague called and asked me if I was interested in doing some contract work for CLSI. When that solidified into a firm offer, I quit my job with SilverPlatter and negotiated a contract arrangement with them as well. In January 1989 I stopped being an employee and became self-employed.

I became a freelancer under ideal conditions that enabled me to avoid many of the problems that other freelancers encounter. I started with contracts with two companies, enough work to keep me busy almost full time. Because I was a known quantity to both of these companies, I was able to command a good hourly fee, and my husband's income meant that I did not have to worry about the dry spells that freelancers often experience. After a year of dividing my time between CLSI and SilverPlatter, I began to branch out to other projects. The contacts I had made during 14 years in the Boston area, working for three library automation companies, were an enormous asset; they enabled me to find work without much of a marketing effort on my part.

Although I enjoyed my freelance experience immensely, I would not necessarily recommend it to everyone. I loved the flexibility of setting my own schedule, not always working full time, and being able to do a lot of my work at home. I also enjoyed the feeling that I was my own boss, and was no longer part of a hierarchical organizational structure. Working for several libraries and companies at the same time enabled me to be more emotionally detached from my work, and not to become involved in office politics. But working on one's own requires self-discipline, and working at home can often be lonely. The flow of work for a freelancer is often variable; there may be times with very little work, followed by times with too much to do.

The variety of freelance work was both positive and negative to me. The varied projects that I worked on included database designs, system specifications, running a MARC output service for a serial subscription agent, freelance cataloging using three different automated cataloging systems, acting as temporary head of cataloging for a college library, and acting as temporary system administrator for a three-library consortium. Although I welcomed the variety, I also sometimes wished I could work on one thing in depth and not be constantly running from one thing to another. I also wished for more focus on my specialty—data conversion.

My happiness with freelancing did not stop me from applying for what sounded like the perfect job for me, dataloads analyst at the Research Libraries Group. RLG, the bibliographic utility that maintains the RLIN database, was looking for a senior technical person with experience in data conversion. Unlike some of the companies I've worked for, RLG provides a career path and appropriate salaries for experienced technical people, without pressuring them to become managers. As a bonus, RLG is located in the San Francisco Bay Area, where my husband and I wanted to relocate.

I joined RLG in November 1994. Despite some trepidation about "giving up my freedom," I find that I am enjoying the more structured life of a full-time job, particularly with RLG's academic environment and great flexibility in work schedules. My freelancing experience taught me how to be intellectually but not emotionally involved in my work. I am once again immersed full-time in data conversion, working with a variety of both MARC and non-MARC data from all over the world. Instead of writing conversion specifications for other people to implement, my job at RLG enables me to do the conversion programming myself and get even more technically involved in conversion work. I feel that all my past experience was the perfect preparation for this job, but also that I still have a lot to learn in the years to come.

20.

Working for a Bibliographic Utility

By Linda Robinson

I have been a librarian for 13 years. For seven years I have worked in libraries, and for six years I have worked for OCLC Online Computer Library Center. OCLC is the largest bibliographic utility in the world, providing more than 20,000 libraries in 60 countries with such services as cataloging, reference, retrospective conversion, and interlibrary loan. In an organization of over 1,000 employees, experienced librarians make up a high proportion of the workforce.

Librarians work in many areas of OCLC including cataloging services, reference services, and the development division; they cover all levels of employment from support staff to vice presidents. Some staff hold both library science and computer science degrees. OCLC builds services for libraries; therefore, experienced librarians make important contributions to the corporation.

Why choose to work for a bibliographic utility? For me the answer was relatively easy. I enjoyed the automation field within library science. I had experience with OCLC products in my positions in public and college libraries. I wanted to be a part of a corporation on the cutting edge of library technology. I felt I had ideas to contribute based on my experience. Since most of my background in libraries centered on technical services and automated systems, I applied for a position in the cataloging services section. Although the choice to work for OCLC was not hard, it was still an adjustment to come from a traditional library setting into corporate America.

How I Got Here

When I entered library school at the University of Texas my intention was to become a cataloger. I had little paid experience working in a library before going into graduate school. As a student I worked in the University of Texas Library acquisitions department. I knew I wanted to work in the library field, but I had only a vague notion of what area in which to work. I knew what catalogers did, so that sounded like a good place to start my education. As I worked through my required classes, however, I noticed that I enjoyed working with computers, automation, and all aspects of the library field related to automation. It never occurred to me that I would be working in a nonlibrary setting within seven years of graduation. My intention was to settle into a university or college technical services environment. That's where I began with my first job.

I accepted a job in a small college library in New Jersey as the acquisitions librarian. This was an entry-level job based on my experience with acquisitions as a student worker. Even in this position, I was able to learn about the local system, about OCLC, and about automation. I showed flexibility and willingness to take on new duties. Soon I was supervising local system data entry. This fueled my interest in automated systems and in the importance of accurate, accessible bibliographic records. They soon promoted me to collection development librarian, reporting to the head of collection development. My duties then included supervision of the automated systems within technical services, troubleshooting OCLC acquisitions and cataloging subsystem problems, and continuation of any conversion projects.

My next position was circulation librarian at a public library in Massachusetts. I wanted to continue to learn about all facets of library work. Therefore, moving from a college library to a public library and moving from "behind the scenes" to public services made sense. I had heard the stories about the difficulties librarians faced when trying to "cross over" from academic to public library settings, but I did not have a problem. Learning about public services certainly put an entirely different slant on my understanding of libraries. It furthered my conviction that access is everything. My philosophy became grounded in the idea that all library employees should be cross-trained—staff gain an understanding of how important their job is in the scheme of things and they gain an understanding of how important others' jobs are as well.

I continued to increase my experience with automation, as this position was not only responsible for the circulation desk, but also for the circulation system and served as liaison to the automation consortium. As in my previous job, the willingness to expand my education and experience opened new doors for me. After one year in this position, a larger public library in the area offered me the newly created position of automation librarian.

As the automation librarian position was new, there were many trails to blaze. I established new procedures. I even wrote my own job description! I was the point person for all automation-related requests, problems, and complaints. etc. I traveled to the eight branches as needed, to train, fix, and troubleshoot. I attended regular meetings of the automation consortium, giving input on improvements to the system and gaining insight into what it takes to make an automation consortium run.

The Move to OCLC

From Massachusetts, I moved to Dublin, Ohio, and accepted my first position at OCLC as a product support specialist in the cataloging services section. Staff in this section supported member libraries by answering calls about the cataloging products, by serving on the development team for new services, and by serving as product managers for existing cataloging products. At the time, PRISM Services was in the middle stages of development.

As mentioned earlier, OCLC views experienced librarians as a valuable commodity. A "Users Council" of practicing librarians participates in OCLC's governance by electing six members of the 15-member OCLC Board of Trustees and by meeting three times a year to provide OCLC with advice and counsel.

From that first position at OCLC, I received a promotion to Product Support Specialist II and then to the cataloging services section as manager. When the position of access services specialist became available, it was a good time for me to make a change. I moved into my current position in the Information Center.

Position Responsibilities

Product Support Specialist I became a member of the PRISM Service product development team. My recent real-world library experience proved to be helpful. There are many facets to product development at OCLC. The goal is to make a product that suits customer needs and is consistent with OCLC's public purposes of furthering access to information and reducing information costs. Our project was to revamp the user interface in cataloging to make it more efficient. PRISM replaced OCLC's original shared cataloging subsystem in 1992.

In order to reach this goal, I had to make sure I knew as much as possible about our customer base and about the product being developed. There are many documents involved in a product development lifecycle, from product idea and business plans to test plans and implementation plans. The product teams are broken into two basic parts: marketing and development. Each part of the team has a development schedule that includes milestones marked by completion of lifecycle documents and completion of components of the actual software.

Product managers wear many hats. They write marketing documents. They review user documentation. They write test plans. They test the software from a user standpoint. They negotiate with the developers and advocate for the users. Switching among these hats many times during a day improves the odds of being a successful product manager.

Section Manager. As section manager for cataloging services, like any library department manager, I had to make sure that the specialists in the section had what they needed to get their jobs done. This meant anything from budgeting for equipment to mediating disagreements between coworkers. There are always opportunities to help pave the road to a successful product introduction. One standard responsibility as section manager was hiring staff and reviewing their performance. I also maintained the section budget and submitted the annual budget requests to my manager. My favorite part was being able to assist staff in making progress on a project. I had to know who to talk to and when and how. Interpersonal communication skills are extremely important in such a job. Each person has a different communication style, and in order to achieve success I had to know what style to use and when to use it. To me, this was always an exciting challenge. Assertiveness and confidence are also important traits for a successful manager. Indecisiveness does not help you or your staff.

Access Services Specialist. The Information Center's mission is to make sure that OCLC staff have the resources and information needed to get their jobs done when and where they want them done. That mission fuels my responsibility too. One of my projects is to create an automation information network to deliver as many of our services to staff desks as possible. In this age of the Internet and hypertext, this project has taken on an exciting, cutting-edge flavor. As with my previous positions, I had to jump into this responsibility and learn as much about the technology as possible. I wanted to make sure I was delivering an efficient, powerful product. Because of my experience as a product manager, it was easy for me to view this internal project in the same way. I can use what I have learned so that implementation of this internal project follows a path similar to that of any of OCLC's external products. Customer service is the goal.

In addition to my automation responsibilities, I am also a reference librarian. Working on both sides of the library—technical and public services—helps improve my skills and insights in both areas. I can then tailor our automated systems to support reference needs. Seeing how technology works, I can steer users to the appropriate services through automation.

How to Succeed in a Corporate Environment

Although one might say I am back in a traditional library setting, I feel there is a significant difference between working in a public or college library and working in any position in a corporation.

To be successful in a corporate setting you must be flexible. The importance of flexibility cannot be overstated. If you are one who prefers an unchanging job, you do not want to work within a corporate environment. If, however, you are like me, and prefer a changeable, flexible work setting, then the corporate life might be for you. Here are some things I discovered when I began working for OCLC and moved away from a traditional library setting:

- Corporations, whether not-for-profit or for-profit, must pay attention to the "bottom line."
- Restructuring and reorganization is a fact of life.
- Those who are willingly flexible will probably succeed, those who are not will not be happy in this environment.
- Ambiguity and change occur when corporate direction shifts. This happens on a regular basis.
- Hard work is to be expected.
- Opportunities to move up as well as sideways are plentiful for those who make a mark.

I made an excellent choice coming to work for OCLC. It suits my personality and my work style. A move from a library setting to a corporate setting should not be considered lightly. I know of a number of librarians who do not enjoy this type of atmosphere. You must be in touch with your own work style, your goals, and your tolerance levels for various situations in order to make an educated decision.

21.

Contract Services

by Sheila Hess

Several years ago I was thrust into my midlife crisis. The family business I had been managing was sold, and, at the age of 49, I had to find a new career. I read *What Color Is Your Parachute*, took the Myers-Briggs test, and finally went to a counselor who helped me realize I needed to find a way to integrate all my experiences so that I could focus on seeking the career that would be the culmination of everything that went before. Obviously, this would take some time, and a lot of thought. One question I kept coming back to was, "What else can I do with my library degree?"

Much of the following article describes my background and experience, what I learned from each situation, and how I integrated the disparate parts into a most satisfying whole. I hope this will be useful to those of you facing similar situations, wondering what to do next and how you can use your library degree to help develop a niche for yourself.

Moving to New York City directly after college, I was alienated by the school system and decided that, instead of being a teacher, I would be a librarian. I went to work for the Queens Borough Public Library as a librarian trainee, meaning I had to go to library school and get my M.L.S. to start the traditional career path. During the three years I was a trainee, I worked in each area of the library, including reference, children's, and technical services, and I did clerical work. I have always been grateful for the chance to see how it all came together.

I went to Pratt Institute Library School in Brooklyn. Riding the subway back to Queens at night I became friendly with a fellow student from Pratt. Although our ages were far apart (she was 60, I was 25), our interests were not and she asked me if I would substitute for her while she went away that summer for six weeks. She was the librarian at the Planned Parenthood national office on Madison Avenue, and I was thrilled with the opportunity to work in an organization with values I shared. Thus I left Queens Borough just after receiving my M.L.S. and spent the summer working as a special librarian. In addition to ordering, checking in, routing, filing, and the other routine jobs the director (or substitute director) of a one-person special library needed to do (in preautomation days), I also spent my time there developing a specialized cataloging/classification system. This was an extremely useful experience in that I learned to evaluate information and determine how each piece related to the others.

At the end of the summer, I moved to Allentown, Pennsylvania, where my husband had taken a job. I applied for the position of director of the Emmaus Public Library, in a suburb of Allentown. I was hired, the first professional librarian in what had been an all-volunteer library. The library had just moved to brand-new quarters and was the community's pride. The volunteers remained; I was the only paid staff member. This was my first management experience, and my M.L.S. was not much help. Not only had I not had any classes, or any experience, in management, but these people were here because it was their community library and they did not depend on me for their livelihoods. I learned a lot about tact, working with people, learning from nonprofessionals, how to build up a library, how to work with a library board, and how to handle sticky situations. After a year in Emmaus, I became pregnant and left the library.

Several years later, having finished childbearing, we moved to New Jersey. There I got the job as branch librarian of a new community library that was to be the first branch in the Somerset County Library System. Not only were there volunteers to work with, but I also had a paid staff of paraprofessionals to manage. Once again, this library was extremely important to the residents who loved living there and were very proud of their community's history. At the same time, we were the first branch in a countywide system that was intent on getting the other community libraries in the county to join the system. This idea was met with a lot of animosity from some of the libraries. It was here that I learned a great deal about politics and the necessity of persuasion, that facts alone are not enough, but need to be presented in the right light. It was here that I first came across entrenched librarians who would fight change because they perceived it as a threat. But it was also here that I learned that most librarians are service-oriented and will do whatever is in their power, regardless of cost, to satisfy their patrons. This service orientation is a lesson that burned into my soul.

Once again we moved, leaving New Jersey to follow my husband's career, this time to northern Virginia. I took a job with the National Organization for Women (NOW), creating and directing a library for the national office in Washington, D.C. As at Planned Parenthood, I needed to find a way to organize all the materials in their specialized fields of interest, and I designed a classification/cataloging system for the files. I found my library degree helped me to organize the information in a logical order, going from the broad to the specific. I created contacts, did research at the Library of Congress and other places, wrote papers, and did anything required to provide the information the staff needed. It was the time of the fight for the ERA and the extension; I learned firsthand about the country's political system, and had a "hands-on" lesson about interest groups, political influence, and the legal and political processes in this country. I learned to lobby those in a position of power—how to appeal to them to do what I wanted. It was very different to be the librarian in an organization at the center of political controversy, never knowing what I would be doing each day, than to be a librarian in a public library with a well-defined role. I was always pleased that I had chosen a profession with so many options.

After three years at NOW, I left and formed a partnership with Virginia Harris, an academic librarian who came to NOW as a volunteer to work on the ERA and never went back home. We formed Harris-Hess Associates, with the intent of working with libraries to provide specialized services. We had to learn to market ourselves, to write proposals, and to figure costs, expenses, and profits. Our library experience got us "in the door," but the rest was figuring out what the library really wanted and giving it to them at the right price—and managing to make money. Our first major contract was a retrospective conversion project with a university law library, and we did very well, expecting that this would continue. We learned the hard way that this business was very uneven—we were either in the chips or eating them. Finally, my own situation mandated that I have a regular income, and I began to think of how to find the right job to use my acquired skills. It was at this moment that I received a phone call from my brother inviting me to come into the family business. And so I became the manager of a hardware/lumber/building materials/door-and-window supply business!

In this new venture, I did not think there would be anything applicable from my library background. However, I soon realized that my experience in creating classification systems helped me in developing product catalogs. Even more, my commitment to public service helped me to focus on the need for satisfying the customer, even in the days before total quality management and reengineering. I thought that I would spend the remainder of my working life here, but we were caught in the building malaise of the late 1980s and, luckily, were able to sell the business. And so I had to decide what to do with the rest of my life.

I wanted to return to the world of libraries, but did not know where I fit. It had been a long time since I had worked in a library, and I could not figure out how to integrate my experiences into something I could sell a prospective employer. Then I saw a help-wanted ad for a project manager with a library degree and business background. It seemed like a perfect fit—I had not even known this type of job existed—and I immediately responded. I got the job, my entry back into the library world (so I hoped), and managed the company's contract with a federal agency library. The contract was to create records for the library's database; my job as manager was to be the intermediary between my company and the library's contract manager, and to make sure that we met the requirements of the contract and also made money. After two and one-half years, I wanted to find a more creative opportunity and, with great good fortune, I happened to read the help wanted advertisements the day that a company was looking for someone to manage its library contracts office. Thus, I was able to move from being the project manager for one specific contract to work for a company with a large library division for library contracting and temporary staffing, in a position that offered me the opportunity to use everything I had learned and to continue to grow.

The company I work for, TeleSec Staffing Services, has been in existence since 1948 and has had a library division since 1972. Many of the people in either the temporary or contracting branches have been with the company a long time, some their entire careers. A company like TeleSec offers many options for librarians—from being a member of the permanent staff to working as a "contract perm" or a "temp." Librarians staff the library division in different positions. For instance, as the manager of the contract services branch, I manage 12 projects, some that are very small (cataloging a small number of selected monographs) and some that are quite large (several multiyear federal contracts for cataloging, shelving, acquisitions, staffing support, interlibrary loan). Another branch of the library division is responsible for placing temporary staff in libraries. The manager of this branch is also a librarian and her specialty is selling customer service. In addition, the library division has a library contracts administrator who uses her knowledge of libraries to write proposals, monitor contracts, keep statistics, and provide support for the parts of the division.

TeleSec also provides choices for librarians who wish to work in a library setting, including working full-time or part-time—in one location or for a variety of clients, working as a "permanent temporary" employee, or working on a "temp to perm" basis. There is a great deal of flexibility—the variety of libraries; the opportunity to work as a "temp" or as a "contract perm" (staying with one contract), or as both at different times; the opportunity to become a permanent employee in a "try before you buy" position. Library contract work provides the opportunity to use all your skills.

Libraries in the 1990s are in a world of restructuring, "rightsizing," and lean budgets. More and more library administrators are considering outsourcing specific tasks such as cataloging, book processing, and shelving. The contractors who take on these projects must have the same professional background and training as the librarians in the institutions who are doing the contracting. Library contracting is probably one of the true growth industries for librarians and I have found it to be an exciting and challenging field, and the perfect answer to the question I had of what else I could do with my library degree.

PART III

Independent Librarians: On Their Own

22.

A Consultant: Bringing Children and Books Together

by Caroline Feller Bauer

It was our senior year in college and we were all sitting around having a cup of coffee and asking, "What are we going to do next year?" One girl said, "I guess I'll marry Tom." Another thought she might go to Katherine Gibbs secretarial school—in those days, even after graduation from the most expensive college in America, becoming a secretary was one of the best options open to women. At least other girls had some ideas. I didn't have the slightest notion about what I was going to do next year or ever after.

On our third cup of coffee, the telephone rang. It was my mother who said, "I just had lunch with the librarian at the United Nations law library. It sounds like a great profession. You can do it part time or full time, anywhere in the world. You can be a public librarian, a school librarian, a law librarian, work for a newspaper or in the library of a large company. The best part is that it requires another degree so you can go to school next year." So here was the perfect solution to the "what will I do next year" dilemma.

Now, many years later, Martha did marry Tom and, at last count, three other men; Ann did go to Katie Gibbs and ultimately into the family business; and I did go to library school. I didn't even wait until fall, but entered in the summer session, not because I was so eager to begin but because my summer job, teaching water skiing, had ended abruptly when I crashed the boat into a dock and I quit before I could be fired.

I cried all through library school. I hated the discipline of Sears, of Dewey—this was long before LC, before databases. My mother promised me a Thunderbird when I graduated, but by the time I finally got my degree, the cute T-Bird had been replaced by a boring sedan. However, I was now a librarian.

My first position was with the reference department at the New York Public Library. We answered questions like "Where was pastrami invented?" and "How do fireflies light?" Next I was assigned to the Central Children's Room. This was so long before the "information age" that one of my duties as a children's librarian was to recopy, by hand, catalog cards to a larger format. I was chastised while working there for not wearing hose during the summer in that stifling room that had no air conditioning. I learned a lot, however, about children's literature and authors, and worked with readers—both children and adults—on a daily basis. I was also the visiting storyteller for the branch libraries.

Subsequently, I worked in two private school libraries in New York City, trying out my ideas for book talks and storytelling on the students. Each of the schools had a lot of books that needed to be weeded. I ruthlessly discarded them to the accompaniment of wails and cries from the administration: "We won't have any books left." True.

My next stop was Colorado, where I was the librarian at a private boarding school. Same problem: many books not worth keeping or even giving away. I'd learned my lesson, however, and crept out in the middle of the night to discard them into the local dumpster. At this time I had opportunities to speak to children at the local public library as well as give book talks at the school. It was satisfying that the listeners always laughed.

At this same time I was the local radio announcer for Aspen, a ski resort—good practice for speaking extemporaneously. Also, I toured the country with a sports show, performing in a kayak—good experience for learning not to be shy in front of an audience. If you appear before 10,000 people twice a day in a bikini, it's really no problem to speak fully clothed to a group of a mere 500.

And then I was a college professor. How did I get the job? I wrote a letter to the University of California Library School, asking about the need for someone to teach children's literature. Nervy, eh? I got such an appointment at the new library school in Oregon. The university and its resources were a revelation. I haunted the graphic arts department and was introduced to all sorts of media ideas. Since you need a Ph.D. to make a career of college teaching, I got one. The degree is in communications, and with my expertise in children's literature and experience with television I took a leave of absence from the university and taught college-level courses on a PBS affiliate. The courses were directed to library school graduate students and education majors. Each of the courses required a "viewers guide" which meant I had to write four books in one year and produce 90 videotapes. One of the study guides led to my first real book.

Once I had a book, a degree, work, and speaking experience I became a . . . ? When people ask me, "What do you do?" I want to reply that "I'm a librarian," but since I haven't worked in a library for many years, I say something like, "I'm an author/lecturer."

What I do now is travel around the United States and overseas speaking to educators, librarians, and children. I used to count how many cities I had visited; now I count only countries. I've lectured in all 50 states and in 61 countries. I give seminars, banquet speeches, and keynote speeches, make school visits, and do author appearances. The ideas I use in my talks have become books, giving me the "I am an author" claim. Sound interesting? Well it is not boring. The drawback is that I like my husband, my ferret, and the beach, but I'm hardly ever home, traveling about 120 days per year.

The consulting game is mostly a word-of-mouth business. You must be seen to get work. People have to know your name and your address so that they can reach you. Once I had a call from a former student telling me that while visiting a librarian in Houston, Texas, she had learned about the "terrific workshop" I put on. She asked if I could come to her town and do the same. "Sure," I said. "Where do you live?" "Saudi Arabia," she said. I've now been to Saudi Arabia three times, presenting to students, staff, and parents around the kingdom.

Someone will see me at a lecture; three years later that same person will be vice president in charge of programs for an organization and I'll get an invitation. I've been in Oklahoma several times to make presentations to early childhood educators, to Maryland to speak at conference luncheons, to Kansas for all-day seminars. In Shanghai, I did a one-day presentation in a school; when the principal of the school returned to the United States, she invited me to spend two weeks speaking to 18 schools in her district in Washington.

I've had to be assertive, too. On my quest to speak to people in all 50 states I've had to create opportunities. With just three states remaining to reach my goal, I found myself in Alexandria, Egypt, in an airport with many other Americans waiting for a flight. I met an educator from South Carolina, one of the elusive states. I sat down next to her and told her what I do. When I returned home I sent her my resume and references and that is how I got to South Carolina.

I write lots of letters, faxes, and e-mail. I respond to people who write with questions, comments and compliments. Everyone is impressed that I answer my mail. I still prefer "real letters" because you can write them anywhere—at basketball games, poolside, or the dinner table. I often take letters that need to be answered, put them in stamped and addressed envelopes, and write the letters on the plane to my next engagement.

To do my work—to be a successful presenter—you need two things: something to say and an engaging way to say it. My lectures are variations on the theme of ideas to bring children and books together for leisure reading. The talks are almost always of the "show-and-tell" variety. I demonstrate how to use puppets, magic tricks, posters, regalia, toys, and other visuals to encourage readers. As you can imagine, this requires much fetching and carrying. I used to travel with six suitcases; now I'm down to two giant cases with wheels. When I hear a lecturer say, "I would have brought the book, but I'm traveling," I'm always tempted to jump up and say "What do you mean you couldn't bring it? I lug stuffed animals to Malaysia and Taiwan."

One of the questions I'm asked by children at author visits is, "How much money do you make?" I know adults want to know this information too, but are reticent to ask. And, I am not going to tell—only the IRS knows. I charge an honorarium, plus expenses, for my lectures. I try to stay competitive with other presenters by asking them what they charge. At this writing I am a bit under the "going rate" but will rectify this soon. A good full-time speaker should be able to gross over $1000,000 annually, especially if he or she is offering products to sell as well.

The best part is that I've made a lot of friends; I've received recognition (a woman on an airplane recognized me and was reading one of my books); I am never bored; I keep searching for new material and so keep up with the publications and the people in the profession; and I had a great mom who suggested library school in the first place.

23.

A Library Building Consultant

by Nolan Lushington

Working as a reference librarian in the Philadelphia Free Library in 1960 prepared me for practically any profession I could imagine. In a great public library you quickly become aware of the exciting variety of problems that a library solves each day for an amazing variety of people.

Coming to the Greenwich (Connecticut) Public Library in the early 1960s as a reference librarian I became aware of some major physical constraints in trying to convert a former department store into a suburban library. The floors were too weak to support the weight of books, and most library users ignored our front pedestrian entrance and came in through the back doors from our parking lot. Librarians at the reference desk were so far away from the books that they jokingly referred to their work as roller skate reference.

Who had perpetrated this farce of a building solution on an otherwise reasonably well-run library? Problems like this really get the mind juices flowing and fortunately I had some interesting people to bounce ideas off: a boss, Jack Bryant, alert to the drama of library service; a staff eager to try new solutions; and an inspiring board president, Marie Cole, whose advice was "don't wait for library patrons to tell you what they want, show them what they can have."

When we got around to tackling some of these building problems in a major way I found an innovative, young architect, Willis Mills, Jr., interested in trying some new solutions. We designed together a book box addition to the library that turned the entrance around to face the parking lot, placed a clearly organized 100,000-volume clear-span bookstack right next to a large multistaffed information center with a backlighted, foot-high "INFORMATION" sign above it that announced its purpose to everyone immediately upon entering the building.

In 1970 I was elected president of the Connecticut Library Association, and the state trustee organization invited me to give a talk on library buildings. Preparing for the talk, I looked in the literature like a good reference librarian and found that with the exception of the Wheeler and Githens book on big library buildings, and a neat little book by Rohlf Myller, an architect, there were no medium-sized, practical manuals on planning small library buildings. I scrambled around and took a lot of slides of libraries and gave a reasonably provocative talk on redesigning libraries as information centers rather than circulating libraries. The result was an invitation to do a consulting job for the village of Washington, Connecticut, way up north in the rural part of the state. My investigations led to the advice that they weed the collection and forget about an addition to the beautiful gem of a building. I thought it would probably be my first and last building consulting job. Fortunately, the trustees felt it was good advice and I was recommended for another job.

In 1972 through the Council on Library Resources I received a mid-career fellowship to study medium-sized, newly designed English public libraries. A month in England on a Britrail pass allowed me to see a dozen libraries and I began to formulate a process for thinking about library buildings based on the user rather than the staff point of view. In addition it became clear that the process of designing a building should start with an evaluation of the library users' behavior. How did the user find a book? What was the book-finding sequence? How was reference service differentiated from book circulation activities? Asking the right questions was the path to rational design, and that path was often littered with the stumbling blocks of dysfunctional architecture, aesthetic barriers to service, and "it's always been that way" attitudes.

Returning to the Greenwich Library, I became involved in a series of seven internal additions/renovations over a two-year tenure as director.

A series of committee assignments with the Buildings and Equipment Section of the Library Administration and Management Association of the American Library Association (ALA) began in 1974, and culminated in my becoming chairman of the section in 1984. This group seemed to be a confusing blend of active, change-oriented consultants and stuffy diehards who were incensed that anyone would challenge the time-tested ways of traditional library design. To think of a small library as a user-oriented information center rather than a fake-Georgian circulating library was not always a comfortable concept for many consultants and librarians in the 1970s. I have never been able to make up my mind as to whether activities in ALA hurt or helped my consulting work.

Most of my jobs have come from word-of-mouth recommendations, or from planning seminars, which I was invited to give starting in the 1980s. These seminars in Arkansas, Pennsylvania, California, Connecticut, Rhode Island, and finally at Harvard University have been wonderfully stimulating experiences with constant challenges from a changing audience.

In 1987 I was fortunate to obtain a position as an assistant professor at Southern Connecticut State University. This made it possible for me to continue my consulting work on a slightly expanded scale, to work with young people going into the library profession, and best of all to work with Dr. James Kusack, a library school professor with a strong background in research and computers and a rigorous intellectual approach to the building planning process. Over the next few years we worked on several consulting projects. We eventually wrote both a book emphasizing the new public library roles as design guides and a library evaluation process as a starting and ending point for the planning process. My vision of the process is described below.

The Library Improvement Planning Process

The library improvement planning process is a highly interactive, complex task involving the library governing body, administrative staff, the consultant, and the architect in a wide variety of interdependent activities. It serves the following varying purposes:

- Identifies overall size and general cost of the project
- Assists staff in determining space needs, capacities, and spatial relationships
- Provides architect with program for design
- Provides staff with a document for the review of architectural plans

The process, in brief, includes these steps:

- Mission, Goals, and Objectives
  — Review and discuss the mission, goals, and obectives of the library
- Community Analysis
  — Analyze library history and community demographics
- Library Analysis
  — Conduct focus groups in the community
  — Interview library and political/economic community leaders
  — Evaluate library use and existing physical facilities in order

to develop library improvement objectives.

Library Building Program Preparation

- Work with the staff to prepare a brief outline program delineating major functional areas and capacities needed.
- Discuss this preliminary program with the library governing body and town fiscal representatives.
- Work with the staff to prepare detailed, functional area sheets for each library functional area. Information will include
  - name function and square footage
  - occupants, equipment, furniture, and storage capacity
  - acoustical, computer, environmental, equipment, lighting, shelving, security systems, wiring, flexibility needs
- Prepare a preliminary library building program.
- Analyze alternatives with the library director to determine how a preliminary program could be accomplished. This may be a renovation of the existing facility, an addition, or an entirely new building.
- Prepare the final library building program.
- Present the final document to an audience to be determined (usually the funding authority).
- Work with the architect on design development and further refine cost estimates.
- Work with the architect on construction documents and bidding.
  - Work with the architect and design consultants on furniture and equipment, lighting, and graphics.
  - Work with the staff and architectural team on moving and installation.
  - Conduct post-occupancy evaluation after the first year of occupancy to determine the changes necessary to respond to new library uses.

I find it difficult to imagine how such planning could be done without library education and experience. Actively experiencing just how a librarian works with a reference question, talking with dozens of library users, watching people use libraries, discussing this use with other librarians, and evaluating library plans with architects are ways to learn this skill.

I have now completed over 150 library consulting jobs over a period of 25 years, and every one is different. The work is constantly changing and evolving. Solutions can never be the same because the community and the ways that libraries are used are constantly changing.

24.

Hedging Your Bets: Working Outside and Inside the Library

by John Cohn

Background

David Genaway has characterized the consultant as the "modern Horatio Alger"—totally reliant on self-generated income, with a livelihood always at risk.[1] This paper is directed at those among us for whom Horatio Alger may not be a role model, yet who are interested in becoming consultants. Its purpose is to highlight some issues important to those who are contemplating doing consulting work while continuing a full-time job within an organization.

Genaway defines a consultant as one who "gives professional advice, analyzes problems and makes recommendations for solving them, provides short-term training sessions, or negotiates the best price from vendors." People go into such work for a variety of reasons. For some it is a way to reestablish a source of income after losing a job. For others it is simply a matter of preference; there are those who favor project-oriented work to the more routinized activity of the traditional nine-to-five jobs.

By the mid-1980s, 13 years after completing library school and six years into the directorship of a community college library, I decided it was time to vary the pace of the work I was doing. Though satisfied with my position at the college, I nevertheless wanted to apply, in a different context, the automation and management skills I had developed over the years. Part of my motivation was economic—I wanted to supplement my earnings in anticipation of having to put two sons through college some years in the future. My primary impetus, however, was simply to expand the range of my professional involvement within a field of work I enjoyed.

Not giving up my full-time job meant having to wedge this new activity into my life without neglecting family or leisure time. I knew that I would have to do the work on vacation time, in the evenings, and on weekends. Everyone handles such things in his or her own way.

To strengthen and enhance what I was preparing to offer the world, I decided to approach a colleague about the possibility of joining me as a consulting partner. Ann Kelsey and I had worked together at the college for two years, and I had come to respect her knowledge of computers, her administrative sense, and her ability to reason clearly and concisely. Ann liked the idea, and we began to plan the creation of an independent consulting firm that we eventually decided to call "DocuMentors." DocuMentors is an independent consulting firm that specializes in planning and implementing automated systems in libraries, media centers, corporate information centers, and consortia. We also provide program development and evaluation, management planning, organizational assessment, and training.

I made the decision to approach Ann after giving the matter considerable thought. I called Ann a "colleague" but she was (and is) the associate director of the college library, reporting directly to me—that is, a subordinate. Thus, although we accomplish our work at the college in what I would term a collegial fashion, we operate in what is nonetheless a traditional, hierarchical, institutional structure. We would, on the other hand, base the emerging partnership on the principle of professionals working together as equals. We did discuss this issue thoroughly before organizing the partnership. Ten years into our consulting work, we believe that the dichotomy has not posed any problems, either at the college or for our collaboration on the outside.

The more critical issue that most independent consultants who are also employees within an institution are likely to face is the "conflict of interest" issue. The rest of the paper focuses on this question.

Independent Work Versus Institutional Obligation

"Conflict of interest" refers, of course, to a clash between public interest and an individual's private pecuniary interest, arising when a government employee's personal or financial interest conflicts or appears to conflict with his official responsibility.[2] My use of the phrase here is in the broader sense of one's personal interest, as opposed to that of the institution, whether the interest is strictly financial in nature or related simply to the commitment of time.

At my institution, every employee periodically receives a memorandum from the human resources department with a reminder about our state's "Guidelines on Outside Employment for Public Institutions of Higher Education" (N.J.A.C. 9:2–10:2). The guidelines provide that full-time employees at public institutions may engage in outside employment only if the outside employment does not:

1. constitute a conflict of interest;
2. occur at a time when the employee is expected to perform his or her assigned duties; or
3. diminish the employee's efficiency in performing his or her primary work obligation at the institution.

There is additional language in the code concerning work that is "regular or continuing," for which written approval is required, and work that is "irregular or infrequent," for which written approval is *not* required. In either case, however, outside employment must meet the three requirements listed above.

The following examples, provided in the statutes, of outside employment that may be classified as "regular or continuing," illustrate the intent of the guidelines:

1. . . . any teaching assignment at another educational institution except for a single or limited number of guest lectures;
2. . . . a clinical or professional practice (for example, in clinical psychology or law);
3. . . . appointment as a consultant to a school district, corporation or other public or private enterprise for an indeterminate period even if actual time demands are intermittent; or,
4. . . . operation, or management of, or employment in any enterprise related or unrelated to a faculty member's professional interest.

This list also applies to management and administrative staff even where, as at my institution, they are not considered "faculty."

What all this means in my state, and no doubt elsewhere as well, is that you must be careful not to let your consulting work interfere with your full-time job. How "interference" is defined will vary with local statute and/or institutional practice. Basically, it is a matter of separating your outside work from what you do on the job. The most obvious way of doing that is simply to make sure that you request personal or vacation leave time to do your consulting work—and to keep careful records of all approvals. Also, it is important to avoid any overt indications that the line between your two "lives" is blurry.

Consider the following true story: Some years ago, a staff member proudly showed me her new business card for some work-on-the-side she was doing. I commended her on the creativity of the card's design. Then I spotted two telephone numbers in the corner of the card. One of them was her personal business number, the other was her college number. I asked her about that and she said that she really did not expect any calls at the college and would not use it in her consulting work. Nevertheless, I suggested that she have her cards reprinted without the college number, a recommendation with which she was not happy, although she understood the problem and reprinted the cards. Several days later, I received a call from the college president. Somehow, he had seen the original card and was concerned. I assured him that the mistake had been corrected, and that was that. You simply must know the limits of your institution in matters such as these.

Another dimension of the conflict issue has to do with how you choose your clients. Our personal rule of thumb is as follows: if the potential client is one with whom we have ongoing, sustained contact as part of our jobs at the college, we will not undertake a separate consultation. For example, several years ago, we did a brief automation consultation for a school district. Our library was not then, nor is it now, involved with that school district, but we also received a consulting request from a public library that was part of the local automated network in which the college library actively participated. That was simply too close for comfort and we turned that job down.

Occasionally, Ann or I will visit another institution in response to a request for assistance, and will do so on college time. This is the usual networking that always occurs between and among colleagues. When the result of such a visit is a request for more time, or a deeper level of consultation than would be reasonable for us to do as part of our jobs, we suggest undertaking future visits, or whatever other activity is requested, as part of an independent consultation. Most people understand this distinction.

Conclusion

Working for an institution is compatible with working for yourself as long as you are mindful of maintaining the necessary degree of separation required. Your institution may, in fact, look upon the outside work you do as enhancing your stature and your worth to the institution. What you want to avoid is a sense that your commitment to the job is less than it should be because you are distracted elsewhere. Much of this may be very subjective and perception-driven, but it is something you must consider if you plan to maintain a traditional job successfully and an "outside" one as well.

Notes

1. "What Makes a Consultant a Consultant?" in *Using Consultants in Libraries and Information Centers*, ed. Edward D. Garten (Westport, Conn.: Greenwood Press), 29–37.
2. *Black's Law Dictionary*, 6th ed. (St.Paul, MN: West Publishing, 1990) 299.

25.

Advice and Assistance to Libraries

by Rhea Joyce Rubin

I'm an independent library consultant. Somehow this job title always requires definition. Whether I'm talking to fellow librarians at conferences or inquisitive seat-mates on airlines, I always have to explain that I am a professional librarian who advises and assists libraries.

In my case, I was originally an outreach librarian and I still work primarily in that area. I usually work with the staffs of libraries to extend their services to people who cannot use them in traditional ways. One such group is people who cannot physically visit the library (for example, those who live in remote areas or in residential institutions). I have established jail library services, worked with library programs in nursing homes, and evaluated staff and patient libraries in hospitals. Another underserved group is people who need library materials in special formats (such as people with disabilities). After the last census, many libraries discovered that their communities included more older adults than they had realized, or than they were serving. I assisted some libraries in identifying the older adults, ascertaining their information needs and reading interests, and planning programs of service designed specifically for them. Since the Americans with Disabilities Act was passed in 1990, I have helped libraries to evaluate their services in light of the new law and work cooperatively with people with disabilities to make necessary changes to ensure program access. I don't "do" computers or buildings—the two areas most often requiring consultants—but instead concentrate on services. About half of my work is planning and evaluation studies in this area; the other half is training staff to work with new patrons or in new ways. I also facilitate meetings, teach short courses, develop bibliographies, coordinate special projects, and assist in long-range planning. My work varies day to day and my projects change year to year.

From There to Here

Like many other consultants, I backed into consulting while working full time. I did not decide to become a consultant initially, but found myself in demand as one because of unique subject expertise. At first, I received requests for speeches, workshops, and classes based on two recently published books. Next I got requests to teach on other topics I knew about. Then I was asked to evaluate or establish services in my areas of expertise. So I took vacation time, and then administrative leave, to do consulting and training jobs offered to me.

I soon found that I knew nothing about the processes of either training or consulting, so I set out to learn. I read, joined professional associations for trainers and consultants, and attended classes and seminars. I knew these were helpful when clients asked me to develop courses or to do studies on other topics based on my successes as a consultant rather than as a subject expert. In 1980 I decided to leave library administration and make consulting my career. I enjoyed using my new skills in consulting, communications, collaboration, and course design. And I liked the independence to select my own jobs, set my own schedule, budget my own resources, and work when and where I chose.

At that time, I was receiving enough requests for consulting to fill about five or ten hours per week—in addition to the 40-plus hours I had been working at my "real" job. A part-time job fit perfectly into my plans to have a baby, so I decided to give consulting a chance. (My husband was working full-time.) The timing was excellent. During the years I wanted to be at home, I worked part-time and when my daughter was old enough to be in school, my work slowly increased to full-time.

Pros and Cons

I love being an independent library consultant. I appreciate working alone (I don't miss supervising employees one bit) and selecting which projects to work on. I relish solving problems and enjoy meeting lots of people. I enjoy the continuing challenges and the frequent travel. In a "typical month" (which is hard to describe since few months replicate any others) I spend five to ten nights away from home, work under two to four different contracts, and spend more hours on the telephone than in any one other task.

Working for oneself does have its drawbacks. The entrepreneurial aspects of the work are my least favorite. I do not enjoy promoting myself, "working a room" at meetings, or writing proposals. I manage to avoid most of this by writing and by involvement in professional associations. Most of my clients for training projects have heard of me through my publications or by word of mouth. Most of my consulting clients have had me recommended by others, know me through professional association activities, or have read one of my publications. I should state that I may be unusual in this regard; most consultants do targeted marketing to reach clients.

Another difficult aspect of working independently is finances. Although people assume that consultants make a lot of money—and some management consultants, for example, certainly do—most have less net income than they would have working in a traditional job. I find that this fact boggles the mind of many, especially people who like to multiply an hourly salary by 2,000 hours to determine that my annual income must be astronomically high.

In fact, being a library consultant is not usually a route to wealth. First of all, independent consultants are not given benefits such as health insurance, whereas library employment packages include benefits valued at 30 percent of the salary. I cannot ethically recommend full-time consulting to anyone who does not receive benefits from a spouse or some other source, as good health insurance is difficult for an individual to obtain and is extremely expensive. Second, every expense—paper clips, electricity, association memberships, airplane fares—is paid for by the consultant. Some direct expenses (such as postage for a mail survey) are reimbursed by the client, but other direct expenses and all indirect ones (such as monthly telephone charge) are paid for by the consultant unless he or she has an institutional sponsor (such as a university). Studies find that most consultants spend approximately half of their gross income on expenses.

Third, only half a consultant's work days are billable to a client. The other half are spent finding work (answering RFPs, giving pro bono speeches, talking to potential clients about possible jobs and so forth) or keeping current. For example, one of my areas of expertise is intergenerational programming; I must stay abreast of that interdisciplinary field as well as my other areas of expertise and, of course, librarianship. The bottom line is that most consultants gross only one quarter of their net income. To further compound the financial difficulties of being an independent consultant, that net income is extremely variable from year to year. Some years more projects present themselves and some years more time is available for projects. And, as I mentioned above, I use my publications as my main promotion tool, but the months devoted to writing are not billable hours.

Another financial complication of working as an independent consultant is that most jobs are paid for by soft money (that is, grants or special funds). I rarely am paid out of a general operating budget; most of my work is paid for by LSCA grants or with money from Friends of the Library or other groups.

A major frustration with consulting is that—by definition—you cannot control the outcome of your work. Consultants have influence but no direct power to implement change. Many times hard work and objective advice is ignored by the client (or the person who supervises the client). I find this a painful but unavoidable aspect of consulting.

A final difficulty of working independently is working alone. This one is easier to remedy, by developing informal networks of colleagues to talk with and by joining professional library and consulting organizations. There are days, however, when I miss the collegial stimulation (and the coffee break gossip) that comes from working in an organization.

Words of Advice

Many librarians toy with the idea of consulting and ask for advice on how to start. I recommend trying it by volunteering to do a needs assessment or an evaluation or a workshop for another library or library association. Do it on your own time, outside of work. Charge nothing (or a small honorarium) but ask to be reimbursed for all direct expenses (such as photocopying). As you work, keep three important records. First, keep a journal, recording your own reactions to the work, any questions you need to resolve later, and ideas for future approaches. Next keep a detailed log of every minute you spend on the project so you have a realistic picture of how long the work takes and how much time you will have to plan for (and bill for) next time. And last, keep track of every direct expense; again this will help you in future budgeting. When the project is over, ask the library director and others for objective and realistic feedback on your performance. Meanwhile, do a self-report based on your journal. Was it fun, stimulating, rewarding? Was it stressful, awkward, out of control? Compare the evaluations, and the question of whether or not you want to continue trying consulting should be clear.

If your experiment is a success and you decide to pursue consulting, follow these five tenets. Start small and build up slowly; do not quit your regular job, but reduce your hours if necessary or take an administrative leave. Find yourself a mentor with whom you can discuss consulting and who can offer advice. Find a source for health insurance. Take seminars in the consulting process. After a year, do another evaluation of your work and your bank account.

If you are a "self-starter" and a good time manager, if you like your work to be varied and constantly evolving, enjoy working with a changing roster of people, can handle self-promotion, and like the collaborative process, you will probably like being an independent consultant. I do.

Although some people claim that "consultant" is a dirty word, and others misuse it by calling themselves consultants when between regular jobs, I am proud of it. I savor the independence, the freedom to choose my work, the travel, and the challenges.

26.

Chance Encounters and Unexpected Opportunities

by Sue Rosenzweig

When I moved to Rhode Island from Chapel Hill, North Carolina, in 1990 I predicted (accurately, as it turned out) that I would be unable to find a position as fulfilling as the one I was leaving; I decided instead to "hang out my shingle" as an independent consultant. I haven't regretted my decision. I get to work on a broad range of projects—most of which are only peripherally related to my degree in library science, even though all of my work experience prior to 1990 was as a professional librarian.

Much of what has happened to me since 1973, when I began my graduate work in library science at Drexel University, has been unexpected, unforeseen, and unplanned. When I began to trace the course of my career for this article, I realized that my path was largely determined by the intervention of specific individuals and/or by taking advantage of opportunities to expand my experience whenever they were offered.

The first person to alter my direction was a fellow student. I had begun my studies at Drexel University intending to become an academic librarian. (My husband is an academic and I assumed that I would always be able to find employment regardless of where we settled. I had already learned, when we lived in Ames, Iowa, that my prior graduate work in international economics was no help at all in finding a job. Knowing that I was interested in working part-time while attending school, the student asked if I would be interested in taking over her job as a library aide in a private middle school temporarily housed about four blocks from where I lived. Within a couple of weeks on the job I knew that I wanted to work with young adults and I immediately added courses in children's and young adult literature and services to my program.

Teaching the course in young adult services was Dr. Ray Barber, who was to become my mentor and good friend. It was Ray who urged me to attend my first American Library Association conference and to join ALA. It was also Ray who involved me in a group of school and public librarians who met monthly to review new young adult books. When I announced in 1980, at one of those meetings, that my husband had taken a job in the research triangle area of North Carolina, several librarians gave me phone numbers of people and places to call for job leads.

I took that list with me and referred to it after finishing a one-year position in a private middle school (replacing a librarian who was taking a sabbatical) and spending one year at the University of North Carolina taking the courses I needed to obtain teacher certification. During the summer of 1982 I was hired as a consultant for a special library within the University; my task was to organize the collection and produce a catalog that would be distributed to all North Carolina daycare facilities. It was at this point that I called the Center for Early Adolescence, one of the places on the list. When the receptionist connected me with the librarian I was surprised because I hadn't thought the center would have its own library. Shortly thereafter the center created a job that entailed reorganizing the collection and setting up a system to support information and research needs of both the center staff and its clients. The combination of my experiences working with young adolescents as a middle-school librarian and organizing a special collection was a perfect match for the position.

The mission of the Center for Early Adolescence was to promote the healthy growth and development of young adolescents.[1] This was fulfilled by advocating for young adolescents and providing information services, research, training, and leadership development opportunities for those who could have a positive impact on our nation's 10- to 15-year-olds. The eight years I spent at the center proved to be exciting and professionally rewarding because, in addition to performing the expected library-related tasks, I had many opportunities to extend my expertise far beyond what my M.L.S. prepared me for. I learned about early adolescent development, effective programming and schools for 10- to 15-year-olds, parent education, and adolescent literacy. I made site visits to school and after-school programs, learning to conduct qualitative research using interviews and observations. I began to give speeches—my first was at the 1983 annual ALA conference—and I learned how to conduct workshops for librarians, teachers, youth workers, and parents. I learned the finer points of training by observ-ing my colleagues in action. I was sent to a week-long training pro-gram, offered by the Grantsmanship Center, to master the art of pro-posal writing and, since the center relied on soft money for funding, frequently read and contributed to grant proposals being prepared by center staff. I was encouraged to take advantage of any opportunity for professional growth that interested me and that would enhance the center's mission. And so I became active in ALA's Young Adult Li-brary Services Association (YALSA), formerly the Young Adult Services Division, accepting a committee appointment almost immediately. My participation in YALSA continues to expand my ever-widening net-work of professionals who share my interests.

My regular duties as a special librarian included responding to many written and telephone requests, from all over the country, for information, putting me in touch with a great network of profession-als working with youth and interested in youth issues and policies. Extensive travel meant face-to-face contacts and I often ended up meeting the very people I had corresponded with or spoken to on the telephone. I created systems to facilitate access to information on over 200 organizations with whom we had contact, and on individuals all across the country—subject specialists, policymakers, and speakers who could further the mission of the center and to whom we could re-fer clients needing their services. I designed a routing system for the 140 professional journals we received and began a process in which center staff reviewed and critiqued videos and films for and about adolescents. All of these activities contributed to expanding an al-ready considerable network of contacts. I discovered that I had a knack for eliciting information from people that went way beyond what was originally requested, and an ability to match people with in-formation and people with people. I also discovered that I derived enormous satisfaction from tracking down the most elusive docu-ments and resources.

By 1987 I was being asked to help other organizations that were setting up similar information systems. Librarians would come and spend one or two days at the center to learn how I had organized the collection and developed the procedures that we were using. I learned that I could teach others what I knew and that I enjoyed teaching.

When I moved to Rhode Island from North Carolina in 1990, I knew that I did not want to work full-time at one job, unless I could find a job similar to the one I was leaving—a very unlikely possibility. I de-cided to try my hand as an independent consultant and left the center armed with a Rolodex filled with people and organizations to contact. By that time most of my former colleagues had left the center for posi-tions as program officers at granting foundations where they continue provide consulting opportunities.

My first contract, which began immediately on my arrival in Rhode Island, was to work with the Indiana Library Federation on a grant proposal. Before moving I had also agreed to become a field associate for the National Center for Service Learning in Early Adolescence (now the National Helpers' Network, Inc.), so I was off and running. I began calling all the people I knew in Rhode Island. Bruce Daniels, a long-time ALA "conference crony" whom I met through Ray Barber, was then the director of the Department of State Library Services for Rhode Island. Back in 1984 Bruce had been instrumental in hiring me to do a workshop for Rhode Island young adult librarians. Once I moved, he invited me to be a delegate to the Rhode Island Governor's Conference on Libraries and Information Services, where I met many local librarians and library advocates. In 1991 I was asked to join the adjunct faculty at the University of Rhode Island Graduate School of Library and Information Studies where I periodically teach the young adult literature course and, when enrollment warrants, coteach the practicum for prospective school library media specialists. I became active in the statewide Young Adult Round Table, a monthly meeting where Rhode Island librarians review books and discuss topics of mutual interest, and I joined state and regional library associations.

Much of my work is directly linked to my library expertise and my knowledge of adolescent development. Workshop presentations on young adult literature, collection development, and reluctant readers are directly related to my library degree. I also do workshops on early adolescent development, effective programming and schools for 10- to 15-year-olds, parent education, adolescent literacy, and service learning. My first consulting job in Rhode Island was to write the $1.2 million Library Power grant for the Public Education Fund of Providence. Obtaining this grant led to many other opportunities in the state and did wonders for my name recognition. I worked closely with the State Department of Education to write two grants for improving middle schools and currently serve as a consultant to the grants. Working with the Roger Williams Zoo, on a proposal that involved hiring adolescents to teach science to children in school-age child care centers, was an opportunity for me to use my knowledge of adolescent development and effective programming for young adults. Because of these successes I have added workshops on grant proposal development and implementation to my repertoire of presentations.

The combination of my subject expertise and library experience has also led to consulting for publishers, grant-giving foundations, and organizations such as the Academy for Educational Development, the Public Education Fund Network, the National Youth Employment Coalition, the Middle Grades Reading Network in Indiana, the Center for Corporate and Education Initiatives at Brandeis University, and Public/Private Ventures in Philadelphia.

What I love most about working independently is the variety of work, the convenience of working out of my home, being in control of my work schedule, meeting new people, and traveling. Fortunately a steady stream of calls has allowed me to avoid the onerous (to me) task of promoting myself and soliciting work.

The downside of life as an independent consultant is the unpredictability of work. Some months are packed with jobs that have tight deadlines and jobs that require extensive travel, while others may be a little too quiet—the "feast or famine" syndrome. I do have the luxury of working as much or as little as I want (I don't have to worry about paying for health benefits or making mortgage payments), but I realize how challenging it might be to make a decent living at this.

There is no question that my library degree provided the basic knowledge and skills on which all my subsequent work experiences were based; however, I also owe the path my career took to both the special individuals I met along the way and those who offered me opportunities to extend my abilities and knowledge in so many directions.

Notes

1. The Center for Early Adolescence closed in June 1995 at which time the collection was assumed by the Search Institute in Minneapolis, Minn.

27.

Independent Information Broker and Consultant

by Camille A. Motta

"How interesting, a librarian! We've never accepted a librarian into this Ph.D. program." I was met with these words of surprise by the director of the doctoral program, as I set out on a new life's direction.

Let me fill you in on what led me to this point in my career, after spending 15 years as a special librarian. Having as a foundation the very traditional education delivered by Simmons College School of Library Science, I entered the profession as a cataloger, first at Harvard (both at Widener Library and at the Countway Medical Library), followed by MIT, then on to two technical services department head positions at the Massachusetts State Library, and finally becoming library director at the Urban Institute, a premier, public policy think tank in Washington, D.C.

Ten years into my stint as director of the library at the Urban Institute, I began to feel an uneasiness about my chosen profession. Personal computers had just about supplanted the mainframes and super-minis of the 1970s and early 1980s. Before the PC, it was OK to rely on the computer science department gurus for computing needs. Before PCs, computing needs were rather minimal anyway, mostly limited to a specific database or a specific application or two. They certainly weren't all that critical to our profession. It was OK not to be too, too knowledgeable about them, and it seemed OK to rely on the "men" in the computer departments when we needed help.

Sometime in the late 1980s, all that changed. An explosion in information, heralded by the online and CD-ROM industries and the coming of the Internet, began to affect how librarians dealt with information. There was too much to collect, it was too changeable to catalog, and it was too diverse to commit to memory. Our roles as collection developers, technical services librarians, and reference specialists were on the line. What particularly brought this home to me, in my institution, was the increasing importance placed on the computer services folks by management. Computer service specialists were "hard to find and recruit," commanded higher wages than members of other professions, and were given special status in an administrative and technical job reclassification. As we librarians struggled to modernize and automate our libraries, we had to contend with these computer services folks in many, sometimes awkward and competitive ways. Even if we got approval for equipment, it had to be purchased, maintained, and set up by these people. Often turf battles ensued. Our expertise was questioned in the face of these all-knowing technical experts, who were now being called in the *Washington Post* help wanted section "information specialists," "information systems managers," and "information engineers."

It was in a climate like this, with library schools closing left and right, and with feelings of uneasiness about a "dying" profession, that I was lucky enough, in 1989, to see a now-famous movie. Yes, I was in attendance at our local library network's annual meeting, when they showed, for all to see, the video "Knowledge Navigator," featuring John Scully of Apple Computer. In this awe-inspiring vision, I found the librarian of the future—an agent who anticipated his patron's needs before they were even spoken, who correctly interpreted the most casually expressed request for information, and who effortlessly located the exact information and delivered it perfectly packaged back to his patron's desktop. This librarian of the future, was not flesh and blood, but a "knowbot"—a computerized agent who navigated the pathways of knowledge in quest of information which he (yes, *he*) was able to discern expertly and deliver efficiently.

Some months later, a second event helped me to identify what skills the librarian of the future might need to possess in order to become/create, the "knowbot." Pat Molholt, then associate director of libraries at Rensselaer Polytechnic Institute, was invited to speak at a local meeting. Pat was, at that time, pursuing her Ph.D. in a field that I knew very little about—artificial intelligence (AI). From the words she spoke that day, I knew that she was also in pursuit of a change that she felt was necessary to make in her life. Change, she felt, was critical, if our profession was to grow and advance in importance. Librarians had somehow to get the technical background required to create the tools that would help users sift and sort the vast amounts of information being generated. Librarians, with their education and skills, had to be a part of the team that designed the expert systems, imbued machines with intelligence, and created the knowbots of the future. Pat believed in this so strongly that she embarked on a degree program that would give her the requisite skills.

Totally inspired and completely in awe, I submitted my application to the Ph.D. program at George Washington University School of Business and Public Management, to enter a field called "Information and Decision Systems." Seeing that this particular curriculum embraced the technical subjects of artificial intelligence and expert systems, and encouraged by the use of the word "Information" in their degree program, I felt that this was a natural step for me. Now, I needed to prove this to the doctoral committee, which only accepted a very small proportion of the students who applied. With some very heavy lobbying on my part and using some very ingenious ways of describing the library profession, I was able to convince key members of the committee of my worthiness. I was able, through my eagerness and enthusiasm, to assure them that this was a natural expansion of what I had learned working in one profession and that, therefore, I showed real promise of making an impact in this new profession.

Five years later, with a very heavily technical course load behind me, and wearing, like a halo, the pride of nearly straight A's, I was certain that the time had come to "cut the cord." Throughout my Ph.D. course work I had continued to hold my full-time library director position. Now, with comprehensive exam time upon me and with the specter of a dissertation in front of me, I longed to proceed full speed ahead, finish the program, and get the degree. Lack of time was holding me up; the full-time job had to go.

Newly resigned from my position, I turned to my academic advisor for counsel. "How about," he said, "if you help me with a consulting position that I have been offered. The task will require a comprehensive review of the literature of the field. I don't have time to do the searching and you have more expertise than I." The consulting job involved working with a team of engineers on expert systems verification and validation—my new field! It was my skills as a librarian that landed me my first paid position in my new field. I worked many long hours in delivering the best search of the literature that was humanly possible. As they gave me more and more tasks, the time period of the original contract was extended—once, then twice. I began to make enough money that I needed to worry about business licenses and self-employment tax. A visit to an accountant assured me that I had to formally define myself as a business. Overnight I became an information broker and consultant. The information broker part was my foot in the past, the consultant part was my foot in the future. The critical leap here was convincing the group of engineers in the team that, after I retrieved the bibliographic citations, I could not only get the articles for them, but I could then read and analyze the articles to come up with a comprehensive review and analysis of the field's state of the art. I succeeded in convincing them, and having done the review and analysis, I now knew as much as anyone about one aspect of my new profession. I became valuable to the team not as a librarian but as a researcher and fellow consultant.

My business has progressed strictly by word of mouth. Not one penny was spent in advertising. I have even had to turn business away. For some clients I do the literature searches, for others I do critical analysis/reviews based on information obtained using my own searches. All of the work that I do involves some aspect of my new field, which is the use of advanced technology in the management, control, and use of information. Everyone I have worked with has regarded my library science skills as important or as an asset to the job at hand. In many cases, these skills have gotten me in the door of organizations doing key work in my new field.

One case in point is the most interesting. Recently I came to realize that I was most inspired by and most eager to pursue a career in medical artificial intelligence. Medical AI often falls into the broader heading of medical informatics. My goal was to find a suitable dissertation topic in some aspect of artificial intelligence in medicine. The best case would be to find a job that would actually pay me while I gathered research for a dissertation. One night while surfing the World Wide Web in search of information on anesthesiology expert systems for a colleague, I came across a remarkable page with the name "Telemedicine Test Bed." Reading the text and following the links led me to a page titled "Validation Efforts." "Wow," I thought, "a way to combine the validation work that I did in expert systems with medical information systems." Moreover, evaluations always make for good dissertations. Continuing to follow the hypertext links, I discovered that the test bed site was located not far from where I lived. I sent an e-mail message to the head of the research division asking if I could come and talk to him.

After several visits and discussions about my background and experience and about my desire to find a dissertation topic in this area, I was blessed with another opportunity which I owe to my library degree. I found out that the test bed had occasional need for literature searching, and the company with which they were familiar charged double what I was charging my customers. "How about giving *me* a chance to do the searches?" I said. "Try me out and see what you think." Two weeks later, I found myself sitting at a table with the communications officer and the head of the research division discussing how I could fit into their work. They decided to give me a small contract for their occasional needs for literature searching. We continued to discuss how I might volunteer to help with the telemedicine validation efforts. We thought of a project that I might be able to do right away—analyzing and summarizing the validation efforts done to date. With a whisk of his briefcase, the research division director said that he would even be willing to pay me for that.

As I walked out the door that day, I felt an overwhelming appreciation for talents that for many years had been taken for granted, both by my employers and, perhaps, by myself. If I had been undervalued as a librarian in my institution, I must have let myself be undervalued. Maybe I even felt it myself—I was *not* as valuable as the computer services staff. After all, only they had the skills that were critical to the work of the organization, skills that no one else possessed. I had to leave my full-time position in order to realize fully the premium skills that I possessed—skills that were highly valued by those who did not have them. I had to leave my institution and strike out on my own to "feel my power" and earn the respect of other professionals.

As I sit here finishing up this librarian-turned-consultant story, I glance at a stack of work sitting on my desk, work that represents my newest contract. If I do nothing at all after this one, I will have received payment back in full for the years of "homework" that I put in as a special librarian. I was recently contacted by the Vice President and Director of AI Technologies (a person well known in AI) at a major international scientific and technical consulting company. The company is well known for its work in advanced technologies, including medical information systems. This eminent researcher asked me to do a literature search for a very technical problem on which he is working. "If you can do this one fast," he said, looking me straight in the eye, "I will contact you for other searches that I know I will need." The beginning of a beautiful relationship, I thought to myself, and one that holds the promise of leading to a real job in my new career—after I finally am the *first librarian* to finish this beast of a Ph.D. program!

28.

An Information Management Consultant

by Ann M. Robertson

"A consultant! Are you playing at working? Can't you get a *real* job?" Those were typical social reactions when I joined the ranks of information management consulting in 1980. An information management consulting job is less structured than most; it produces a great variety of tasks; it provides the opportunity to work with people of diverse backgrounds on various levels within an organization; it presents numerous personal growth opportunities; and, best of all, it still involves dealing with information. For me, it was a *real* job then, and is even more so 15 years later.

Information management consulting involves helping businesses not only to analyze their business practices in light of information creation, flow, and communication, but also to identify, organize, manage, and retrieve the information they need to operate efficiently and profitably. A librarian is the ideal person to provide this expertise. Library schools teach how to systematically approach evaluating, modifying, and creating information systems, how to identify solutions to problems by conducting in-depth research, how to obtain information rapidly on a myriad of subjects, and how to organize large amounts of data logically.

The role of an information management consultant in the marketing, sales, development, and implementation of a project is a function of the size of the consulting organization for which he or she works. I have been lucky enough to work in two small businesses where I have been involved in all of these activities.

Developing advertisements, brochures, and handouts targeted to specific business services or industries; attending, networking, and exhibiting at conferences, workshops, seminars, and social affairs; and presenting papers, being on panels, giving speeches, and writing articles are the formal marketing activities in which I have been involved. Most librarians have developed exhibits, bulletin boards, newsletters, and promotional materials. Librarians are famous for their networking skills and always enjoy attending and participating in conferences, seminars, and workshops. Staffing an exhibit booth and hawking your services at a trade show are very different, however, from visiting a booth as a potential client. It takes a great deal of self-confidence, not to mention physical stamina, to spend hours on end selling your organization's services and your abilities to deliver the desired result. Working a reference desk provides you with some of these skills.

The most beneficial marketing leads come from word-of-mouth references and responses to Yellow Pages advertisements. Reference interview skills are employed in determining potential problems and in selling services. Marketing and sales in the information business usually have a long lead time. Once a prospective client has been identified, the information management consultant may be involved in the actual sales call and proposal preparation. The ability to sell oneself as a competent professional with the skills required to solve the identified problem(s) is required. Written communication skills are a must for preparing succinct proposals.

When the client signs on the dotted line, the information management consultant may be a member of the project team, an on-site supervisor, or the project manager. In some instances, the consultant will be involved in the selection and supervision of the project team, in client reporting, and in project billing and collection activities. Personnel selection and supervision, report writing, and purchasing are activities in which most librarians are regularly involved. For me, the most fun and challenging part is the actual consulting work.

Consulting projects usually begin with a needs assessment study, the first step of which is to gather information about the client's organization, its current information creation and management practices, its identified problem areas, and its information requirements and expectations, both current and future. This usually is accomplished through doing research on the client; interviewing employees, individually or in groups; observing activities and processes; quantifying the documents in-house and in storage; and reviewing and evaluating the information storage and retrieval systems. The second step of the study is to analyze the data gathered. It is also the time to identify new areas of information or new types of technology requiring research prior to developing recommended solutions. The third step of the study is the development of recommendations and an implementation plan. Recommendations are informally presented to the client contact for technical and political input. Refinements are made and a formal briefing presented to client management. The fourth step of the study is the preparation and delivery of a formal written report detailing the scope of work, the methodology used, results of the interviews and observations, recommended solutions, and a suggested implementation plan. Often the consulting company is involved in the implementation project, sometimes as the turnkey operator, the project manager, or the client advisor.

The skills employed to perform a needs assessment are ones librarians use daily. Reference interview skills (listening, asking pointed questions, building trust between the patron and the librarian, and so forth) are extremely useful in the information gathering and presentation stages. The librarian's ability to look at information problems from the user's perspective is extremely beneficial in the information gathering, analysis, recommendation, and implementation stages. Research skills are required for gathering and analyzing data. Acquisition, classification, cataloging, and indexing skills are helpful in the analysis, recommendation, and implementation stages of a project.

Attitudes and abilities play an important part in being a successful information management consultant. First you must have faith in your ability to take on any job. In challenging situations, you must be able to seize the moment, step up, and make decisions or definitive recommendations. You must be willing continually to spend time educating business people about your skills, their relevance to accomplishing specific jobs, and the value you add to their businesses. Good communication skills, verbal and written, are essential. Reasoning abstractly "under fire," but explaining things in layman's terms without using jargon, is a talent you must develop. Being able to accept criticism and deal with change is very important. Time and energy are required to attend workshops, meetings, conventions, and networking activities in order to build your professional and client contact base. You need to be a self-starter who enjoys work.

In this information age, librarians can play a prominent role in all areas of business. Your opportunities are only limited by your imagination, the level of effort you are willing to expend, and the amount of time you have available each day.

29.

An Itinerant Librarian[1]

by Susanne Bjørner

Many of my colleagues, both former and current, believe that I have left librarianship and taken up a new career. I haven't; I've simply transferred my work from a single organization bounded by walls, with a defined mission and user population, to one defined by multiple and varying clients and by my responses to them.

Nearly 12 years ago I left my last full-time institutional library job—inspired and made confident by the personal experiences related in the first edition of this book. I wanted to move back to direct contact with the public that I had served in my previous 15 years of work in school, public, and special libraries. I also wanted to regain the sense of wholeness in relation to the information cycle that I had experienced in many of those positions. Almost all of my jobs had been in small, usually one-person, libraries. I was accustomed to providing answers for people, to developing support mechanisms for information management that worked (whether or not they were according to code), and to overcoming personal, institutional, and technical obstacles that hindered information use. With the flourishing of the online database industry in the 1980s and my own competence in using personal computers, I was confident that I could keep myself occupied with interesting work.

Computers

Computers were not a part of the curriculum during the years 1969–1971 when I earned my M.L.S. degree at Simmons College, but I attended professional school part time while holding down a full-time paraprofessional library job at a computer company. My nondegreed library manager and a clerical colleague had developed a circulation system for the library using an 80–column keypunch card. Library computer applications were underfunded, however, and not taken seriously, and I came away from that experience frustrated that small libraries, the kind I made my career in, could never afford access to mainframes and the new minicomputers.

I withdrew from automation in libraries. MARC's early adolescence passed by without my knowledge, and academic and special libraries' pioneering efforts with SDC and DIALOG seemed a world away when I scanned the professional literature. I next gained exposure to computers in 1980, when I took a job to start up a library and I was presented with an Apple II+ instead of a clerical assistant. I was motivated to get that machine working to do catalog card production, bibliography creation, and database searching through BRS. In addition, I used its word processing, database management, and spreadsheet applications for general office functions. Since the agency I was working in was responsible for curriculum development, I also had the opportunity to observe how microcomputers could change education through improving educational administration and learning experiences for students.

When the chance came in 1983 to apply what I had learned about microcomputers to libraries on a statewide level, I took it. By now I knew that this new personal computer would transform the way people dealt with information. Assisting people with their information demands was what I had been doing all along as a librarian. If there was to be an information revolution fueled by personal computer development, I was determined that librarians would be a part of it.

My job as microcomputer specialist for the state library agency let me encourage use of this new tool by librarians throughout the region. The job reintroduced me to the issues, technology, and uses of large computers for library circulation and cataloging. I also worked to promote the expansion of public library services to include offering direct access to electronic, as well as print, information.

Places

I left that position concurrent with a change that moved me to the north country of New Hampshire, where my family roots are, an area with many mountains but few libraries or information-intensive businesses. There was no institution that could afford to hire me and provide interesting work, so I took the advice of two books I remembered from my public library days: *Go Hire Yourself an Employer* and *You, Inc.* My professional roots were in reference service and in small libraries so I was used to going outside the library to answer the questions. It was natural, therefore, to focus my work on what was beginning to be called information brokering—providing information from the online databases of such vendors as DIALOG and BRS. I realized that not only did my suppliers not have to be where I was, but neither did my customers. Today, 12 years and a few locations later, geographic independence is still a primary factor in my choice of work.

One cannot be totally independent, of course. An early assignment was as a temporary, part-time database searcher for the fee-based search service at MIT libraries. The customer specified that this work be performed on-site, in the presence of clients, for three days each week. This association made good business and professional sense, so for six years I commuted once a week to the job, and then went home to work independently the rest of the week.

The steady MIT work substantially affected the development of my independent business. Originally I had thought that "The World of Information" (the least limiting business name I could think of when it became clear to me that I needed to have a label) would grow as it developed a client base of customers with needs in information retrieval. I also offered services in database design and development and workshops to teach various aspects of information management. I expected that those activities were really adjunct activities that would provide additional, but only supplementary, revenue. To have focused on the information retrieval part of my business while providing that service at MIT would have been a conflict of interest, so I redirected my independent work to other information activities.

Services

I began writing for online industry publications. I also took on consulting assignments in software design, database development and data transfer, survey development and analysis, and technical writing and editing. I continued and expanded my efforts to teach information management skills to librarians and others in business and the professions. All these activities, in addition to the work at MIT, were focused on an information cycle that I had verbalized in my first service brochure, in which I offered assistance in the identification, location, organization, delivery, utilization, and communication of information.

That information cycle is what still guides my work selection now. Since 1991 I have been working independently and full time from a base in rural Connecticut. During this period I have reinstituted information retrieval (identification, location, and delivery of information) as a service, both for a few clients directly and as a service provider to other information retrieval companies that are better at marketing information retrieval services than I am. I write extensively for the electronic information community, with continuing columns in *Online* magazine and *Link-Up*. I conceived, compiled, and edited *Newspapers Online* (Needham Heights, Mass. BiblioData), which was published in its third edition in 1995. Few of my clients are local; they may be across the country or across the world. Electronic mail, fax machines, and overnight couriers make it almost as easy to be productive in remote locations as directly on-site with the client.

I am a consultant to information providers, corporations, and libraries on projects relating to electronic information and I do customized training for information management. I also take assignments as a temporary staff member in a library or information center periodically, so that I can keep up with what is happening in information management in larger organizations and institutions more typical of the market than a single-operator company. Those assignments may be on-site with local corporations, or they may be for specified periods of time some distance away. For instance, in 1995 I spent five months at the National Technical Knowledge Center and Library of Denmark.

The delineation of the information cycle is important to me because it provides a construct within which I can define my professional and business interests. Since I have, over time, worked on a wide variety of projects and products (within different industries, at different stages of development, and for different players), I run the risk of getting too diffused. The cycle definition helps me focus on the activity in question and the ultimate use of the project in which I am engaged. I find, too, that I need a variety of activities throughout the course of a week. If I season what is primarily a week of writing with a little research, or manage to take a little break from a consulting project for some research or training, I maintain my sanity. Some good synergies result, too, that benefit my clients as well as me.

Scheduling

Scheduling is probably the hardest part of running my business. Working on my own I don't have to settle for doing just one thing at a time. Unfortunately, doing several projects at once can also produce stress, and that stress gets more than a little wearing at times. So I strive to minimize the number of major projects I work on at any one time, and achieve diversity from sequential rather than simultaneous jobs.

It's always hard to say "no" to an interesting project. Frequently, good possibilities come up at the same time, and many are projects that are time sensitive. My first task, after determining that I would like to work on a project, is to understand the time requirements: total staff hours and duration. Most jobs become characterized as those that do or do not fit into other. A "fit-into" job is not a negative reflection on interest, budget, or other; it's an indication that scheduling is more flexible.

Ideally only a single, rigid-schedule job is on the calendar at one time. Sometimes, however, a client starts to talk about a project far in advance, but when the project finally comes in I may be committed to another project. Renegotiating schedules is sometimes possible, but too often in these cases I find myself with "freelancer fever"—working more hours than I really want.

Sometimes when I am otherwise committed I refer a client to a colleague with whom I am familiar through the extensive business and professional network that has developed among information providers. I am actively involved with the Association of Independent Information Professionals (AIIP), the Special Libraries Association, and the American Library Association's Independent Librarians Exchange Round Table (ILERT), all of which provide opportunities to meet and maintain referral and support relationships with hundreds of colleagues.

I've learned not to worry about projects that don't materialize, as long as I haven't invested too many resources in their development. Nor do I worry any longer about the few times when the telephone doesn't ring—I treat it as a blessing. I have good relations with previous clients and with professional colleagues, and I know that something will materialize soon. I already have too many ideas for work and too little time to develop and market those ideas.

Rewards

There is great curiosity and wide misunderstanding about the financial rewards for independent information professionals. All too often outsiders tend to assume either that information brokers are "making a killing" or that they don't make a living wage. Although both extremes may be true, they are the exception.

When I first started out, I was determined to make a salary that was the equivalent of the librarian's salary I had taken home in the past. I've succeeded in that goal. I have also spent vast amounts of time and money (more than any previous employer could contribute) toward my professional development and travel.

What you earn as a self-employed information professional depends first and foremost on what you set out to earn. We can already see several relatively young information firms that have grown large enough to employ and pay salaries and benefits to several people. Some have grown attractive enough to merge with or be sold to major players within the information industry. I believe that more will achieve this level within the next few years.

Other self-employed information professionals, and I am among them, choose to stay small. We are often motivated by rewards that are more important to us, at least for now, than money: flexibility in work hours or location, professional ideals, the challenge of something new. Regardless of the choices you make, I believe that it is important to recognize that financial and personal priorities almost always change over the years. Accordingly, services, place of business, form of business organization, even employment status may change.

If circumstances ever require you to return from freelancing to what many call a "real-world job" (but what I tend to think of as an "old-world job"), there is still an important benefit from a period of freelancing—the knowledge and competence you have developed that enable you to define your skills, analyze a market, and sell your value to an organization. In other words, you can always find or create a job for yourself. In an era when lifetime employment and long-term employer commitment have disappeared from the workplace, that confidence may be the most important job benefit around.

Notes

1. Parts of this essay were originally verbalized by the author for "Who Are These Independent Information Brokers?" in the February/March 1995 *Bulletin of the American Society for Information Science.*

30.

An Independent Information Professional

by Reva Basch

"You're talking to a desperate woman; when can you start?"

With those words, my career path veered sharply into the unknown. The speaker was the director of research at Information on Demand, a pioneering company in the for-profit research business. I was a modestly experienced librarian, newly relocated in northern California and looking for work. I had heard of Sue Rugge and her innovative attempt to provide research, reference, and document delivery services, for a fee, beyond what libraries could afford to offer. The idea intrigued me—entrepreneurial librarians, a library without walls. When I called the San Francisco Bay Area Special Libraries Association jobline and heard that there was a vacancy at Sue's company, I didn't hesitate for a moment; my next call was to Information on Demand itself.

The jobline came through for me; within a day or two I was happily occupying a desk at IOD, calling experts in Texas, Arkansas, and Oklahoma to determine the market for water-pumping windmills. I was in my element. Apparently my supervisor thought so, too; the position, originally intended to be a temporary one, solidified into a permanent, full-time job. I joined Information on Demand as a research associate in the spring of 1981. My career path to that point had been relatively conventional, its linear progression bumped occasionally by the exigencies of marriage, cross-country moves, and a year-long flirtation with the restaurant business. My undergraduate degree, like that of many of my colleagues, was in English literature. I earned my M.L.S. degree in 1971 from the University of California at Berkeley. The year I attended Cal was the year the School of Librarianship became the School of Library and Information Science. I avoided the two or three courses then offered in computerization and information theory; I elected to take children's literature instead of online bibliographic retrieval. Computers, anything smacking of mathematics and automation, were anathema to me.

When I entered library school, the profession was wide open; jobs were readily available and the prospect of unemployment almost nonexistent. A year later, when it was time to start looking for a job, the economy had taken a downturn and freshly minted graduates in all fields were having trouble finding work. Many of my peers took paraprofessional positions just to survive, or abandoned the profession entirely. I had wanted to work in an academic or special library. The University of California, the largest academic employer in the San Francisco Bay Area, was not hiring, and the competition for jobs at other institutions was fierce, so I focused my attention on the corporate sector, copying telephone numbers from local business directories and cold-calling to ask whether the firm had a library and, if so, where to send my resume.

Finally, I struck gold. Cogswell College, a small, private, two-year school that awarded associate degrees in electrical, mechanical, and civil engineering, had just received a grant to convert one of its machine shops into a library. They were at the point of choosing carpets and draperies when my call reminded them that they would need a librarian as well. Timing was all; the job was mine.

I brought with me not only my newly acquired skills in cataloging, classification and collection development, but the Gaylord and Brodart catalogs as well; we would need shelving and, I pointed out, a card catalog. The school administration had, of course, been unsuccessful in finding a supplier among their regular office furniture dealers.

My first job out of library school, then, was both a start-up and a one-person operation. I did original cataloging of their collection; labeled, stamped, and glued book pockets; acquired new books and periodical subscriptions; set up a circulation system; and staffed the reference desk. It struck me at the time that library school had really been vocational school; this job called for the direct application of most of the skills I had learned. Many of the students were immigrants or first-generation English speakers, and I spent considerable time talking to them about their lives and the intricacies of American culture. This was the early 1970s, in San Francisco. There was a lot to talk about.

I stayed at Cogswell for a year, then moved back east, where I was hired as an assistant librarian at a large engineering/construction firm. My experience at Cogswell got me in the door, but this felt like my first "real" job, a supervised staff position. During the five years at this job, I honed my subject cataloging and reference skills, and gained experience in supervising both clerical and professional staff.

I also learned about corporate politics and the need for librarians to form alliances with heavy users of their services and to maintain visibility throughout the organization. I sat in on staff meetings, conducted orientation sessions for new employees, and produced and circulated a mini-newsletter describing new acquisitions and services. When my boss left the company, I moved into her position as supervisor of library services, and onto the front lines of justifying to my management the very existence of the corporate information center.

This was a disheartening experience. As library director, I reported to the manager of employee training, who in turn reported to the head of the human resources department. My ultimate supervisor was not a library user, did not understand the services we provided, and therefore considered the facility to be marginally useful at best.

I had been reading about DIALOG's interactive online search service. Unlike the batch-process information retrieval methodologies I'd avoided studying in library school, this seemed dynamic and immediate. I could clearly see "my" engineers making use of citations and abstracts from the NTIS and Engineering Index/Compendex databases. I lobbied hard to bring DIALOG in-house, but the human resources director was adamantly opposed: the corporate mainframe had screwed up their first attempt to computerize the employee benefits statement. I was to have nothing to do with computers.

It was at that job that I first heard of Sue Rugge. Subconsciously, I filed that knowledge away for future reference. At the beginning of 1979 I left my job at the engineering firm and took some time off from the information profession to attend restaurant school, move back to California, and investigate other career alternatives.

The following year I drifted back into the library realm, creating a position for myself as a technical information specialist—part librarian, part records manager—for a small engineering consulting firm in San Jose, California. Here I was in another start-up, one-person library. I had the opportunity to take DIALOG training and did a limited amount of online searching for the engineering staff, but once I had established the information center and documented its systems and procedures, the job became stagnant. It was from that perspective that I made the call, that spring day in 1981, to Information on Demand.

The five and one-half years I spent at Information on Demand proved to be pivotal. They provided both the model for my own business and the expertise I needed to operate it. As a self-taught online searcher, I was minimally competent when I joined the firm. My supervisor gave me useful feedback and provided, as much by example as by direct coaching, countless valuable tips on how to plan a search and execute it in the most efficient manner: make notes offline before you begin, string commands together with semicolons, browse titles and indexing terms to refine your strategy rather than printing the entire answer set at once. The two of us handled all the online work, which ensured ample opportunity for me to hone my database searching skills.

Along the way, I also refined and deepened my manual research abilities, learning my way around the University of California library system, including some out-of-the-way small collections. I was able to apply the basic reference sources I had studied in library school, as well as some esoteric ones, to real-life research scenarios. I learned how to develop a list of experts to contact for information that was not available online or in print, how to approach them, and how to conduct a productive telephone interview. Since many of our projects involved a blend of online, library, and telephone work, I developed a sense of the "gestalt" of secondary research—the tradeoffs between time and money spent, the most efficient ways of tackling a problem, how to estimate and track labor and expenses, and knowing when to stop. Perhaps most important of all, I trained myself to conduct a reference interview that would elicit not only a list of search terms but also the context. The key question, I learned, was "What do you want to *do* with the information?"

Through direct client contact, I acquired another set of skills at the managerial level that stood me in good stead later, when I started my own business. These skills included the ability to explain a complex process—what the research staff would be doing on behalf of the client, and what the client could expect to receive—in an honest yet reassuring way; to do an on-the-fly yet accurate estimate of labor and direct costs; and to close the sale. Operating in IOD's fast-paced, high-volume research environment, I had learned to juggle priorities, stay within budget, meet deadlines, and switch my own internal gears as required, from the designer sunglasses market to chronic canine hip dysplasia to soil liquefaction in earthquake zones.

Hired as a research associate, I was promoted after a couple of years to assistant director of research. When my supervisor left, I assumed her position as research director. The corporate culture, meanwhile, had shifted following the firm's acquisition by one of Robert Maxwell's U.S. publishing entities. I found myself doing more administrative work and less hands-on research. Before too long, I was ready for a change.

My career swerved again in mid-1986, when the "desperate woman" who had been my supervisor at Information on Demand recruited me to work for her new employer, a software development branch of Mead Data Central (now LEXIS/NEXIS). I was lured by the promise of a programmer-scale salary, significantly higher than the librarian-level income I was earning at IOD, and by the possibility of working in a completely different environment and learning something new.

My position at Mead Data Central involved working closely with the software engineering staff on user interface design. Our mission was to develop friendlier, more graphically based front ends for the NEXIS service. I applied my experience as an online searcher to a seemingly endless round of decision making about how menus and submenus would be organized, what commands and system options would appear on each, how to word each menu item so that it was concise yet unambiguous, and where the escape key would take the user at any step along the way. I learned to write detailed, logical explanations of how the product would operate, and what would happen from the user's point of view at every stage of interaction with the system.

Although I did not learn programming, and could not write a line of code if my life depended on it, I did come to appreciate the interaction between product design and the software development process. A new feature or a system change that users think is "nice to have" might involve a trivial programming change or it might require rewriting large chunks of the operating system. My exposure to the supply side of the information industry tempered my impatience as a user to the sometimes glacially slow rate of change in the online services I used. This more balanced perspective helped, too, when database producers and online services began to approach me with consulting assignments.

The two years I spent with Mead Data Central also fed my curiosity about personal computers. I developed my basic computer skills and became comfortable using this fundamental new tool of my trade. I invested in a home system that mirrored the capabilities of the one I used at work. Gradually, through exposure and use, I acquired a sense of good and bad software design, what worked well and as expected, and what didn't. I became adept at word processing and at configuring telecommunications programs. I gained the confidence I would need, very shortly, to function fully in this new digital environment.

During this time—starting with my departure from Information on Demand—I was doing occasional freelance searching for clients who managed to track me down. The volume of research requests built through word of mouth to the point where it appeared that, with a little marketing effort, I might have a viable business. This realization coincided with new management at Mead Data Central and the withdrawal of the one-day-at-home working condition I had negotiated. The prospect of operating from home full time became very attractive.

Aubergine Information Services, nascent when I left Information on Demand, emerged as a full-time business when I left Mead Data Central in 1988. Thanks to a couple of regular clients—one of them Sue Rugge, who by now had started the Rugge Group, a consortium of independent research professionals—who fed me a steady stream of online search jobs, I was able to invest almost immediately in the office equipment, reference books, and training I needed. My client base grew, and I found myself tackling projects in virtually all subject areas.

As the business grew, I supplemented both my income and my rather passive, word-of-mouth marketing efforts with writing and speaking engagements. I began to write for information professional publications such as *Online* and *Database* and to give talks at national and regional conferences. This kind of exposure led to consulting assignments with database providers and most of the major U.S. online services. I also worked on marketing pieces as well as system and database documentation, drawing on the technical writing skills I'd acquired on the job at Mead Data Central.

I started exploring the potential of electronic mail, not only for practical applications like delivering search results and communicating with clients, but as a supplement for the face-to-face social interaction missing in a one-person, home-office operation. I discovered the world of computer conferencing and was fascinated by the phenomenon, as well as the feel, of these emerging online communities. This interest became a strong thread in both my professional and my personal life; my involvement with electronic communications led me to explore—just ahead of the rising curve of public awareness—the Internet in its various manifestations.

Meanwhile I was solidifying my network of professional contacts and building visibility through participation in Special Library Association chapter activities (including chairing the fund-raising and program committees) and, more germane to the entrepreneurial trajectory on which I seemed to have launched myself, the Association of Independent Information Professionals (AIIP). I joined AIIP in 1988, the year after its inception, and, at the first annual meeting I attended, volunteered for three committees. This was most uncharacteristic since I tend not to be a joiner. My enthusiasm for AIIP was a clear indication of my commitment to independent research and consulting.

AIIP grew rapidly, from 27 founding members in 1987 to several hundred today. I served on the board for three years, including a term as president in 1991–1992. AIIP has proven to be an invaluable source of leads, referrals, and collegial expertise and support. It holds an annual meeting and publishes a substantial quarterly newsletter, but the heart of the group lies in its members-only electronic forum, currently on CompuServe. There we share tips for effective searching, describe new print and online sources we've discovered, talk about how to deal with clients and vendors, and indulge in banter and non-work-related conversations, as office workers do, around a virtual watercooler.

Although I still do online research on a regular basis, the focus of my business, Aubergine Information Services, has shifted away from on-demand searching and toward writing and consulting. This has been a natural evolution, and it pleases me a great deal. I continue to work for a small stable of regular research clients, and I take on new projects when I find the subject or the prospective client interesting. I refer routine jobs, such as mailing list searches, and projects that are not strictly online-based or that require a specialized subject background to colleagues who are ready to handle them. The searching I do keeps me in touch with database developments and system enhancements in the online realm. It helps me maintain the perspective of a working searcher, which is useful in some aspects of my writing and consulting work.

My early interest in the Internet and virtual communities has moved from an incidental involvement to the foreground of my professional life. Much of my consulting work is concerned with the interaction between the Internet and our traditional online vendors, and with the potential of the Internet and the World Wide Web as an electronic publishing medium. I still write for the online professional journals, and have published two books, *Secrets of the Super Searchers* (Pemberton Press, 1993) and *Electronic Information Delivery: Ensuring Quality and Value* (Gower, 1995). Currently, I am expanding my range and repertoire to include the popular computer press and some general publications as well. I write articles about all aspects of electronic information gathering, and about life online in its various manifestations; another book based on some of these issues is taking form in my mind.

What I find particularly satisfying about my career today is the synergy among the three major facets of my business—research, writing, and consulting. Each component feeds into, and is fed by, the others. I am deeply involved, both personally and professionally, in the changing nature of "online." This is rich and largely uncharted territory; I see no end to my exploration.

A classic old science fiction movie ends with the line "Look to the skies." When people ask me about establishing a niche as an independent information professional, I tell them, "Look to the 'Net." Online searching, electronic publishing, commercial transactions, and many forms of fundamental human interaction are migrating to the Internet. Understanding this medium is a professional plus now; in a very short time, it will be essential.

31.

Solving Information Chaos

by Katherine Bertolucci

I organize information. My consulting practice, Isis Information Services, provides advice and practical knowledge on creating, organizing, and maintaining subject-based collections. For almost 20 years, I have worked with corporations, charitable groups, and individuals in establishing custom-designed information systems. I have been a consultant, an employee, and a volunteer. Whatever the business arrangement, my contribution is clear. I am there to solve information chaos.

Shortly after learning how to read, I started arranging books on shelves and creating notebooks full of important facts. Even so, at the University of Chicago Graduate Library School, I was an exception. Unlike most of the other students, I had never worked in a library. The University's Regenstein Library continues to be the only traditional library in my career; this fact has been, I believe, a great advantage in my approach to information management.

Since graduating in 1977 I have devoted my activities to subject-based collections. Because the University of Chicago training was primarily theoretical, I have the background and the freedom to create new ideas and procedures appropriate to special collections and libraries. I am not beholden to any sacred library tradition. In my opinion, each collection deserves an individually designed system based on the requirements of the subject and of the people who are working in that subject.

My first job after graduation was for an advocacy group that promoted alternative agriculture. It set a pattern for me of clients who are highly productive researchers, with large collections of information. In this project, I organized the materials for quick access in a manner that encouraged the evolution of new ideas. The best classification systems are research tools in themselves.

Following this first assignment, I made several career decisions in a self-identified direction. First I moved from the country to the city. Then to gain computer experience, I took a temporary paraprofessional position at a television station. After completing the assignment I began looking for a project that met my planned career parameters. Perusing library employment advertisements, I identified those that involved organizing a collection from the beginning.

I was looking for professionally creative projects, with clients whose goals I supported. This has been an important principle in my consulting practice. Information management is a crucial component of any successful business, and my goal is to contribute to the achievements of my clients. As a result, every library that I have designed is still in operation.

After the television station, my next two positions provided opportunities to use some of the University of Chicago theoretical training. First was a save-the-whales organization with a large collection of books. It seemed that the Library of Congress classification system would be appropriate so I investigated that option and made an important discovery: major classification systems organize the whole of human knowledge, so they're a little sparse when it comes to detail in any one subject area. I organized the whales materials by type of whale. Later on I worked for a geothermal exploration and development company. Instead of investigating LC, I investigated the actual materials in the collection. They logically fell into an organizational scheme; in this case the major division seemed to be geographical. Another classification system would have put the seismology in one section, hydrology in another—data about one geothermal exploration area would have been distributed all over the library. Instead, for classification purposes, I made the science subordinate to geography.

When the geologists were working on a project, materials about an area were already collected by the system design; the system itself enhanced and streamlined their research. I had made a logical shift in the information paradigm—let the information and the use of information determine the system. With standard classification, the system is the primary component and the information must be fitted to it. With custom design, the system fits the information. The materials and researchers' use of them are primary, with the system supporting and encouraging efficiency. It is user friendly.

Expanding the definition of information, I took a job with a manufacturer of consumer products and organized a massive collection of such merchandise as plush animals, clothing, and toys. As information professionals, we sometimes assume basic levels of organizational knowledge are the norm. This may not be the case; I introduced this company to the concept of an inventory. It was a fun project and it was my last actual job. All subsequent projects have been in the consulting model.

At this point, instead of looking at the librarian ads, I needed to start serious marketing. My professional associations helped. Because I work in a number of different subject areas and types of special libraries, I belong to many professional groups. These include the major associations, any subsections for consultants, and both subject and geographic groups that change with my various assignments. Through this network I consulted a number of directories and started learning how to write 100-word descriptions of what services I offer. I also signed up with a library personnel agency. Most important, I took Amelia Kassel's marketing course for information brokers.

The best marketing technique is word of mouth. It takes a while to build a reputation, but at a certain point the referrals start coming in. A personal friend recommended me for a project in her office, the AIDS division of a county health department. This was a very personally satisfying assignment. It involved a circulating library of AIDS education videos and a distribution method for brochures. Our clients were community activists. There was a sense of purpose in the entire office and, for me, the idea that information can save lives was very stimulating.

Another referral came from a former client, for whom I had done a small project. As chief librarian for the Oakland Unified School District, she recommended me for a project within the district offices. Thus began one of my most challenging assignments. I was presented with several rooms full of totally unorganized books in ten different languages, eight of them Asian. I considered the Dewey Decimal System because it is so widely used by school libraries. This, however, was not a school library; it was a curriculum library for teachers of students with limited English proficiency. Many of the materials were produced in other countries or privately published. We were looking at a lot of original cataloging. I would be there for the first year or so, but ultimately paraprofessionals would have to sweat over those Dewey classification schedules. In addition, my clients required that the library be open and circulating during the organization project. I decided to arrange the books by language. This was an obvious step, but it seemed a major accomplishment when I was able to direct a teacher to the Spanish section. I then organized each language by the curriculum areas defined in the state education code. This was about as consistent as I could get in the classification system because each language had different strengths and approaches to the curriculum areas. I set up a system of alphabetic codes for the facets of the call numbers and mapped the classification hierarchy on a spreadsheet. The paraprofessionals picked it up very quickly and a number of teachers complimented the organizational method.

One unique aspect of this library was the computer requirement.

Circulation was paramount. We had teachers checking out 40 books at a time. In many special libraries, circulation is merely a matter of knowing who has what, and staff members can usually keep a book for as long as they want. In this library however, we needed all schools to have access to the best teaching materials throughout the school year.

We chose a software system that is marketed to school libraries and gave the circulation component a good workout. Overdues were such a problem that I recommended fines, a very controversial suggestion; after a few years they finally accepted my idea. It works and the money buys new books. The software easily computes the amount due and performs all the other intricacies in a complex circulation environment.

As every reader of this book knows, computers are an important tool of modern information management. I have been using them for a long time; the geothermal company started out with a CP/M system. I have used multiple operating systems and many types of programs over the years. One of my skills is the ability to evaluate a project and objectively select software. Again, the information and the client's use of information are the primary components—the software should serve the project, not the other way around.

As a consultant, I maintain an impartial relationship with the software vendors. It is rare that I will select the same software twice. To me the reason is obvious—every project is different, with unique requirements. In addition, software packages are constantly being updated and new programs come onto the market. I start each assignment with an open mind. I know what I've used in the past, I know what's on the market, and I know what my client requires.

For example, in a current project for a biotechnology company, the major focus is serials control. I didn't even look at software that had been satisfactory in the past—it lacked the serials component. Two other projects, a wildlife organization and a major pet food company, are using bibliographic management software for two entirely different reasons—we chose two entirely different packages. Software selection is a matter of defining the information environment, looking to see what's currently on the market, and selecting the best fit.

I am now seeing some changes in the types of projects offered to me. Along with creating libraries I am also redesigning libraries with established systems. Frequently these are collections that were organized by nonprofessionals or that are inadequately maintained. The goal in this type of project is to examine the current system and determine what to keep and what to improve.

Sometimes a very simple change can be a great benefit. I once redesigned a filing system on early childhood education. The files were strictly alphabetical. I looked at the files and realized that there were three major subject areas. So we moved the files into the three areas, maintaining the alphabetic system within each area. This gathered similar material together yet retained the familiarity of the old system.

I am also consulting in the adoption of second-generation software systems. In these assignments, a library has been established and cataloged onto a system that is no longer adequate, so the company seeks advice on the newest systems. As in most other projects, the software selection is usually part of a complete redesign and update of library operations.

In my consulting I have created a work environment in which I operate to my highest capacity. I have constant intellectual stimulation. My time is my own. My work is very creative and makes a positive contribution to the efforts of my clients.

The work environment is constantly changing. Different industries operate in diverse ways. A school district is separate from a scientific research company, which is separate from an advocacy organization. Since I work with multiple organizations at any given time, there are a lot of personalities involved. Switching gears can sometimes be disconcerting, but as a consultant I thrive on change.

In any given project, I am the expert. Generally I am the only one who knows anything about libraries. I supervise myself. Since I am not working with other librarians, I have to create my own network to keep up with the overwhelming changes in our profession. I do this through my professional associations and also through my directory listings. The listings are primarily a marketing tool, but they also let other professionals know about my service. I have received many important invitations through these directories.

Several years ago I met with my marketing instructor, and several others, to form the Information Group International, a consortium of information professionals with different areas of expertise. We support each other and collectively promote the group and our individual businesses. This has been an invaluable source of professional motivation.

As a librarian in private practice, I have had many wonderful experiences. There are opportunities to gain new knowledge and to participate in other professions. Private practice has provided me with the opportunity to make an important contribution to my clients and to the community.

32.

Multiple Hats: Library Consultant/College Instructor

By Denise K. Fourie

I can't say that I purposely set out on an alternative career path. More accurately, I found myself on it after moving to a small town and I have since worked diligently to make it a viable employment choice. Two motivating forces contributed strongly to my career change: a desire to leave the big city and a feeling of burnout with traditional public library reference work.

The early years of my career found me in suburban municipal libraries—working the reference desk and dealing with the wide range of personalities (some sane and many quite insane) that step up to that information counter with their queries. This experience gave me a strong foundation and I have used many aspects of that traditional background in my current work as a consultant, educator, and contract librarian.

But at the time, after five years of public library reference work, I began to feel trapped, wishing for a more creative role than that of "a polite waitress serving up short-orders of information to customers," as a sarcastic colleague once put it. Skills such as planning and developing information services, evaluating products, designing floor plans, and even selecting equipment and furnishings, all seemed overlooked and underutilized in my role as a traditional, busy reference librarian.

Beginnings

Coincidentally, at the same time that I was feeling stifled, my husband received a job offer that gave us the opportunity to relocate from the Los Angeles basin to a more rural area three hours north.

Although happy to be in a more country-like setting, I soon realized that there were a very limited number of library employment possibilities. Consulting seemed like a potential alternative—that is, acting as an independent contractor who would advise clients on varying aspects of such library and information services as the development of print, multimedia, and electronic collections; organization and layout of facilities; classification and retrieval options; public relations; and staff training. Besides making recommendations, I was also prepared to do the work involved and serve as a contract librarian when appropriate.

Serendipity and personal connections led me to my first two consulting jobs setting up small, in-house libraries for large companies. Ironically, both of these jobs were located back in Los Angeles. This type of contract position with a fixed budget and finite number of billable hours became typical. Early on, I supplemented my income with a variety of part-time jobs including writing, substituting for local librarians, and serving as a seasonal tour guide at a historical state park.

Home Office

After the first few projects, I realized that if I were going to continue in business for myself, I needed to set up an office. Using a room in my house was the most cost-effective approach. Business cards, a checking account, separate phone lines, brochures, ads in the Yellow Pages, voice mail, a computer and peripherals, and a business license all followed. Today the home office is often portrayed as an envied work arrangement. Ten years ago it was still considered a questionable venue for business. Warning: there are still people who think having a home-based business means you watch daytime TV, eat bonbons, and are available for long, rambling phone conversations!

Variety of Projects

While library/resource center start-ups and reorganizations have become my specialty, I've taken on many other types of interesting projects including online searches, research on the history of landmark buildings, research and photo selection for books, archives development, and the compilation of annotated bibliographies for scientific reports. I usually work as part of a team with the client's staff; occasionally, I work with another librarian/information manager as a partner. Clients have included corporations, such as William Morris (a talent agency) and Pac Tel (a regional telephone company); local school districts; planning firms; colleges; and government agencies, including Hearst San Simeon State Historical Monument.

Getting Work

Jobs are landed through a combination of word of mouth, networking, advertising in area Yellow Pages, and some limited marketing. After initial meetings or inquiries, I must prepare and submit proposals, which are always time-consuming and often expensive to put together (and the hours are uncompensated). And, of course, I don't always get the job. Besides working independently, I now also subcontract with a well-known library personnel firm in California as one of their consultants. This always means travel to urban areas—usually developing library service plan proposals for high-profile corporate clients. These assessments require strong writing and other communication skills, and a knowledge of library/information management trends and products. The key to all this is the ability to manage and plan for personnel and budgetary resources. Today, consulting and contract work represent about 60 percent of my employment.

I have chosen to live in a small town. If you live in a metropolitan area and pursue this type of consulting, you should have the potential for a much larger volume of business. The information field is a growth industry, so it is likely that the demand for such service will increase, especially with the emphasis on integrating the Internet and other online services into all work environments. Continued rapid advances in digital technology keep making it easier and more efficient to "telecommute" with both local and out-of-area clients.

Teaching

That 60 percent consulting and contract work dovetails nicely with another alternative path that I have taken—that of college instructor. Several California community colleges offer vocational education programs in library technology—practical, work-oriented courses for library and information center support staff. These courses tend to be offered evenings and weekends, since they are geared for students who are retraining, exploring new career options, or seeking continuing education.

Cuesta College's former library director, Mary Lou Wilhelm, showed a lot of faith in my abilities (I had never taught before and had no formal teacher training) when she hired me for that first semester. I was diligent, however, and prepared thoughtful lectures and multimedia lesson plans so that my course load and the scope of my classes each grew. Teaching continues to be enjoyable and a challenge. Typical responsibilities include preparing lectures and assignments, evaluating and counseling students, and designing new courses (including an internship practicum and an Internet course). I am often hired for additional writing projects on a contract basis.

Membership in Professional and Community Associations

For self-promotion, to keep abreast in the field, and for your own sanity, I strongly advise that you join many professional and community organizations. The American Library Association roundtable group ILERT (Independent Librarians Exchange Round Table) is really a one-of-a-kind gathering of other professionals in nontraditional careers. It's comforting to find a group of active professionals who share our special niche. California's state library organization has no counterpart, but there are plenty of opportunities to serve on meaningful committees in your area of interest.

Don't overlook participation on local library boards, Friends' associations, and community organizations. These are groups that will welcome your expertise and often provide business connections for you.

Reality Check

No article on alternative career options would be complete without a summary of the personal attributes and technical skills required to work in this manner. My advice is to review these checklists and take careful stock of your individual situation before jumping ship. Notice, not surprisingly, that the advantages mentioned below are often the flip side of a disadvantage.

Skills Needed as an Independent Consultant

- self-discipline
- initiative

- ability to deal with irregular income
- ability to sell/write about the often intangible products libraries and information centers provide
- base in traditional librarianship to be familiar with vendors, equipment, standard practices, reference titles, etc.
- good personal networking with colleagues in a wide variety of library environments
- willingness to travel (often without direct compensation)
- desire to keep current in the field—to have an awareness of new developments, products, trends, technologies
- willingness to try new things ("never turn down a combat assignment")

Advantages to an Alternative Career Path as an Independent Consultant

- always dealing with something new
- exposure to a variety of information/library/archives environments
- no need to ask for time off as long as you can juggle your work contracts
- flexible schedule
- adaptable to different lifestyles
- satisfaction in having others ask for your advice
- confidence-building (you realize your skills are much broader than a cookie-cutter want ad for a librarian)

Disadvantages to an Alternative Career Path as an Independent Consultant

- start-up costs
- unpredictable income stream
- anxiety about the continuity and economic feasibility of work opportunities
- irregular schedule: light at times, firm deadlines at others
- no paid benefits (sick time, vacation, health insurance, etc.)
- being a bill collector
- small amount of anxiety with each new job
- people (especially traditional librarians) are not sure what you do for a living
- feeling that your time and efforts are fragmented, divided between several projects at once
- may be hard to move back to a traditional institution—they often don't place value on nontraditional paths

33.

Freelance Information Management

by Darlene E. Waterstreet

While trying to decide what to write for an update of my article in the first edition of *What Else You Can Do with a Library Degree*, I happened to be listening to Glenn Yarbrough singing "Where's Forever Gone?" and thought, how appropriate! It's hard to realize it's been over 20 years since I decided to experiment for six months or a year with freelance information management, and 15 years since first writing about it. It can hardly be called an experiment anymore, since I've spent more time as a freelancer than in all other full-time jobs combined—and also enjoyed it more. So let me give you a little background, and a few opinions on the advantages and disadvantages of freelancing.

With an undergraduate degree in business administration, and a number of years of data processing experience, I received my master's in library science from the University of Wisconsin–Milwaukee (UWM) in 1968. I spent more than five years working for the UWM Library, first as head of systems and data processing, and then in reference. The first of these positions had the great advantage of putting me in contact with all the functions of the library. As a systems analyst, I studied and charted procedures in technical services, collections development, and circulation; made suggestions for their improvement;

and initiated automated systems where practical. Later, my request
for a transfer to reference was approved, so I also had a chance to get
reference experience.

I left UWM at the end of June 1973. For some time, I had been considering a move, and had given a great deal of thought to a research
business of my own. I had sent out feelers to a number of Milwaukee
businesspeople, and one of these contacts led to the offer of a job as
information specialist for an advertising agency. This intrigued me,
since my undergraduate degree had included a major in marketing,
and it promised more security than striking out on my own. (Which
proves how wrong I can be!) I enjoyed six months as an advertising
agency information and research specialist, but was shocked when,
on December 31, 1973, the agency merged with a larger one. On
January 2 I found myself out of a job, since the larger agency did not
believe it needed a library.

At this point, I began to reconsider the independent information research possibilities. I had experience in both academic and special libraries, plus data processing experience, degrees in business administration and library science, a reasonable amount of money in the
bank, nobody except myself to support—and no job. This latter point
is important because I expect it is much harder to leave a job, no matter how frustrated you may be in it, and strike out on your own, than
it is to try the same independence when there is no job to leave. I told
myself independent information research was worth a try for six
months; if it was obvious that I had no future in information research, I could always look for another job.

And so Badger Infosearch was born, located in Milwaukee. "Infosearch" was, obviously, a contraction of "information research" which
was what I expected would be the primary function, although this has
turned out not to be the case. For those interested in the administrative details, Badger Infosearch is not incorporated, and has never had
any staff except myself. I decided at the outset that I would be a one-
person operation, and have never expanded. I want to do the actual
information management, not all the administrative duties that running a larger company involves. Although I considered renting office
space, I decided against it and have never regretted working out of my
home.

One of the early problems I encountered was the question of rates.
Was each job worth the same amount per hour? If so, what should the
rate be? I had some facts on rates charged elsewhere, and thought
most of them were too high. I decided very early that I would rather be
fully employed at lower rates than spend time looking for clients who
were willing to pay high charges. In spite of this, I found some people
were unwilling to pay even a reasonable, lower rate for information
work. One prospective client, a professional man, wanted someone to
weed, organize, and catalog an entire special library, which at that
point consisted of a lot of boxes and stacks of books. After telling me
in our preliminary conversation that his wife was currently attending

library school he did a double take on hearing my rate. He exclaimed, "That much to organize a library? I can get a secretary to do it for about four dollars an hour!" (Remember, this was in the mid-1970s.) I tried to point out some of the decisions and procedures requiring more than a clerical background. Apparently I was unsuccessful, because he never called again. Perhaps he compromised by getting his wife to do it, for four dollars an hour. My rates have risen over the years, but they may currently be too low because it's been a long time since any prospective clients have questioned them.

Between the jobs that were coming slowly at first, I decided to keep busy and fill a gap in Wisconsin reference materials by compiling an index to the biographies in the *Wisconsin Blue Book* (the state government manual). While the income from the index, which I published myself, was not great, it was reasonable, and I later published a similar index for Michigan. The main thing this project accomplished, however, was to help me become familiar with indexing. When a friend in a special library asked whether I was willing to take an indexing job that had been offered to him, I thus had at least some idea of where to start. But I had to decide if I was in the research business exclusively, or if I was willing to branch out into other types of information work.

I decided that I had no objection to doing something with information besides searching for it, if the client was willing to pay my rates. After doing a sample index of a small part of the papers (a set of board of directors' minutes), I gave the client a price quotation, which was accepted without any hesitation. It was the first time I recognized that my library degree had much broader applications. Incidentally, this index has been a continuing project, and I still do periodic updates after 20 years.

I realized that I was not doing as much short-term business research as I had expected. Instead, I was developing a service for a variety of clients involving various forms of research, and doing absolutely no research using fee-based online databases. I mention this only because many people, including librarians and library school students, still equate freelance information work with database searching.

Several of my current projects involve helping to build company archives. Perhaps the interest in corporate archives stems from the approach of the end of the century, but whatever the reason, I find these jobs fascinating, especially one involving a family-held private company in a planned community, where the archives involves company, family, and village materials. Unfortunately, I have not been trained as an archivist, but I have plans to take an archives course soon. In freelance work, one never stops learning.

After more than 20 years, I believe that freelancing has both advantages and disadvantages, but the former far outweigh the latter. The main advantage is independence. For most clients it is only the results that count, not the procedures you used to get them, nor whether you worked four days or seven last week. This independence, however, is countered by a lack of security. There may be times between clients when you would trade your total independence for one old-fashioned library payroll check. And these times still come after many years in business.

Another important advantage is the variety of work involved. Related to the variety itself is the experience it provides. If freelancers ever should look for a traditional library job, they would be able to offer prospective employers a much wider range of experience than most librarians who have spent their professional career either moving up within one library system, or moving to similar jobs in different libraries. There is a continued need for freelancers to learn new skills and new areas of information for different projects—in fact, you need to learn a fair amount about the client's business even before getting the job. I can give you a quick summary of insurance, brewing, plumbing, electric utilities, and on and on—but I could not give you the in-depth information on any of them that a special librarian in that industry could.

A recent advantage of freelancing is the fact that, in this era of downsizing (or reengineering, or whatever the need to decrease staff happens to be called at the moment), many companies are willing to pay outside consultants rather than hire full-time employees—because the companies don't need to pay employee benefits, or make long-term commitment to a project. This has made my business boom for the last few years.

For anybody considering starting a freelance information service, there are at least six required assets: competence, capital, contacts, patience, willpower, and an innovative outlook. It also doesn't hurt to have a little luck!

Competence implies experience. I would not suggest that you go out on the day you receive your M.L.S. and start a freelance service. Competence, if you are freelancing, also implies the ability to handle your own accounting, your own advertising and public relations, your own secretarial work, and your own janitorial service—unless you have enough capital to pay for these services.

Capital is needed for expenses and supplies, as well as for groceries during times when there is no money coming in. Starting to freelance while employed part-time is a possibility, but I would doubt that you can give enough attention to the freelance business if you are holding down another job.

The more contracts you have made, both in the information field and in the area in which you wish to specialize, the easier it will be for you to get started. The information contacts will usually be quite willing to steer business your way, since they lose nothing by doing so. I have made valuable contacts from my participation in the Special Libraries Association, having been both president of the Wisconsin chapter and chair of the national SLA Consultants Section. Anyone thinking of becoming a freelance information manager should consider joining this SLA section, which actually includes members from many nontraditional types of librarianship and information businesses. The contacts among your potential clients are most important. And once you have a few past clients, they can do a lot of good— if you make sure they are satisfied clients.

Patience and willpower are necessary in order to keep you from giving up if the going is rough, and to make you organize your time when the jobs start coming in. An innovative outlook is necessary to get into this area of the information business in the first place. You will also need an innovative outlook to recognize the opportunities that appear every day—opportunities that are overlooked by a good many people who would be quite capable of turning them into jobs if the thought ever occurred to them. And, finally, you may need an innovative outlook to come up with something you can do when there are no clients begging for your services. For instance, in addition to the Wisconsin and Michigan Blue Book indexes, I have done an annual index to proceedings of insurance associations and a book of trivia quizzes on the Green Bay Packers.

Badger Infosearch has weathered the problems and become a reasonably successful freelance operation. I'm still not sure where forever has gone (or at least the last 20 years), since I've never found the time to do all the things I was planning 20 years ago, but I'm still very glad I didn't go out on January 2, 1974, to look for a new job. Freelancing is still a lot more fun than working for a living!

34.

The Information Guild

by Alice Sizer Warner

I call myself "The Information Guild." I am self-employed, a sole proprietor, working out of our home in Lexington, Massachusetts. I work as a teacher, a writer, and a consultant. My library degree is from Simmons Graduate School of Library and Information Science.

In the late 1970s I had the fun of writing a chapter for the earlier edition of this book, about "what else" I was doing with my library degree. I described my beginnings as a school library volunteer, and how this experience drew me to a Simmons degree so, presumably, I could get paid for what I'd been doing for free.

At Simmons, I inevitably learned there was a lot more to our field than school libraries, and the result was that a Simmons classmate and I essentially created our own jobs by forming an information company, Warner-Eddison Associates, Inc. My chapter about "what else" told of our clients, our company's structure, our employees, and the birth of our firm's library software.

I left that company in January 1980, just as this book's predecessor was going to press. I had absolutely no idea what I wanted to do next, proving the old saw that one doesn't really know what one's options are until one explores one's options. I was offered two opportunities in Washington, D.C., and another in New York City. None seemed quite right; I turned them all down and kept exploring.

I finally had time to attend a luncheon meeting of a group I had helped found: the Women's Network, based out of Middlesex Community College here in Massachusetts. At that luncheon, the Middlesex continuing education dean asked if I would be interested in teaching a course about women running businesses. Although my primary qualification was that I had made every business mistake that could be made, I accepted the offer on the spot and created "Women and Business Ownership," a one-day, bring-your-lunch Saturday course. Then we added another course, this one about home-based businesses. Both ran every term for years. These were my first teaching experiences, and I've been teaching ever since.

During the Warner-Eddison years, my partner and I had written a small book about libraries and volunteers which was published by the Bowker Company. In the early 1980's, while I was struggling with Middlesex courses, I was asked if I would write a sequel. "But I've already told you all I know about volunteers; I can't tell you anything more," I replied. So we agreed that I'd survey what was currently happening among volunteers and public libraries and report on that. We'll never know how many questionnaires were actually distributed. Bowker and I sent out a finite number, based on a library's minimum book budget of, as I remember, at least $50,000. However, questionnaires begat sons and daughters of questionnaires; recipients all over the country made copies to send to other, smaller libraries not on our mailing list. Replies began coming in, and I was entranced. No one had ever before asked these libraries about their volunteer programs, and telling me all about it gave almost as much pleasure to the tellers as it did to me. But I had a book to write, so I stopped opening the mail after reading the first 500 questionnaires and got to work. I wrote the book, and then opened 250 more questionnaires and made the book better. *Volunteers in Libraries II* came out in 1983. It was my first solo book experience, and I've been writing ever since.

These, then, were my early experiences at teaching and writing. At Warner-Eddison I had been consulting all along, and presumably I could keep it up. So the decision was made to create the Information Guild as the umbrella under which all three activities—teaching, writing, and consulting—could come together. What does being the Information Guild mean? What is my life like?

My first traveling/teaching job was to Fredrickton, New Brunswick, in the Canadian Maritimes, where I taught a one-day seminar for the Canadian Association of Law Libraries. I taught in an amphitheater and we had fiddlehead ferns for lunch. Much travel has been for the Special Libraries Association, especially to their annual meetings and for their regional continuing education efforts. Courses have explored entrepreneurship and intrapreneurship, charging fees, marketing, budgeting, and mainstreaming. For a while I was traveling so frequently that I settled into a suitcase routine, using the same clothes again and again—outward bound, wear the blouse and the pants and the blazer; at the hotel, wear the dress to dinner; for room service breakfast, wear the nightgown; to teach, wear the skirt and the other blouse and the blazer; coming home, switch the skirt for the pants.

Class handouts and teaching notes always travel on my back, in the red knapsack.

My first graduate-level library school teaching was at Syracuse University in 1983, where I gave a two-week summer school course on how to be an entrepreneur. Then I developed another graduate course, on library budgeting and fiscal management. This has led to appointments at Michigan and North Carolina summer schools, as well as to my becoming a long-run, adjunct professor at Simmons Graduate School of Library and Information Science. I'm currently in a mode of "if it's spring and it's Wednesday, call me Professor."

As for writing, I have produced a regular column called "What Do You Want To Know?" for the newsletter *Information Broker* since it started publication in 1983. I try to turn out at least a handful of articles for library/information journals each year. As a public service, I regularly write a neighborhood newsletter which is being archived by our public library as "social history."

When I produced the book on volunteers, I became the proud owner of an Apple II+ computer. The next book, *Mind Your Own Business: A Guide for the Information Entrepreneur* (1987), was for the publisher of the book you are now reading, Neal-Schuman Publishers.

"MYOB" was written on the same vintage computer, except for the chapters on marketing and selling; those chapters were written, literally, in pencil on dimestore theme paper while I was encamped far from home near an offspring who had been badly hurt in an auto accident. Our son fully recovered. And when I went to enter my penciled scrawls into the computer, I found that I changed not one word—and, incidentally, neither did Neal-Schuman's editors. Next came, again for Neal-Schuman, *Making Money: Fees for Library Services* (1989), and this was followed by *Owning Your Numbers: An Introduction to Budgeting for Special Libraries* (1993), put out by the Special Libraries Association.

I am currently working on two books, and both are being written in unorthodox fashion. The first is a childhood memoir called *Bethany*, and for the first time I am writing without knowing who the publisher (if any) will be. I write at this book, using a new laptop computer, only when we are living in our camper at a very special campground on Mount Desert Island, Maine; wallowing in memories and being on vacation seem to go together. I also am working on a how-to-do-it book on library budgeting for Neal-Schuman, and this book is being written on the laptop in the laundry room downstairs; somehow, segregating myself while the washer sloshes and the dryer thumps is creating the right atmosphere. Only time will show whether these methods work!

The third part of my business, consulting, has been primarily for large companies. For instance, I created a library where none before existed at the financial office of a Canadian manufacturer. Most volumes in that library cost $8,000 to $10,000 each, so lavishing expensive attention on a few hundred items made a good deal of sense. Another example: I was called in by a major U.S. corporation with plants worldwide, and was asked to "Look at our information stuff and tell us if we're going into the year 2000 all right." I spent a great deal of time listening to people as I didn't want anyone to say, "Why didn't she ask me?" Results? We automated as much as we could, and I traveled a lot to check on far-flung sites. A small collection in Wales (Great Britain) was cataloged long distance. And a high point for me was a three-day marathon in the Texas panhandle when five of us created an instant laboratory library using old-fashioned, assembly-line techniques. Incidentally, I had asked my client to hire Texas-based librarians for me, and I was told "Aw, we wouldn't know what to say to them; you hire them." And I did so, from my home office in Lexington, Massachusetts.

Other consulting involves the design and start-up of fee-based library services. I have worked with universities whose libraries were developing fee-for-service departments. I recently assisted a large association whose library was to start charging fees. My job was to help staff overcome reluctance at collecting money for what they'd always given away for "free."

So this is what I do as the Information Guild: I teach, I write, I consult. I write about what I teach about and what I consult about. I always insist that my pupils, and my clients, know what their goals are. Goals can be grandiose, goals can be modest; without goals, no plan can be made to reach them.

When I started the Information Guild, two goals were foremost for me: I didn't want employees (I no longer wanted the pressure of having to earn money in order to pay salaries), and I also wanted to develop something, or a combination of somethings, that I could do for the rest of my life—an adjustable "job" from which I'll never have to retire.

I think I have done that, I am doing that. I enjoy every minute; I have the best of all worlds. I am very lucky.

35.

My So-Called Library Life

by Mary K. Feldman

I came into the library world a little late, after dropping out of college with World War II as an excuse. There was a hiatus in my education while I married, had four children, operated as a suburban mother and as a volunteer in the local library, and even worked part-time to shelve books and work on the circulation desk. The librarian encouraged me to go to library school, but I didn't really think I would do it. In 1962, at the age of 42, I went back to college to complete (almost to start over) my college career, and went on to the library science degree from there. I suspect I was one of the first of the "older women" to go back to school at that time—certainly I was the oldest person in all my classes!

My purpose was to become a children's librarian, in a school; I had my children and possible vacations in mind. When I finished the degree, that original plan seemed rather naive. I wound up, instead, as head of technical services at Trinity College, in Washington, D.C., a small Catholic college for girls, which had no automation at all (this was 1965), and was organized by the Dewey system. My boss was Sister Helen Sheehan—I could have had no better mentor or boss. She encouraged me in all kinds of library activities, for which I am grateful.

When Sister Helen retired, I looked for another job, and with the assistance of my other mentor, Dr. Elizabeth W. Stone, I went to the U.S. Department of Transportation (DOT)—a fortunate choice, because they had some automation and were interested in more, and they used the Library of Congress classification system (with some variations of their own). DOT was one of the libraries that comprised the first FEDLINK experimental group to use OCLC outside of Ohio, and that again was a fortunate thing for me—to be in at the beginning. Because it was the beginning, and because Dr. Stone had become dean of the Department of Library Science at Catholic University, I was asked to speak about OCLC a few times, and when the University got some money, I was asked to give a short course on it, which gradually grew into a somewhat longer course. My part-time teaching career went on for several years.

At Trinity I had done some reference work, and I moonlighted elsewhere as well on reference. At DOT, after a period of cataloging, I was promoted to the reference section, so I had that experience as well.

When I left DOT as a result of a reorganization and reduction of the Department, I was close to retirement age. Nevertheless, I went to CUA to work at the National Center for Family Studies. At Sister Helen's encouragement, I attended the first ALA preconference on automation in 1965, and I had always been interested in that aspect of library work. I had acquired a computer (a CPM KayPro 4), and did some work on it for the National Center for Family Studies. Other people had suggested me for word processing, so I input a couple of chapters for a book.

After a year, the Center was no longer funded, because of policy changes. I kept on with part-time work, now using an IBM PC. I input three book manuscripts, handled some mailing lists, and did OCLC reconversion work and cataloging for various clients in the area. That is what I still do.

I came into the field with very little in capital—only my computer and the retirement funds I received from DOT, Social Security, and TIAA/CREF. It helped that I owned my home and a car, and that I was able to work very flexibly (since I had recently acquired both a library science degree and a divorce, and the nest was rapidly emptying).

I cannot emphasize too much the value of networking—and of belonging to library organizations. In my library career I have belonged to many library groups, both local and national, and have held offices in several. People knew me because of this involvement, and because I was editor of the District of Columbia Library Association newsletter, *Intercom*, for many years. They could not miss my name, since they saw it every month.

Some of my work is cataloging for libraries in the Washington area that do not have sufficient cataloging to hire a full-time person. I may go to the site, sometimes I pick up material for later delivery, or sometimes material is delivered to me for the client to pick up later. I have dealt with several federal libraries, for some on a continuing but occasional basis for a few years, for others only when the backlog gets big enough that they need someone to clean it up or when a new shipment of books is received. This has been mostly OCLC-related work, though some of it has been Bibliophile work, and I am currently working with two libraries that use WordPerfect and Inmagic. I have also produced card catalogs for small libraries (very small, most of them), using Librarian's Helper, and have organized a couple of libraries from scratch, in one case using Microdis. One of these was a complete disaster—I color coded it, and learned when it was finished that one of the persons who was supposed to use it was color-blind! Lesson: Find out everything before you start.

As for charging for your service, I am not a very good example. I suspect I charge too little. A very successful contractor once said, in a conference that I attended, that the way to price yourself is first to decide how much money you want to make and then how many hours you want to work (not forgetting about holidays and such). Then you should halve the hours to determine your base figure, because, he said, you will find that you need about half your time to sell yourself and get more work to do. I have never had to advertise my services—all my work has come from word of mouth, recommendations from people with whom I have had other contacts, or library organization connections. My income is enough to keep me going, though without the additions from retirement funds it would not seem very significant. I will certainly never be rich.

I have worked with medical libraries, law libraries, college and university libraries, small museum libraries, and corporate libraries; have used WordStar, WordPerfect, dBase, Inmagic, OCLC, Bibliophile, Lotus Notes, Microdis; and have used both Dewey and LC classification systems. For two libraries I developed thesauri especially for them. Occasionally I give a lecture, mostly on MARC or OCLC, sometimes just on general cataloging. My current projects are for a health library, a restaurant association, a college library, a medical library, and a special corporation library. I am having fun!

36.

Freelance Grant Writer/ Project Director in the Wonderful World of Humanities

by Deborah Bowerman Brennan

During my ten-year career as a professional librarian in my local public library, I had the opportunity to do just about everything—from leading the preschool story hour to being the director. I enjoyed it all, but, once my children were raised and educated, I decided to take some time off to see what I wanted to do with the rest of my life. As fate would have it, at the moment I was making that decision, things in the public library world in Rhode Island were getting more interesting.

The Rhode Island Department of State Library Services had sent a state contingent (which included Peggy Shea, from the Department; Thomas Roberts, Executive Director of the Rhode Island Committee for the Humanities; literature scholar David Stineback; and librarian Lauri Burke) to a workshop to learn more about a new American Library Association and National Endowment for the Humanities project called *Let's Talk About It*. The meeting was designed to help each contingent create a grant proposal that would support a statewide reading and discussion series. The group returned home with a nearly completed proposal and a need for a project director to complete the plans and carry them out. Peggy Shea knew that I was available and interested and, as they say, the rest is history. I was about to embark on my new career—that of freelance grant writer/project director.

What had prepared me for this career? My library skills proved indispensable—conducting research, locating resources, identifying experts, and compiling bibliographies. A knowledge of who would be in our audience and an understanding of their interests proved equally invaluable. It helped that I am a "self-starter" and capable of being very organized (though anyone seeing my desk and office might think otherwise). I also like to write and I enjoy the process of "playing with numbers" to create a budget. Finally, my training in library administration had honed my management skills—I was ready and able to run a complex operation on a shoestring.

During my years as a library director, the part of the job I had enjoyed most was putting on public programs. They were much more fun than worrying about the union or whether or not the air conditioning was going to work. I did not see public programming as mere fluff. Those programs were an extension of books on the shelves, capable of bringing information to the general public in a different and, perhaps, more accessible format. Also I had seen the public relations value of those programs, when articles in the local media called attention to the library and its services, in reaching nonusers and getting them in the door. I believed that once they saw how friendly and helpful we were, they were sure to return. During my tenure, we had some real success in generating local programming, but preparing and presenting each program was extremely time-consuming.

A National Endowment for the Humanities grant to the Providence Public Library led by Christie Sarles and her staff, had introduced me to the joys of prepackaged, ready-to-go, statewide programming. Using input from librarians and the expertise of humanities scholars from local colleges and universities, *A Lively Experiment*, as it was named, offered a potpourri of free programs about Rhode Island history to public libraries around the state.

A Lively Experiment was such a welcome addition to local library programming that, when it was over, librarians begged for more. It took several years, but, finally, with the success of the Department of State Library Services' proposal to the National Endowment for the Humanities, *Let's Talk About It* brought statewide programming back to Rhode Island. The fun was about to begin, and this time it was I who would welcome local librarians and their patrons to the wonderful world of humanities programming.

Working closely with Peggy Shea from the Department of State Library Services, I helped take the *Let's Talk About It* reading and discussion series to 12 libraries around the state. With additional funding from the Rhode Island Committee for the Humanities, we even hosted a series for the inmates at the local prison. *Let's Talk About It* was a huge success. Our audiences loved having the opportunity to hear college professors speak about books. At the same time, the professors enjoyed having the opportunity to work with out-of-school adults who brought their life experiences and mature ideas to the discussions. As one scholar said about the audiences, "They keep us honest." This interaction between the scholar and audience became the cornerstone of all our future projects.

At the same time that we were involved in setting up *Let's Talk About It*, Rhode Island was gearing up for the celebration of its 350th anniversary. Fay Zipkowitz, Director of the Department of State Library Services, invited me to volunteer as the chair of a committee dubbed Librarians for the 350th, whose mission was to ensure that libraries would be an integral part of the statewide celebration. In a number of exciting brainstorming sessions, librarians developed a variety of projects—including a plan for a Rhode Island bibliography, a reading and discussion series devoted to Rhode Island authors and settings, and, important for me, a multifaceted series of public programs on Rhode Island history.

Peggy Shea and I, along with a small planning committee, wrote what proved to be a successful grant proposal to the National Endowment for the Humanities, with me serving as the project director. Using as our title the intriguing question *Is There a Rhode Island Style?* we offered exhibits, concerts, demonstrations, and panel discussions, as well as straightforward lectures, to libraries around the state. Rhode Islanders are proud of their history and they flocked to programs on topics that ranged from the decorative arts and architecture to the role of women in the history of the state—all presented by humanities scholars eager to interact with out-of-school adults in the public library setting.

Let's Talk About It and *Is There a Rhode Island Style?* were followed by a succession of statewide programs carried out under the aegis of the Department of State Library Services. We then enlarged our vision by joining with colleagues from the other New England states to form the New England Council for Programs in Libraries. This ad hoc committee, composed of state library representatives like Peggy Shea and freelance project directors like me, had as its primary goal the development of proposals to bring free programs to libraries in the region. Secondarily, it would help ensure that we freelancers remained employed. The council prepared a successful proposal to the National Endowment for the Humanities submitted under the auspices of the New England Foundation for the Humanities. *Sharing Humanities Programs in New England Libraries* had freelancers as state coordinators responsible for organizing the public reading and discussion programs presented by the local libraries. We also developed a second component of the project, *The New England Book Bag,* a regional resource network to share the multiple copies of the books each of the states had generated as a result of the *Let's Talk About It* and other reading and discussion series.

During these years of statewide public programming, as part of each series we included evaluation forms that encouraged audience members to offer suggestions for future programs. Rhode Island being what it is, a thin shell of land surrounding a very large body of water—Narragansett Bay—it was inevitable that people would request a series on the bay and its place in the history of the region. Using the input of librarians, scholars, and everyone else who cared about the bay, five years and hundreds of ideas later, the "megagrant" *What a Difference a Bay Makes* was born. With generous funding from the National Endowment for the Humanities and the Rhode Island Committee for the Humanities and with matching funds from a local foundation, the Department of State Library Services together with the Rhode Island Historical Society and libraries in the Narragansett Bay region presented more than 100 programs, reaching thousands of Rhode Islanders over a two-year period. As the project's director, I had the fun of putting it all together—with a lot of help from my friends.

What a Difference a Bay Makes brought historians and folklorists, archaeologists and Native Americans, authors and artists, musicians and boatbuilders, philosophers and fishermen to libraries for performances, discussions, lectures, workshops, and tours—all dedicated to Narragansett Bay and its indispensable place in the life and times of those within its reach. So that all this wonderful information would not be lost, we then spent six months compiling a project anthology based on the presentations, copies of which were donated to each library in the state. *What a Difference a Bay Makes* went on to win a coveted Award of Merit from the American Association for State and Local History.

That was in 1993. Since then, circumstances somewhat beyond my control have put my career on hold. But my peers continue to take reading and discussion series and other exciting humanities programs to audiences around the country. Many of them are now reaching an exciting new audience. Adult new readers are experiencing for the first time what our other audiences have started to take for granted— the thrill of having college professors listen intently to their ideas and opinions.

How do you get into this freelancing field? I would urge any of you with an interest in the arts and humanities to work with like-minded individuals in the community to develop grant proposals. If you are willing to volunteer your time, to gamble as it were, then all you have to do is offer your services to your local library or humanities council. You might want to get your feet wet with a small project for which you are paid only an honorarium. While it is true that soft money is getting softer, local and national arts and humanities councils are there to help you. And remember that there is corporate money available as well.

Writing a proposal is easy—*if* you treat it as a team effort. Have brainstorming sessions involving everyone who knows something about the topic, along with the library staff likely to be interested in presenting programs. Use your scholars to write the sections of the proposal that require subject expertise. Take your ideas to a funding agency that shares your goals and is interested in your topic. Once you have identified likely funders, if you follow their application instructions and use any advice they offer, you are sure to succeed. And a final caveat: Once you have the money, make sure you leave plenty of time to plan the programs. As anyone in the business can tell you, there is a version of "Murphy's Law" for planning: Everything will take twice as long as you thought it would.

The real fun begins when you hold the programs. You will spend your time with wonderful people, you will learn about interesting topics, *and* you will get paid for it. You will also have the satisfaction of knowing that you have helped the local library in its efforts to be the cultural center of the community.

Because of my grant-writing and project-directing experience, I have been invited a number of times to serve as an evaluator for other humanities projects (on topics ranging from Victorian book design to the Coptic religion in Egypt). Perhaps the next one will be yours!

37.

Librarian, Vendor, and Information Adventurer: Life with My M.L.S.

by David Jank

I can still remember the moment I decided I was going to library school. I didn't care how long it would take or how much it would cost. An M.L.S. degree was just the right thing for me.

I was hoping I would land a job as cataloger at my local public library, where I had been employed all through high school and college. Secretly, I had calculated that by the time I finished my master's degree, our cataloger would surely be retired, they'd have to give me the job out of loyalty, and I could settle down into a career for life and never have to commute to Boston again. That was 20 years ago. Not surprisingly, this scenario never came to pass.

I coveted the NUCs, the LC schedules, and even story hours, and because I was told I couldn't touch any of them without my professional degree, my only mission was to get that piece of paper so I could get the job I wanted. Once I did, however, the wealth of knowledge and skills I acquired suddenly made me a hot item in areas I had never even expected. In fact, ever since I finished my M.L.S. I have never worked "in" libraries at all, at least not in the sense in which I grew up thinking of them.

I think the most valuable lesson I have learned as an information professional is that the overall management of information itself, rather than the production of that information, is at the heart of a librarian's talent and skills. The library and information services industry has likely been the service profession most significantly impacted by technology in the last two decades. While countless other professions are also finding themselves in the wake of technological change, no profession has been so redefined as ours.

Indeed, the very tasks on which I had assumed I would build my professional career are simply not in demand the way they were back then. I am convinced that the reason my library degree has served me so well is not because librarians per se are in such great demand, as any number of reengineering victims can attest. Rather, it is because of the expanding number of service providers marketing to the library and information profession, and the growing number of management executives who now realize the value of information manipulation and the expertise of those who can do it. Information manipulation promises challenging opportunities for the entrepreneur, while the expertise serves as a not-so-subtle reminder of the precious market commodity our skills represent.

At the time I finished graduate school, the library automation marketplace was exploding. The early 1980s was the romantic era of this technology, and professional librarians with even a semblance of computer literacy were hot properties in any library or information center. More important, however, the growing technical savvy of professional librarians dictated that all vendors, from book jobbers to software designers, needed to "get smarter" about our profession if they hoped to maintain any reputable market position.

This is when I entered the picture. Once I landed a job as a "systems specialist," which basically meant I knew what a disk drive was, I was on a roll. Coincidentally, I had been fortunate enough to serve in a graduate school internship that afforded me a limited, but valuable, number of opportunities. This combination of technical skills and information industry knowledge was then a rare one, and to an extent, it still is.

Vendors appreciate people with these skills because, with such employees, they are better able to provide quality service to libraries and information centers. Similarly, such skilled job applicants have a real advantage in the library marketplace. For my part, I opted for the vendor life throughout most of the 1980s, as it afforded me not only practical opportunities to develop business skills, but allowed me to make what I felt were the most valuable contributions to my profession—helping to shape and design the technology that librarians would be using in the future.

When I worked in a traditional library setting, I found myself agreeing to have my library serve as a test site for any number of computer products. Managerially, this proved a very wise decision, in that my employers were able to take advantage of new, cutting-edge technologies at minimal, if any, cost, and vendors benefited from receiving input from their client base at the product design level. The camaraderie I developed with my vendor colleagues provided a nurturing environment in which I was able to explore new career opportunities.

I started working for vendors as soon as I discovered how much fun it could be. I had always assumed I would never be "techie" enough for them. Little did I know that, across the board, most of them were desperate to find library specialists who could shed some additional light on their tasks at hand, and who could serve as liaisons between their own technicians and their endusers. What better source for the creators of library products than members of the target groups to which they market? I had, it seemed, uncovered some gold in them there hills.

The opportunities for library professionals in the vendor community are virtually unlimited, and I have always encouraged my colleagues to explore them. These are not limited to technical environments either. For library professionals who are also skilled writers, researchers, editors, speakers, teachers, or managers, creative employment options in the information services industry can be limitless.

I have always been impressed by the willingness of library vendors to go that extra mile in getting smart about the market they serve. Most do an exceptional job, and librarians benefit from having the opportunity to "infiltrate" their ranks. I have worked on product design, network development, data processing, and quality control, and all without having a degree in computer science. I have provided technical writing and documentation support, as well as database design and systems training, all of which have been targeted to the library profession. Such experiences allowed me the flexibility of migrating between positions in libraries and with vendors, and all of the positions, I believe, were a direct result of my having earned a professional library degree.

Ultimately, these experiences led me to make a three-year sojourn back into a traditional library setting, but in a nontraditional role. Although I was again in a library building, I was doing something I never imagined likely—serving as a manager in a large, metropolitan data-processing setting. Again, while this was not something I had ever envisioned happening, I grew to realize that it was a logical extension. Librarians, I have found, just seem to know technology as it applies to libraries better than technologists do.

As the library profession has been redefined by technological advances, so too has the computer industry itself. No longer are computer science specialists trading in their degrees for instant employment. There is a growing movement in the high tech arena to consider vertical market expertise as much as, if not more than, technical skills when recruiting new employees.

Management information systems (MIS) and other subdivisions of the data-processing industry are of prime importance today in all professions, and the library community is no exception. For the technologically astute information professional, any MIS, technical support, or training position is prime territory for career direction, especially in the area of technical support for libraries.

While my formal technical education has been minimal (computer courses here and there), my understanding of information technology has its foundation in my solid library school education. I have learned many technical skills over the years, but I apply them because of the fundamental learning I received from a traditional, liberal arts under-graduate education, followed by a professional degree in the study of the industry that I serve.

Although I have an unfinished doctorate (which is likely to stay that way) I still consider the M.L.S. my most significant educational achievement, not so much in its content as in its focus. Our profession is a dynamic one, and we need to be dynamic in our own professional growth in order to serve it.

While librarians intuitively have a knack for finding and managing information, I have come to believe that expanding employment opportunities especially exist for those of us willing to step in and advise clientele on how to use and manipulate this information themselves. I do not view this as a departure from traditional library functions but as a logical evolution of them. The library degree, when viewed not as a set of skills but as an industry specialization, is a valuable one.

I can never be sure where I will ultimately go with my degree, and that is what makes things so exciting. With the exception of my very first professional position, not one job I have ever held actually "required" the M.L.S.. All of them, however, were offered to me not explicitly because I had the degree, but because I had developed, as a result of earning that degree, an analytical understanding of how this industry works. Invariably, those who recruited me would always make a comment to the effect of "Gee, I never knew librarians knew how to do that," and over time, I found myself replacing my indignation at such comments with the realization that I was part of an industry whose future was uncharted. Librarians alone have the power and ability to chart it, and we should do so vociferously and enthusiastically.

The journey on which I am now embarked is one of market research and analysis: gathering information, synthesizing it, and presenting it in an appropriate fashion to those who need it. Twenty years ago, I would have written that off as a job for "one of those M.B.A. types." Instead, I have discovered that my technology, research, and information management skills and expertise are providing seemingly endless opportunities for me, "one of those M.L.S. types."

I had not realized just how much need there is for market researchers and writers who are adept at gathering, processing, managing, and disseminating information about anything at all. It seems to me that we librarians constitute the most logical pool of resources to meet these needs—and for the adventurous at heart, the possibilities in this arena appear to be endless.

In essence, I have taken a quantum leap in my professional career.

I have decided that it is possible to take my library and information know-how, leave the physical library environment as I had known it, and strike out into areas where I suspected there would be some need not for librarians per se, but for people who knew how to manage information, in any form and in any setting. We librarians will always be able to fill that void provided that we are willing to take risks, to pursue individual metamorphoses, and to view our professional degree not as a certification of skills but as a qualification of education and expertise.

I attribute most of my success to a certain willingness to try anything, provided it is related to information services. I am grateful to my library school faculty who taught me that anything can be done with this education; I am grateful to those library and information professionals who were willing to take a risk and let me try anything on the job; and, most of all, I am grateful to have worked with so many businesspeople who realized the worth of having a "librarian-type" around.

38.

An Unfinished Odyssey

by Sally Pore

When I received the letter from Betty-Carol Sellen asking me to contribute a chapter to the second edition of *What Else You Can Do with a Library Degree*, I was sure there was some mistake. After all, I had read the first edition and I knew that the contributors were people who had "real" jobs. I saw each of their stories as a success story. A success story, I thought, would hardly describe my situation. I spoke with Betty-Carol who confirmed that she did, indeed, want me to contribute a chapter to the book.

So, what else can you do with a library degree? I am still in the process of discovering the answer to that question. Since I don't yet have a complete answer, I can only share with you my journey as it has unfolded thus far.

A career in the library field was to be a second career for me. Although my career goal in high school had been to be a librarian, I got sidetracked along the way, earned a master's degree in speech pathology, and spent 17 years working as a speech/language pathologist. On bad days I would invariably say, "I should have been a librarian."

In the fall of 1990 I finally did something about it and applied to a graduate school in library and information science. That fall I went to the campus, had an interview with one of the faculty members and then a second interview with one of the administrators. Both people seemed very enthusiastic about my entering the program, and, when all of the i's were dotted and t's were crossed, I was accepted. I began in January 1991.

My particular interests in the field are in the areas of information research and writing. I very much enjoy the process of searching for information and I also enjoy the process of compiling information and writing. In graduate school I was most fortunate to have a wonderful advisor, and he encouraged me to think in terms of becoming a reference librarian in an academic library. It didn't take a whole lot of encouragement—it sounded great to me. That vision of "Sally the Librarian" was mighty close now.

I completed the graduate program in June 1992. That was three years and 98 job applications ago. In addition to the 98 openings to which I have applied, I have made 146 other contacts. The vision of "Sally the Librarian" seems a little less clear now.

Before I tell you "what else I have done with my library degree," it seems important to tell you, briefly, why I believe I am not working in a library somewhere. I have a disability—I have cerebral palsy and both my mobility and speech are affected. That, I have come to believe, is very simply why I am not employed in a library. Although the library school accepted and welcomed me enthusiastically, people out in the profession are not interested in hiring persons with disabilities. I can only hope that administrators and faculty members in library schools and those in the profession will soon begin to speak with each other.

So, what do you do with a library degree, no experience in the field, and no job? I began by looking around for some volunteer work that might give me some library-related experience. I was fortunate to make contact with the New Hampshire Historical Society, and for about a year I worked on indexing projects for them. I also made contact with the local public library and I have, on a volunteer, as-needed basis researched and responded to questions that they have received regarding local history.

But if you are looking for work, you don't just go off to your volunteer duties. You network, and you network, and you network. After I had been out of school for about a year and one-half (a very long time when you need work), the networking paid some dividends. The president of an advertising agency spoke with someone at the Historical Society about writing a company history and was given my name. An attorney contacted a law librarian about work on a major bibliography and was given my name. Because I had made contacts at the State Library, they printed my flyer in their newsletter. This led a woman working on her master's thesis to call and ask me to type the thesis, and also led a law librarian to call to ask if I would do some newspaper photocopying.

Very occasional photocopying of newspaper articles for the law librarian has led not only to a new friendship, but also to a small but more frequent job. I now photocopy for her and another law librarian in the state all of the Supreme Court opinions as they are handed down.

Typing the master's thesis turned into a project of typing two complete drafts; it also led to an ongoing friendship. Deadlines had to be met at several points along the way. Although I wasn't able to do much editing because of the nature of the project, the little I did whetted my appetite for doing more.

Compiling the bibliography for the attorney has called for several skills. My first task was to locate a database program to meet all of the project's requirements. After one false move I found Procite, which has been a godsend. Next, within the Procite program I created three different authority files which speed data entry. The database is being created for publication, with entries indexed by field of law practice. As data are entered I am continuously making decisions about where to place any given title and when to add additional fields of practice that hadn't been thought of previously. There are currently 1,400 records entered, with probably a few more thousand to come. A word of advice for those constructing their first major database: Make rules, write them down, and stick to them. As you work over time you will forget whether you are entering numbers as words or as numerals, or whether you are using commas or semicolons between phrases. Making such rules at the outset will save major editing time later.

The most challenging and significant project so far (in terms of amount of time spent) has been that involving the history of a company more than 100 years old. Although I was contacted initially about researching and writing the history, after receiving several boxes of the company's archival materials, I first devised a classification system for the materials. This involved creating a classification system by subject, rearranging the materials into the new system, and preparing a listing of the contents in each subject area. Work on the actual history has involved researching available materials, listening to and taking notes on taped conversations of recollections of present and former employees, preparing and submitting outlines of the text, writing drafts of the text, writing cutlines for photographs, and meeting frequently with the editor/coauthor of the project. With each of these activities I am calling upon and using skills I learned in library school—organization and classification skills, research skills, writing skills.

I have also been able to combine my interest in writing with my experiences in the area of rehabilitation at both the personal and professional levels, and I have had articles and book reviews published in journals of nursing, rehabilitation, and speech/language pathology. Writing for health-care professionals is an ongoing interest.

In the time since I began thinking about writing this chapter another short-term project has come my way. I have been asked to research possible funding sources for a new program that a nonprofit organization hopes to initiate. This raises the possibility of providing the same service for other agencies and organizations.

For a long time I considered that the task of searching for full-time employment was my main job, and I would work on the freelance projects only after all of the contacts had been made and the resumes had been sent out. Recently, however, there has been a shift in my thinking. I am realizing that I *like* what I'm doing. I enjoy working on both the legal bibliography and on the company history. I'm realizing that it's actually very convenient and comfortable for me to work at home. I believe my real strengths and talents are in the areas of research and writing, and it just may be that I can make better use of those strengths and talents by working from home than I could with a "regular" library job.

Of course, coming to such a decision is not something to be done without a great deal of thought, and as I write this I have made no final decision. How do I know that I can generate enough business and enough income to support myself? In truth, I don't know. The few marketing strategies I have tried up to now have generally not been successful. I am going to have to learn still more skills—how to market, how to determine realistic price quotes for projects, how to allocate time between several ongoing projects. "How to market" may be a challenge, but I worry that "How to market with a disability" may be a significantly greater challenge. In searching for all of these answers I will again turn to my network of contacts.

What else can you do with a library degree? So far I have discovered that you can generate indexes, compile bibliographies, research, write, and edit. I believe there are several other things you can do and I am anxious to try them. Some of these include researching information for authors, writing text for promotional materials, working with businesses and agencies to develop strategies for compliance with ADA, and working with companies to prepare annual, semiannual, and quarterly reports.

I gave this chapter the only title I could—An Unfinished Odyssey. When I began my journey into the world of library and information science I did not expect to be sitting at home three years after completing the program. At this point I am not where I expected to be, and I don't know if I am where I should be. But I have to acknowledge that, although I may not be doing as much work as I would like, because I went to library school I thoroughly enjoy the work I am doing. We will just have to see where the next bend in the road leads.

PART IV

Independent Librarians With Companies of Their Own

39.

Developing an Enterprise: Library Personnel and Information Management

by Carol Berger

When I decided to start my own business in 1982, I intended it to be a "company." My vision was to employ a large number (then unknown) of librarians and other experts who could help others in the profession when the need arose, preferably by filling in during short stints on demand. This was underscored during the first few months of testing the idea through some market research and later while implementing it when real customers actually came along. I learned that what I wanted to do could not be done alone, nor could it be done without a central command capability that had to be very well organized and documented. Once the structure was down pat (at least in my mind), everything else fell into place and the enterprise began.

I founded C. Berger and Company (CBC) after having worked as a librarian for over 15 years in a variety of settings and in several parts of the country. CBC is a library personnel and information management consulting firm. We provide support services in the form of temporary and contract professional and clerical workers; executive recruitment for permanent supervisory and management-level professionals; library/records/information center setup and maintenance; and such related services as cataloging, indexing, and looseleaf filing. Although personnel operations are available in only six states, other services are supplied nationwide. CBC's customers include major national corporations, publishers, and manufacturers, as well as universities, law firms, government agencies, trade and professional associations, and large and small public libraries. We receive calls for interim directors and children's librarians and for custom database development, library design, and outsourcing specific functions or entire operations. In a nutshell, C. Berger and Company is the librarian's librarian.

A company with so broad a scope is a far cry from my childhood dream of becoming a high school teacher. That dream was why I had attended the Catholic University of America, pursuing a B.A. in English literature in the 1960s. By senior year I'd narrowed my goal to a position in suburban Virginia so that I could share space with my college roommate who'd received her commission as a speech therapist there. To tide me over, I obtained part-time work at the District of Columbia Public Library's Carnegie building, a job I pursued at the suggestion of the senator from Connecticut who referred me there when I approached his office for employment. As a reader's advisor at the DCPL, I received hands-on training at the information desk, directing curious (or lost) patrons through the building, the collections, and the old and new card catalogs. I was also submerged into the reference room resources and subsequently assigned to provide quick reference assistance for phone and walk-in inquiries. By the time I got my college diploma and learned that I needed certain additional education courses to be certified as a teacher, I accepted a transfer to the Chevy Chase branch of the library and the challenge of being a young adult advisor, which increased my growing interest in the profession.

Like many others, I turned to library science as a career because of the encouragement of a mentor. Our branch librarian knew everything—she could answer any question, could recommend the perfect book from our collection for every need, and could charm every patron. She was patient with children and employees and advised me that I had a gift I should pursue, especially since I could apply to the Graduate School of Library Science at Catholic University without taking the GRE. Once I was accepted, I was further supported when she rearranged work schedules to accommodate my classes on alternate mornings and evenings for three semesters. I would probably still be there if I hadn't asked to be transferred to the library's centralized technical services department. That opportunity was reserved for professionals or for typists, so I moved into the private sector, where I have since spent most of my career.

When starting in library school, I focused on public library course work, but after changing jobs and learning more about the variety of special libraries (and the positions within them), I broadened my studies as well. From the public library I moved into the library of a government contractor—from young adult work to cataloging engineering books and indexing government documents. Next was a very brief stint in a high school library, where I discovered I didn't belong, even though the commitment would reduce my federal student loan. Then it was on to another engineering firm library, and from there to a position as the librarian in a small company that provided information management and indexing services under contract to the federal government, publishers, and other commercial firms. And while still in Washington, I became library director for the trade association of the airlines. By this point in my life, I had three children, a husband who had taken a new position with a firm in northern California, and a thesis and comps still left for that M.L.S.

During the two years that I did not work while on the West Coast, the library profession exploded in new ways. DIALOG was born and OCLC was formed. Sophisticated networks and cooperatives flourished. Our next family stop was suburban Chicago, where I easily found a part-time job as a contractor to close down the library in a food company. Next was the opportunity to develop a library for the National Live Stock and Meat Board (and learn about online tools firsthand). It was here that I enrolled in the M.B.A. program at the University of Illinois, with the approval of my employer, so that I could become the board's expert in computer applications. My last "real" job was as head of the research library at Beatrice Foods Company, where I was introduced to RLIN and personal computers, while still continuing those business school studies. In fact, it took me six years to earn that degree in addition to working full-time, commuting, and mothering. Midway, I received an M.L.S., finally, by taking the long overdue comprehensive exam.

Cutbacks at Beatrice included my position as well as those of three assistants in the library, and I faced unemployment and many questions about the future. Did I really want the hassle of constantly justifying a library's existence and its need for funding in the corporate sector? Was I up to the one-hour-plus commute each way into the city? What other options were there for using my library skills, business training (with MIS and marketing concentrations), and professional connections cultivated through Special Libraries Association and American Society for Information Science memberships? What did I *need,* that no one else provided, when I was working as a librarian? How could I supply those services to my peers?

Even before that fateful day at Beatrice when we parted company, I was forming the concept of C. Berger and Company. As a consultant for the local SLA chapter, I had worked with several organizations that were considering if and how to set up libraries in-house. In addition, my research indicated that there was a firm in the East offering services very much like the profile I drew up. When my suggestion to open a branch of that firm in the Chicago area was rejected, I began looking at ways to do it myself, taking a temporary firm as my model. With the blessings of a U.S. Small Business Administration SCORE advisor, a skeptical husband, and supportive friends, I ventured into the unknown. The journey began in the basement of my home, and has ended in an airy, 2,800-square-foot facility with a support group of over 125 employees. It has been an exciting time that has utilized skills acquired from every job and probably every class I ever attended.

Running a business can be an exhausting as well as a rewarding experience. You can't have too much self-confidence, time, or nerve; your skin can't be too thick, especially when it comes to selling or marketing your services or product; and you can rarely refuse an offer to speak to groups, or join or head committees when you start out. Networking and working a room become second nature and business cards fall like raindrops from the pockets of your suits, briefcases, and portfolios.

But most entrepreneurs find that it's worth the effort. They receive great satisfaction in being able to build on their organizational, communications, and interpersonal skills, while flexing creative muscles at a whim. Some are great project managers, software specialists, or technical wizards. Others excel as online searchers or teachers. All are salespeople—convincing potential customers, employees, suppliers, bankers, and others that they will succeed. The final reward is not the vacation you can afford to take or new car or computer you can buy, but the pleasure of realizing that you *did* succeed after all, whether as an individual or as the member of a self-made company.

All it takes is a vision, unlimited energy, and the ability to infect others with your enthusiasm—an easy recipe for any entrepreneur!

40.

An Information Broker

by Deborah C. Sawyer

Why I Went to Library School

I only decided to go to library school in the fourth year of my B.A. program. Having taken a degree in linguistics with courses in Russian and Chinese, no one career path beckoned over any other. I had more ideas about what I *didn't* want to do; I remember sitting in my college residence room, sobbing while a well-meaning girlfriend exhorted me, "But just think, if you went to law school, you'd be a lawyer!" But I knew I didn't want that.

It was from this same room, however, that I had been watching the new John P. Robarts Research Library being built kitty-corner from my University of Toronto residence building. This is what planted the seeds of an idea, which took root: If I went into librarianship, I would be able to work with all subjects, rather than having to specialize in one, such as law. This is what decided my career choice.

Why I Chose an Alternate Career

It didn't take long, after I started library school, to realize that a traditional career was not for me. Before actually enrolling, I had thought I would become a children's librarian (and I even applied for some positions in this area). But it only took a few hours of cataloging and reference classes to make me realize my career path probably lay elsewhere. To sum up why I changed my mind about traditional work: RULES! I knew there would be too much bureaucracy in a traditional library setting. And, there was certain pressure from the faculty, given my background, to specialize in an area such as Slavic bibliography. Such a narrow focus was just what I had wanted to avoid.

I did take a range of courses to give me a firm grounding for traditional work. As well as cataloging, basic reference, and subject analysis, I took business, legal, and science librarianship; government documents; a trio of audiovisual, children's, and young adult's literature courses (the idea of children's librarianship was still there); plus a course in archival science. As it happens, several of these courses turned out to be valuable preparation for what I now do.

How I Got Started

My first position after graduation was as the editor of two bilingual reference publications, the *Canadian Education Index* and the *Directory of Education Studies in Canada*. This work involved skills above and beyond what I had learned in library school, notably editing and print production. Indexing and the role of language in indexing were two library skills that came into play, however, along with my earlier background in linguistics. It was from this base, three years later, that I moved into doing some indexing contract work for my own company, Information Plus, which I started in February 1979. For six months, I did such contract work on the side, quitting my full-time job the following October to devote myself exclusively to my own enterprise. In this way, the indexing skills I had honed at my full-time position provided the bridge into the world of self-employment.

How I Got to Be Where I Am Today

Indexing might have been the bridge, but it was only the starting point. Along the way I have added a great many more skills to my repertoire. Probably most important are the in-depth interviewing skills I gained as a freelance magazine writer (in the early years of self-employment, one turns one's hands to many things)! Learning how to gather information from people, to get them talking, to get them to share their wealth of knowledge has certainly been the key success factor in what I do now.

In this sense, library school education, by itself, is not enough for the work I do today, which is conducting in-depth custom research to support corporate decision making. By "going with the flow" of client demand, my company evolved from indexing (deciding where information is to be put or how it is to be accessed) to researching (knowing how and where to retrieve information or, simply, getting the information back out). There is a continuum, however, between indexing and researching and the early library school and university foundations, that has been important. And, of course, hard work, sacrifices, and the willingness to take risks are all vital.

As a result, my companies (the original company founded in Canada and a second one, also called Information Plus, started in the United States in 1990) work with corporate clients, supporting decisions about acquisitions, new business development, competitive strategy, and a range of other issues. I have a paid staff at each location along with the usual accoutrements of office space, equipment, and an in-house library. To serve our clients better, each office specializes in the country in which it is located; the U.S. office handles American-focus research while the Canadian office concentrates on topics centered on Canada. Together, the combined efforts cover the North American marketplace and serve clients both domestically and overseas. (It was partly to develop this reach and partly to serve existing U.S. clients better that I opened an office in the States, under the auspices of NAFTA.)

I'm pleased to say that my original goal, to work with a range of subject matter, has also been met. The projects we handle cover a wide range of topics: diabetes and the cost impact of diabetes on the prevention-diagnosis-treatment spectrum; best practices in physical distribution; trends in offset printing as they affect demand for ink; competition and the competitive view of the future in hospital-based coagulation testing; future trends with CD-ROM; an investigation of market potential and acquisition candidates in the office coffee services business; trends and competition in the artificial sweeteners market. Over the years we've done hundreds of projects, all varied, often breaking new ground. We frequently answer questions that no one has ever asked before, necessitating real sleuthing to find the information.

We've also developed enough strength to branch out into related markets. We publish a bimonthly newsletter, *Information Solutions*, and off-the-shelf reports, and we offer seminars such as *Prospects!* aimed at new and smaller businesses.

How Can You Do the Same?

First, it is essential to realize that an M.L.S. (or equivalent) degree alone is not enough in this business. An M.L.S. is but a starting point, although a good one if you take a range of literature courses and learn how information is created and who creates it. Knowing how business works is essential. Get some hands-on, private sector experience in a nonlibrary position in a for-profit enterprise. Yes, even if you take orders at a pizza parlor or ring up the cash in a hardware store, when it comes to serving business, you'll be light-years ahead of your classmates who have only library experience to draw on. Read business books, learn how business people think. Break free of the idea that online databases are it; one of the biggest limitations in any librarian I have hired is an overreliance on databases. It is for this reason that we currently do not have any librarians on our staff full-time. Bibliographic and database sources are a small slice of the information pie. Learn how skip tracers do their work. Learn how private investigators do theirs. Learn about quantitative consumer research methods. It doesn't mean you have to do the same but, if you are from a library background, you need to understand just how much more information there is, and how to find it, than you learned about in library school. Get some selling skills. Take marketing courses. Learn about new uses of information, such as database marketing. You will need encyclopedic knowledge to succeed in this line of work.

Conclusion

It is probably true that librarians who become entrepreneurs are, first and foremost, entrepreneurs who would have gone into business for themselves, no matter what profession they had chosen. In today's world, a logical step for someone with a library degree is to go into private practice as an information broker. Once upon a time, such an option did not exist, but today librarians can become entrepreneurs—now, that's the difference!

41.

Library Solutions

by Anne Grodzins Lipow

With a 30–year-old library degree followed by an amazing variety of positions in a single library, in 1992 I started my own business—Library Solutions Institute and Press. As I write this nearly four years later, it is a thriving enterprise and still growing. I'll begin this short story by describing what Library Solutions is all about; then I'll explain how it came to be; and I'll end with some thoughts about work in a library setting compared with the entrepreneurial experience and its relationship to library education.

About Library Solutions

Library Solutions operates in two streams of activity: Library Solutions Institute (LSI) offers training programs worldwide, and Library Solutions Press (LSP) publishes those training programs in book form.

LSI programs fall into two categories: staff development institutes, workshops, and consulting projects geared to library operations, and Internet training workshops for organizations of all types (including, for example, libraries, businesses, conventions, professional organizations, and schools).

The library staff development institutes are two- and three-day intense conferences—scheduled over two or three days in a retreat environment—that provide a forum for structured learning and discussion for up to 60 participants who wish to grapple with issues in librarianship that have no easy answers. Through a combination of presentations by experts, plenary and small group discussion, practical exercises, and useful handouts, the aim is to arm the participants with skills and ideas that enable them to contribute significantly to the shaping of the profession. Following are descriptions of two institutes:

"Rethinking Reference: New Models and How to Get There" addresses issues of change in reference services required by user needs, technological innovations, and budget reductions. The faculty are acknowledged leaders in the profession in areas of library administration, education, and reference services.

"Building Partnerships: Library and Computing Professionals" is intended for managers in academic libraries and computing centers who see a critical need for their organizations to work together in new ways and who want to grapple with the issues in a stimulating environment. The goal of this program is to build effective leadership in reshaping services and organizational structures in their universities. The program brings together several experts in both fields who will teach and lead discussions in the whys and hows of working collaboratively.

The workshops for library staff focus on building specific skills needed in today's libraries—for example, reference interviewing techniques, how to deal with difficult clients, methods for managing and supervising in a "team" environment.

The Internet training workshops are presented by instructors who are both Internet authorities and master teachers. The workshops are directed at two types of audiences: Internet learners and Internet trainers. Topics include basic Internet skills; mastering particular Internet tools and functions (for example, HTML, file transfer); finding information and resources on focused subjects (such as health and medicine, business and law, K–12, science and technology); and training-the-trainer programs.

LSP converts the live Internet training programs into written, self-paced instructional handbooks. Most titles are published in two versions: the book-alone edition for the learner, and the PLUS edition for the trainer. PLUS editions come with diskettes containing presentation slides, and may also have the lecture notes, handouts, special tips to the trainer, lists of Internet addresses, and other material that would help a trainer prepare a similar workshop. LSP also publishes the proceedings of its institutes. At the close of 1995 LSP could boast of 16 titles, and several more planned for 1996.

How It Happened

My ability to launch this enterprise was made possible by the special way in which my library career developed, along with a lucky coincidence of events. My entire in-library career was spent working at one of the finest libraries in the world, the University of California at Berkeley. Over a 30–year period, I had managed several departments, including a small acquisitions unit, the interlibrary loan service, and the systems office; I developed and headed a department that provided such nontraditional services as a campus document delivery service, a seminars program for faculty in how to use library resources (including the Internet, which was a resource used in academic institutions long before it was available to the population at large), and a computer reference service. In the final six years of my tenure at Berkeley, my job title was Director for Library Instructional Services, which included responsibility for developing and coordinating staff training programs as well as user instructional programs. As a bonus, I was often called on to work with other libraries (not only academic libraries, but public and special libraries as well)—some wanted help in designing and developing programs similar to those I had developed at Berkeley, others hired me to provide training programs directly to their staff. Thus I acquired my understanding of the workings of libraries and a competence in training and development, and considerable experience applying the two areas of knowledge in relation to the evolving Internet.

Then in late 1991 came a big moment of decision when the University of California statewide system, needing to reduce its operating budget, offered a major financial incentive to its long-term employees: if they retired as of March 30, 1992, they would receive lifetime income and benefits that greatly exceeded what they would receive if they retired many years later, plus a lump-sum payment worth six months of salary. I was eligible for this special package, but leaving a wonderful position in a great university library with its outstanding staff is not something one rushes to do. Having learned at Berkeley everything I know that made me a good consultant and trainer, I knew that without the first-hand contact with the day-to-day issues libraries face (including that important information one picks up through informal conversations at the water bubbler) and lacking handy access to journal literature, my knowledge and skills would quickly become obsolete. But luckily there were ways I could maintain these critical benefits. Through continued occasional work with staff at the University, as well as a "retainer" type of appointment for staff development services with the local public library consortium (which later led to special contracts with library organizations and projects), I would have the regularity of in-person contact I needed to keep abreast of issues. And by joining several electronic library discussion groups via the Internet, I could eavesdrop on the day-to-day concerns of my colleagues. I therefore accepted the early retirement offer and used the lump-sum payment to set up a home office with the requisite computer equipment, fax and copy machines, furniture, business phone, and a countless other such start-up necessities. (I had never before been able to "work at home" so knew that I needed a very separate and unhomelike space for my office.)

As the months wore on, hundred dollar bills seemed to fly out the window to pay for business cards, brochures, books on "how to start your own business," Internet services, promotional activities, and special services related to my particular line of work. I had to learn a lot in areas that were quite unfamiliar to me (and that are not taught in library school)—for example, the world of publishing, hiring salaried employees, hiring trainers on a contract basis, how to price products and services, business tax obligations. Since there was no longer a guaranteed monthly income (except for the retirement income which was far too little on which to run a business), I had to figure out how to manage cash flow problems—how to pay my ongoing business expenses (which include paying author royalties, institute speaker fees and expenses) before (sometimes months before) the client pays me, or even how to ensure that the client pays at all.

In Retrospect

The switch from being a library employee to being my own boss turns out to have been the right move for me. Not that I was unhappy with my library position. On the contrary, I loved going to work every day, I was stimulated by the issues we struggled with, and I liked feeling very secure in the foreverness of the job itself. Whenever I read about or observed firsthand the inconsistencies and unpredictability, sometimes even cruelty, of the entrepreneurial world, I felt smug and relieved to work in a parklike, intellectually stimulating atmosphere where money and material goods were secondary to the job of developing minds.

In this new life, I work more hours than I did in my library position (for which I frequently put in 10- to 12-hour days). How right was my self-employed friend when she warned me about starting my own business: "It's great," she said, "you're free to work any 18 hours a day you choose!" But every hour I work it is more like play. The source and nature of the personal pleasure I'm deriving in this new life are different from those of my library days:

- All decisions are mine to make; I don't have to ask anyone for permission. I like that a lot. I can accomplish a great deal more in a shorter period of time because of it.
- There are no distracting committee meetings to attend. All of my time can be spent in activities that are fully relevant to my work and goals.

- My income depends on people liking my services and products. I very much enjoy seeing and hearing the positive responses of my clients and purchasers of my publications, and being able to change and improve as I hear criticisms.
- I'm constantly learning something new, and I am free to follow a learning path, uninhibited by concerns of the consequences to "my job responsibilities" or to my coworkers or to "the library."

I'm less happy about having employees that I know are dependent on me for their income. But since I have the best staff possible, it's a small discomfort to suffer.

Best of all, the personal satisfaction I get from the knowledge that people are choosing my services or products and telling me they are benefiting from them is incalculable. It is something like the good feeling I got as a reference librarian when a student said "You've saved my life . . . " or "Thanks a million, I've learned so much." But now that feeling is multiplied tenfold, because what my clients get from Library Solutions is not available anywhere else. Then add the journal reviews that use superlatives to describe LSP publications (such as Karen Schneider's words in *American Libraries*, "Everything Library Solutions Press does is stupendously useful. . . . "), and the special awards (I am the proud recipient of the 1994 RASD Mudge/Bowker award for excellence in reference service, largely based on the "Rethinking Reference" institutes that I organized, and LSP's publication, *Crossing the Internet Threshold*, now in its second edition, has been nominated for the 1996 American Library Association/G. K. Hall Library Literature award). Top it all off with seeing some of our Internet titles translated into several languages (including Spanish, Turkish, and six East European languages), and you can practically see that cloud I walk on every day.

One more observation. No one chooses the library profession to become rich. Since I care little about money per se, or about most of the things it can buy, librarianship as an occupation—with its compensation deriving from the satisfaction you feel when you help others find the information they need—was very appealing to me. Throughout my career in the library, I was never disappointed. The "psychic" rewards were plentiful. Now that I've turned my work into a business, the revenues are, by any objective standard and, certainly in comparison to my library salary, enormous. What surprises me most is how pleased I am about this income—not from the standpoint of the money itself or what it can buy, but from what it represents: a concrete affirmation by each client, one by one, that my work is worth exchanging for that sum of money which symbolizes the relative value of my work. For me, such direct and immediate endorsement (or rejection) is a more powerful measure of quality of work than the "thank you" at the service desk or the annual merit increase in salary bestowed by the library administration.

Could I have done the work I am doing now just out of library school? No, not with the education that came with my degree. In those days, the only job library school prepared you for was working in a library. There was no automation, no multitype library consortia, no rapid change, no distance learning and remote users, no competing information resources, no variations in organizational structures, no felt need for staff training. So there weren't the opportunities that exist today. Students graduating from library schools now are prepared to work either in libraries or in organizations that sell services to libraries

I've often been asked, "Don't you regret not having left the library earlier?" My answer is a resounding no. While much of what I do today I could have learned in today's library schools, I know that, at least in my case, the in-library work was an indispensable part of the preparation process. I am very sure that I could not have built the company I now have without the knowledge I gained from working in a library—and much of that knowledge can still only be gained in a library. Also, had I tried this venture earlier, the timing would have been wrong—the world didn't need my skills badly enough to support a practice until just a few years ago when training in general became a high priority for libraries and when the Internet in particular gained a mass presence.

I've also been asked whether or not I could ever be happy working in a library again. Without hesitation my answer is yes. Libraries, with their honorable mission and diversity of functions and work environments, are some of the most fertile places today for innovative and exciting developments that would keep any smart, flexible, and service-minded person who thrives on uncertainty happy for years to come.

Finally, there's the issue of what to label me. I learned (when someone asked me how it feels to no longer be a librarian) that we seem to reserve the word "librarian" for library-degreed people who work in libraries. I feel strongly that I am still a professional librarian who provides a service to libraries and to people and organizations beyond libraries. In the current debate over what to call us (whether to keep the word "librarian" or change to something like "information specialist/consultant"), I tend toward the camp that believes it's time for a change. But however that issue settles, I want the word for my professional designation to be the same as that for people who ply this trade inside library buildings.

42.

Corporate President

by Gloria Dinerman

THE LIBRARY CO-OP was founded on the theory that the business of information science demands the service of experts. We retain special consultants who can advise, put together, take apart, move, direct, organize, report, codify, inventory, catalog, or perform any other library related skill required to serve the needs of our clients' universe.

IF TIME MEANS MONEY, there is a place for us in your corporate, academic, municipal or school planning. Library projects that require efficiency and coordination are handled with exceptional attention to every detail. Our placement services supply temporary or permanent professionals whose skills will often surpass the parameters of the job description. Seminar programs reflect new trends in current technology and are designed to stimulate your imagination and intellect.

FOLLOW OUR ABC'S OF IDEAS. If your special interest is not listed, please help us to expand our service by forwarding your questions. In the purest sense of the word, our "CO-OP" means people working together for each other. Join us.

—from the Library Co-Op descriptive brochure

My interest in libraries began with reverence and awe at the age of five. Twelve years later, my first job at college was to manage the picture rental department which was housed in the library. With a salary of $3 per hour I got my choice of prints and photographs.

In the early 1960s during breeding and bottle years, I did a major library project under the mantle of the League of Women Voters. The project was a merger of eight independent libraries into a single organization. After two years, the venture was finally completed and my idealistic image gave way to the disconcerting fact that librarians could be diligent, selfish, demanding, discerning, unreasonable—in other words, human. My library involvement continued, and in 1980 I became a trustee of the second largest public library system in the State of New Jersey and remained in office until 1991.

What makes my story different from that of most librarians is that my degree was earned *after* I went into the library business. Until 1982, when the Library Co-Op was incorporated, I had worked for two governmental entities and one major Wall Street brokerage house all in a middle management capacity, and I was the victim of downsizing three times. Enough!

After my third downsizing experience, with morale and self-esteem as low as the underside of an earthworm, I decided to work on my own. I might fail, but I couldn't be fired. My intelligence, personality and my luck would be the driving forces toward business and financial independence. Since personnel management and organizational ability were my strongest assets, I gravitated toward the consultant end of human resources which included recruiting, staff development, training, and writing procedures and manuals. I was hired mainly by nonprofit organizations to work on a contract basis doing executive recruiting or organizing personnel departments. Through a series of related library contracts, and because of the persuasive efforts of some professional friends, I was strongly encouraged to focus my accumulated experience exclusively on librarianship. On November 15, 1982, two actions changed my career—the Library Co-Op, Inc., was registered with the Middlesex, New Jersey County Clerk, and I enrolled provisionally in library school. Enrollment was provisional because I had to take the Graduate Record Exams before I could be officially accepted. Imagine the trauma! The stress! The terror! My whole new career hung on the passing of three hours of testing. But the degree was an absolute necessity to *legitimize* my business. I acquired the sample exams, shut off my phone for a week, and got into the same study mode that was successful 25 years before.

The exams were passed; school was open to me; potential public and school librarians overwhelmed the classes; automation was in its infancy. The makeup of the classes is mentioned because the curriculum emphasized academic and school courses. Special, governmental, and institutional libraries were virtually ignored as the concentration of scholarly efforts focused on basic reference and cataloging. My business instincts knew that change in information delivery was advancing like a foot soldier and if success was to be my objective, my goal, my rising star, I had better develop myself and my company as leaders in automation, rather than follow a reactive path and wait for my classes to catch up with technology. In addition to school, I took 40 hours of online searching from a corporate teacher—not that I ever wanted to pursue the search and research avenue of business, but I had to know how before I could supervise people who did.

Starting my corporation was not easy. My office was in my home, school took up half my time, marketing took the other half. I joined every library organization in two states, went to as many meetings as possible, sold myself and my ability, made friends with anyone who could be helpful in using our services, took any small job that came my way, and got myself known—selling Gloria Dinerman was my aim. I was too new to sell personal skills. I sold confidence, background, and the conviction that I would see any assignment through to its successful conclusion. Five years of working in the canyons of Wall Street, plus a certificate from the New York Institute of Finance set me apart from my competitors. I could sell a business concept with professional skill.

So many librarians who go into their own business forget that it takes more than a talent for DIALOG or STN or LEXIS to be success-ful. To make the market work for you, you have to act rather than re-act. Be aggressive in developing leads and convert those leads to sales. Research talent is not enough to bring in accounts—neither is knowing a central core of possible clients. Many of my friends who have been in and out of business have failed because they expected their accounts to last forever. They forgot to keep on marketing even when they were busy. The relationship between company and em-ployee is far different from the relationship between company and consultant. The day you stop marketing is the day that business starts to decline. You can't count on anyone but yourself. You have no friends in the workplace—only clients.

If you can't market, if you don't have the money to advertise, if you fear rejection, if you have problems making decisions, if you don't regularly read the financial section of your major newspaper, if you don't know how to manage your cash flow, if your energy is low, if you are easily satisfied, if opportunity is hard to recognize, then stay away from entrepreneurship and devote your hard work and good inten-tions to an employer.

If you can think on your feet, if you can ignore adversity, if you can stretch your imagination to provide new ideas, if you believe in your-self, if you can handle loneliness and lowlifes, if your positive attitude glows regardless of disappointment and market changes, then you are ready to go on your own.

Do you know where your consumers are? Who needs your services the most? Do you know enough about the business of your prospec-tive clients to be able to show them that you understand their con-cerns?

For client development, start with your strongest field of experience. Mine was school libraries. Yours may be medical or pharmaceutical libraries. What does your type of library need from you? Who will give you the work order? Most business is not continuous and you must always seek new leads. You cannot be shy about requesting referrals from a satisfied customer.

The Library Co-Op now has a staff of eight, including myself. There are 25 additional special consultants who may be called on to do specific assignments on an "as-needed" basis. Staff development was the easiest part of building my corporation because of my heavy experience in recruiting and a native intuition that guides my selection of a mix of people. Three positions have turned over in 13 years, four if you count one retirement.

Many people have asked if I could recommend courses that would be helpful in business and my response is generally "no" because librarians have unique problems and cannot conform to prescribed models. Courses on being generally successful that are peppered with do's and don'ts of running a company may serve to assist people who only need technical or economic knowledge. The temperament of a librarian is one of service, not business. What attracts people to the profession repels them from the economic side of corporate stress. When librarians underprice their services, companies cannot help but take advantage of the bargain. No one has yet determined what an information professional is really worth, but there always seems to be an entrepreneur who will underprice the market just to get started, and the market varies from every area of the country to the next.

When we provide temporary professionals for our clients, we are under the constraints of a pricing structure that is dictated by the client company or institution. In other words, we really do not have the independence to set our own fees. If we try to negotiate a fee and the company is unwilling to pay, it will go to another agency who will work for less. The cost figure for research and writing that comes from our clients is generally set at about $35-37 per hour. We recently received a request for a writer—a non-M.L.S. person who could disseminate information and abstract it into simple language and also prepare some technical instructions for the use of a new product. Many of our librarians can write well, and we had no problem filling the request. We have worked for this client for ten years and they knew the high-quality people we provide, but the requesting department was not the library and our allowable charge was $50 per hour, not $35. I don't think that means that the company placed less value on retrieving information than in writing it up. I do think that pricing is based on supply and demand—and librarians are in long supply and are not too demanding.

This leads me to pay equity. Should a paraprofessional be paid the same as a professional librarian if the paraprofessional is doing professional work? When we negotiate salaries or even when we help to write a job description, the question of professional/paraprofessional will very often be a point of discussion. I have participated on panels and lectured on the topic of pay equity and I have taken both sides of the argument. In my own staff, three of us are professionals and five are not, and my pay scale will give a higher starting salary to the professional. But raises and year-end bonuses are meted out on an equal percentage basis. Everyone knows and participates in library work. If you expand beyond a one-person operation, the first decision that has to be made is about salary. The Special Libraries Association publishes a good survey every two years, with figures broken down by geographic area, by type of library, by title, by age, and so forth. Reading the survey is an excellent place to start when deciding what to charge, what to pay for help.

There is a maxim in our office, "Don't Say 'No' to Anything," and this has been the basis of our success. Last year, following the belief that automation consulting was a good adjunct to existing services, we formed a new division called Laird Consulting that spans the universe of all client/server architecture as well as library applications in particular.

A nonlibrarian who is an automation expert and sales manager heads the division. Librarians join prospect calls to form a team effort to give the client the benefit of technical knowledge and information management. So far it has worked well. We market to the medium-sized company that can now afford and appreciate an automated information center.

Following are some suggestions from the librarian as a corporate president:

- Unless you have six months to a year of income stashed away, or unless you have an outside source of funds for living expenses, don't even think of starting your own business.
- Get clerical/paraprofessional help as soon as you can so your time will be spent on assignments and marketing.
- Direct mail marketing works as long as you develop your own list from contacts, directories, and associations. The advertising statistics cite a 5 percent response to be excellent. Mine is between 15–18 percent.
- Follow up solicitations with a personal call.
- Surround yourself with intellectual equals. Being in business is lonely. You need objective mental stimulation.
- Keep every deadline. Return every phone call.
- Don't undercut the competition unless you want the job for a special reason. Convince clients that they get what they pay for and quality is less expensive in the long run.
- Begin by keeping accurate records of your completed work (for example, job type, beginning date, time to complete, charge-related expenses, profit). Refer to these records when estimating a job. You will make mistakes, but if you are smart, you won't repeat them.

- Clients will be frustrating, unreliable, slow paying, inconsistent, fallacious, and dogmatic. Expect erratic behavior and be pleasantly surprised if you're treated well.
- Don't let personal feelings interfere with your goal. Thin skin is not becoming in business.
- Read the trade journals, such as *Information Today, Library Journal,* and *Compuserve Journal.*
- Acquire a basic knowledge of the Internet.
- Don't be an information junkie, be a knowledgeable reader.
- Be prepared to work 7 days a week, 12 hours a day. There is no substitute for drive.

To readers of this chapter, I wish success. It's not easy but it's worth it.

43.

Contract Cataloging

By Joni L. Cassidy

According to the 1986 study "The State of Small Business: A Report to the President," the number of women-owned small businesses increased annually by 9.4 percent from 1977 to 1983. This increase was well above the annual 4.3 percent increase in men-owned businesses.

The delegates to the White House Conference on Small Business that same year provided a snapshot of trends and issues that are shaping small business. On average, compared to 1980 the businesses represented at that conference were smaller; most had fewer than 25 employees and more of the businesses were in service industries (47 percent compared with 39 percent in 1980). I find it very exciting to be part of this "economic trend," even though I didn't start out my library career in the entrepreneurial sector.

I was a "library baby," starting out as a page in high school, and moving up to circulation clerk and then technical services clerk through college and graduate school. I hold an associate's degree in business administration, a bachelor's degree in fine arts, and a master's degree in library science (1978). Hence, today I'm an entrepreneurial librarian who enjoys doing her company's advertising and public relations work.

My first professional position was setting up the federally funded Job Information Center for Eastern Long Island (New York). I purchased the furniture; did acquisitions, cataloging, and processing; provided reference services and resume counseling; and lectured extensively throughout our service area. In short, I was a regular "one-woman traveling band."

When my job center was not funded early in 1981, I moved to audiovisual and young adult services. My responsibilities included cataloging audiovisual and young adult titles. The year 1982 brought me to New York City and the Mercantile Library, a 162-year-old private lending library. I was the head of public services and supervised a staff of 14.

In 1983 I added law as a subject specialty to my cataloging skills as the cataloger for the New York County Lawyers Association, the city's downtown bar association. It was about this time that I realized that cataloging was the part of each prior position that had given me the most satisfaction.

Through my contacts with law firm librarians, I discovered the need for good cataloging in the private law sector. For many reasons, the Library of Congress Cataloging Distribution Service doesn't meet the needs of a law library as well as it meets those of public and small academic libraries. And, although many law collections are represented in OCLC and RLIN, those records require significant editing for quality and consistency. A law library still needs a skilled cataloger to enhance the records.

So, in answer to that need, I founded Cassidy Cataloguing Services, Inc., in 1985 after 18 months of informal contract cataloging projects for various law firm libraries. One such project was at a Wall Street firm that subscribed to OCLC. Even though the environment there was not a comfortable one for me, I welcomed the opportunity to learn online cataloging from an excellent law cataloger. During that period, most of my work was done from home with an electronic typewriter, and one part-time clerk to assist me on-site.

A year later, the company was automated by my husband, Michael, then a full-time theater lighting technician working for Cassidy Cataloguing in his "spare" time. The law/business bibliographic database he set up in 1986 has grown to more than 90,000 records and serves as the heart of the company's activities today. By 1988, in-house and client demand for technical computer support led to his full-time commitment to the company and its future growth.

We opened our first office in Manhattan in February 1989 when an excellent law cataloger left a Wall Street firm to join our staff. The office was one 250-square-foot room. We moved over the next four years into two successively larger offices in the same building. Then, early on a December evening in 1993, a staff member and I were robbed at gunpoint and tied up in our own office. We left the Big Apple the following month for safer, larger, commercial space in New Jersey. Clearly, one of the advantages of self-employment is the ability to make decisions of this kind. You have the power to establish your own quality of life and working environment.

With a full-time staff of 9.5 (2.5 catalogers, 1 copy cataloger currently in library school, 2 paraprofessionals, 2 clerks, 1 systems administrator/CFO, and me, the administrator/CEO), our company provides cataloging and other technical services to over 50 law and corporate libraries. In addition to the private law firms and corporations we provide services to, our past and present client list includes three law schools in the Northeast, one of the Smithsonian museums, and the New York Law Institute.

Most of the actual cataloging and computer work is done in our New Jersey office, where catalog and shelflist cards, book catalogs, and labels are produced. Our staff works on-site at one-quarter of our client libraries, comparing their holdings to records in our database for full retrospective conversion projects. For titles they don't find in our database, they photocopy title pages and record the bibliographic details needed for original cataloging. Then they return to the library at a later date to file cards, attach labels to books, and so forth. Records are delivered to the library on disks in USMARC II format. As the labeling progresses, we shift and rearrange the books into correct classification order. We provide maintenance cataloging services to most of the libraries for which we have provided retrospective conversion.

We are one of the few companies in the United States that provide this specialized service to law libraries, cataloging being an area of librarianship that few librarians choose as their specialty and law being a subject area familiar to few catalogers.

Cassidy Cataloguing has worked to attain a reputation for high-quality cataloging in the law library community. My staff and I have lectured extensively on the successful application of national bibliographic standards to the private firm setting and, I believe, we have been instrumental in the widespread acceptance of those standards by making high-quality records available to firms too small to add a cataloger to their staff. In addition, we are active in professional associations, both national and regional, supporting a strong commitment to continuing library education in the area of technical services.

To that end, we have sometimes functioned as a learning incubator, hosting "guest catalogers" who work full-time for a law firm and part-time for us fine-tuning their skills.

In 1991 we were invited to participate in a joint venture with Gaylord Information Systems, a division of Gaylord Brothers. Gaylord introduced a new database of detailed MARC cataloging records for the specialized subject areas of law and business on compact disk. Records are accessed using Gaylord's CD-ROM MARC Cataloging System, "SuperCat." These records are contributed by Cassidy Cataloguing Services, Inc., and updated quarterly. Our records were chosen for this new product along with the cataloging records of the National Library of Medicine, the recognized authority in medical cataloging.

In 1993 we expanded overnight from a regional to an international service area by altering our methodology to provide contract cataloging by mail. Three-quarters of our clients contract for services of this kind. That same year, we went into the union list business, compiling and maintaining serials holdings for regional groups of law libraries.

On the subject of going from "librarian" to "independent contractor," I'll say this: As in the case of any crisis in your life, you'll be amazed at what you can do when you have to do it. Another small business owner wrote, "If you want to grow as a person and you want to really test who you are, you start your own business."

Certainly library school prepared me for the cataloging and technical services work that's the heart of our business, and I manage all our various projects, making any policy decisions that are required. My education, graduate and undergraduate, helps me to supervise our staff, advertise and promote our services, write professionally, lecture nationwide, and do my own research. Most important, my degree lends credibility to our company and the services we provide. That is to say, people trust us with their libraries and I believe that is the key to our success. But, nothing except experience will prepare you for negotiating with clients, dealing with accountants, lawyers, the IRS, bankers, insurance agents, long-distance carriers, software vendors, landlords, suppliers, and all the other folks who will interact with your business. I am lucky in that my husband was willing to take responsibility for all our financial affairs (money in/money out) freeing up my time for client development, project management, and staff supervision.

The ideal situation is to start a business doing something you do well and that gives you some pleasure. Start it part-time while you have a "day job" to fall back on. The security of knowing you have a paycheck coming in will free up your mind for creative business development and allow you to take some risks. If possible, work a while for an independent contractor providing services to the market segment you wish to tap.

Be active in professional associations, attend meetings, work on committees, speak at conferences, run for elected office. These activities can go far in establishing awareness of your services. Most importantly, you will gain acceptance as a professional peer. If possible, you want to present your services as a way of extending, or enhancing, an existing library staff, not as a way of replacing them. "Outsourcing," the use of outside contractors, will be most successful, in my humble opinion, where it is used in conjunction with in-house staff to provide expertise in a particular area or to add extra hands for labor-intensive projects such as retrospective conversion, barcoding, or reclassification.

There are no limits when you run your own business. You make your own hours. Sometimes that equals all your waking hours. Your income is limitless, too. It has no ceiling, but it also has no floor! If it's your business, the gains *and* the losses are yours. There is also no limit to the sense of satisfaction and pride when things go right, you know that clients appreciate the work you're doing for them, and your staff shows you that they share your vision and they're playing on your team.

44.

Good News for School Libraries

by Lorraine Knight

How to title this chapter—services to school libraries, package what you preach, libraries as production lines...? I have some dilemma but I do have good news for readers with a school library background, our jobs are not on the line if we go independent! It is an opinion I formed after a year's leave of absence, touring the United States and "thinking about things."

Like many of you, I was dismayed by the contradiction that in an age of database management, the original database makers, librarians, could be asked to leave their jobs or that the perception was out there that professionals could be replaced by technicians. Some misunderstanding, I thought, and set out to prove it in my own way. The problem was that media specialists were being asked to function as technicians and not as professionals. Then, after spending hours of their "professional time" doing clerical work or providing a break for overworked elementary school teachers, they could be asked to leave because they were only "baby-sitting" or providing clerical services—a classic catch-22 situation. The dilemma I discovered stateside was the same as we in Canada were experiencing in spite of a strong tradition of the "teacher-librarian" who develops a library program and is a contributing member of curriculum teams.

In Canada, too, millions of dollars were being spent on automation projects that quite often went awry. I had been involved in one, the automation of the largest school district in Canada, a project that was on the point of collapse when I left in 1993. At that time UTLAS (University Of Toronto Library Systems) was being bought out and, I strongly suspected, was no longer interested in the school library market. In York region alone, over 100 school libraries would be dropped in the middle of a district automation project that had been ten years in the making. The new high school collection I had just established, including over 700 fully cataloged films in video format, would no longer be supported by an automated catalog. The integration of our CD-ROM network with the rest of the collection would also be lost. Concurrently the board positions of elementary and secondary library consultant and director of technology (A-V) were being "temporarily" disbanded.

I did not have answers when I left in 1993, but I certainly knew the questions—why were we paying so much for cataloging to be a "contributing" member of UTLAS? Why didn't we have a COM catalog? Why couldn't we get copies of our database in standard MARC format? Why couldn't we have an automated catalog more suitable to the needs of a school population—particularly when so many excellent products were on the market?

On the year's leave of absence, automation software became my first topic of research. I discovered *Library Technology Reports* and read all I could about the top 20 integrated packages for PCs. I began to visit sites when I could—Eloquent Systems in Vancouver, British Columbia and Data Trek in Carlsbad, California. I also planned to visit Nichols Advanced Technology out of Edmonton and La Crosse, Wisconsin, but the trip proved unfeasible.

Databases of MARC records on CD-ROM became my next target of investigation, as did the alarming statistics of technicians, catalogers, and library consultants necessary when a school district became independent and created databases of its own from licensed or purchased MARC records on CD-ROM. For certain, at the end of my research, I would know how to set up a technical department for a school system or district, but would they be interested? In a time of cutbacks this hardly seemed the answer, but independence did. I was determined to put the control of their databases in the hands of school personnel. Little could I have imagined that this would demand my independence as well.

Confirmation of my suspicions came when I discovered my home province of British Columbia had no job openings and that jobs were in short supply in other provinces and in many states. No jobs but enormous problems—there was a contradiction here somewhere. Could it be that the bureaucracy itself was looking for answers?

As I have always told my students, formulate the question and you're halfway to the answer. In this case, the answer came from my future partner, Sheila White. Sheila and I had recently completed a

successful library project by combining our separate areas of expertise—Sheila, as production director for a sheltered workshop, and I as
head librarian for a school in the planning stages. What had happened was this: The school was under construction so I had all the
resources, films, books, and CDs sent to the workshop. Sheila made
sure the shipments were received at her tractor-trailer bay; checked
in by her shipper; and stored on a warehouse pallet (which later grew
to be three, four, and then five warehouse pallets). When all shipments were received, I headed a team of disabled workers, who
stamped, labeled, security stripped, and barcoded the resources. They
took pride in every detail of their work since it was the first time they
had been trusted with anything other than screws and paint cans. Finally a collection worth $100,000 was delivered to the new school on
five stretch-wrapped pallets that were forklifted onto waiting school
dollies. There were no losses and the database that resulted was 96
percent accurate on a first run. We thought we really had something,
but the time did not seem to be right for anyone to understand it. So
Sheila and I decided to join forces, buy an R.V., and travel for a year.

The brainwave came in Arizona. First of all, we love Arizona. There
is something unique about the geography of the state. And it appears
that Arizona people loved us because they were the first to listen to
what we had to say about libraries, conversion, and curriculum-based
media centers.

We formed our own company and called it Library Conversions
Limited Company—not because we thought we would be doing conversions, but because "accountability" was a name that had already
been taken. (We originally chose "accountability" because, by the time
we were finished, we planned to prove the accountability of our programs by the increased use of the library by teachers and students.)
For me, "conversions" would do because we would also be "converting" attitudes about the purpose and uses of libraries within the
school system.

We went on an advertising blitz and sent pamphlets, brochures, and
sample programs across the country, following up with a phone campaign. We were put on hold several times, but because we were local
and there was a need, the Peoria School District, one of the largest and
most progressive in Arizona took us on. Oddly enough, they did so because they really thought we were a conversion company—and now we
are. We go in with our production crew to create the individual school's
database, and the district licenses the database. Sheila's production
techniques have enabled us to create a database of 10,000 cataloging-
in-hand items in one week—in other words, we can turn over one elementary school library in a week.

The control of their database is in the hands of the school just as I
had envisioned, and the five or six disks of records we deliver at the
end of the week provide a jump start for library automation. Instead
of waiting for years for the completion of district automation, large
school districts are saved the inconvenience, frustrations and duplica-

tion of costs (not to mention the inaccuracies) of a procedure that occurs over time, and we have the potential of more than enough work to keep our crews busy for years.

Professionally, I have a great deal of satisfaction knowing that we provide an invaluable service and I work closely with Sheila to establish high standards for the quality of the records we deliver. I am also enthusiastically involved with the creation of MARC records using the new data elements for curricular information that have recently been defined by the Library of Congress. Library Conversions has its own USMARC Code for Organizations granted by the Library of Congress and we plan to push our cataloging standard to be recognized across North America.

We see the company developing with job opportunities in all areas—for catalogers, for consultants, for production directors, and for teams of workers, but most importantly for the benefit of the schools. We envision franchising our business and its procedures and approaches, so that what we do can be duplicated wherever there are librarians and production managers willing to take the plunge for independence.

Our combined efforts have created the total package for school libraries—including a teaching package for database research techniques which I was able to write and copyright on that fruitful leave of absence. When the schools are ready, we will be able to give full library services. For now we "act on demand" to provide any service, technical or professional, required by the schools.

I learned an important lesson on that leave of absence—there is no sense going against the flow. If there are technical directors in charge of libraries, don't tell them they need to establish a library services division with a coordinator of school libraries—ask them what they want. If the answer is "my machines, your people," don't look now—you have a business. The consulting will come later as you develop more and more expertise.

Look for a partner when starting a business venture. Choose someone with business experience and stay away from another academic. I find my limits are constantly being stretched by Sheila's understanding of production-line techniques, as are hers by the need for a semicolon in place of a period, but we understand that our complementary skills are the reason for our success. It is, however, an enormous leap with unimaginable stresses coming from everywhere all at once, so steel yourself.

Most schools have an immediate need for MARC records for their collections. Providing them is what we do now and we may always do this in some fashion. What we are really about is finding resources to fit the curriculum—providing for teachers the capability to search by learning objective, and for students the database and database skills to find the answers to their questions.

45.

Steps on the Way to a Company of My Own

by Daniel Boivin

When I heard about the idea to publish a book on librarians' experiences outside traditional fields, I thought it was a great idea. Too often these days we see other professionals applying for and winning jobs where librarians would be more qualified but are not recognized for their varied skills.

When I was asked to write about my own experience, I was surprised because I never realized that I was doing something quite different from most of my fellow librarians. When I thought about my responsibilities as account manager at DRA Information, Inc.—my most recent job before becoming the proprietor of my own company—as compared to other librarian jobs, I realized it was different. Everything I learned before working at DRA, however, has been quite useful. Let me describe what has been my own career progress.

In 1983, I was in the middle of trying to decide whether to complete my B.Sc. degree in geology or to start something new. Before giving up on geology, I had the good fortune to meet someone with the geology degree who was about to complete his master's degree in library science. We had a long discussion and one of his statements was well noted by me: "With your B.Sc. degree, you won't have any trouble finding a job in library science." He was there to prove it, having to choose among three different jobs and the semester was not even completed.

So there I was, two years later, at the Library and Information Science School of the University of Montreal. I was quite excited and enthusiastic. My decision to go to library school seemed even more justified and appreciated when, a month later, I obtained a part-time job at the Polytechnic School of the University of Montreal. My B.Sc. degree was already working for me.

From that point on, I never had difficulties finding work. In 1987 I completed my master of library and information science degree and also had a job offer—a one-year term at the Laurentian University. This job, the Dr. P. E. Filion Graduate Librarian Fellowship, had been created by the director of the library, Roy Bonin, to offer to a new graduate a real work experience in all the different library divisions (public services, technical services, and management) so that the graduate could eventually find a permanent job elsewhere. Also, it was acceptable to the institution that one could leave before the end of the term if a permanent position was offered elsewhere. It was a good opportunity for me as a new graduate.

I had to move from Montreal to Sudbury for this job and my family was a bit sad to see me go so far away from home but it turned out to be a good choice. Five months later I was able to find a job at the Canadian Institute for Scientific and Technical Information (CISTI), National Research Council Canada, in Ottawa.

I was hired to work for the CAN/OLE CAN/SDI division as an automated services librarian. My responsabilities were to work on SDI profiles for CISTI's employees and customers. These profiles ran on different databases (such as INSPEC and Chemical Abstracts) offered by CISTI. I was also involved in doing a few other things, but, because my experience as a librarian and my knowledge of the different databases were still limited, I was not given much responsability initially.

This was also a great experience, but because it was on a six-month contract basis and because it was not certain to be renewed, I was still looking around. Luckily enough, CISTI then had three openings in technical services for catalogers. Catalogers—ugh! This is what I thought.

In library school, I had taken only one course in cataloging and one course in indexing (they were mandatory). I was much more interested in online searching and library automation and I had specialized in those two areas. But there I was, faced with the possibility of a permanent job—but as a cataloger.

What do you think I did? Well, everybody needs to eat, right? Plus, I saw it as another experience and maybe a stepping-stone to another job within CISTI. So, of course I went for it and got one of the three openings.

During my 30 months of experience at CISTI, I spent 16 months in cataloging. This turned out to be one of the most important job experiences I've had. I was fortunate enough to be trained properly in how to catalog and classify different types of documents. CISTI was an excellent place to start a career—they took the time to teach us, which eventually meant for them that we were better catalogers and that the catalog reflected the enhanced quality of the staff.

I believe that this experience continued to be worthwhile in my most recent job as an account manager for DRA. I often got technical questions on how to catalog and to index materials, what MARC tags are supported, and so on. Without that experience, I wouldn't be as successful as I am today. I believe every librarian should have a good background and understanding of technical services. This will always help you, whether you are a reference librarian, systems support person, database designer, or manager.

My eight remaining months at CISTI were spent within the CAN/OLE CAN/SDI division again. At that time this division was going through the development of what was called CAN/OLE II. They needed additional staff to maintain the service as some of the staff were working on the new project.

Having already worked in that division, I was "borrowed" from cataloging for an eight-month period. This time I had to accomplish other duties and had more responsibilities, such as helping customers with their online searches and giving brief presentations to visitors. This was really what I wanted to do.

My future wife, however (there is always an "if" or a "however" in personal stories), was still living in Montreal and we had been commuting for almost three years. We had mutually agreed to try to find jobs in one city. I eventually got an interview for a six-month maternity leave replacement contract with the MultiLIS Division of Sobeco Ernst & Young (MultiLIS is now part of DRA Information in Canada). The interview went well and I had the job. But, I was in quite a dilemma—should I leave a great permanent job for something unknown and short-term, and be with my sweetheart, or should I keep my permanent job and look for something else?

Well, I went for it. It looked like a very exciting job and something that could turn out as a great opportunity. I started as a support person for the marketing division. My responsibilities were to help answer requests for proposals, to prepare demonstrations, to assist during presentations, to staff booths at shows, and to answer general requests for information. As time went by I got more responsibilities and I soon became an account manager for the Quebec market. Five years later my territory was Quebec, part of Ontario, and the Atlantic Provinces. Eventually I had additional responsibilities such as preparing software, services, and hardware quotes, as well as handling contract negotiations, written communiqués, and publicity.

It was a very demanding job and environment but also very rewarding. I often worked long days and on weekends and I was frequently away from home. These demands, however, can almost become benefits. You get to see other people, and different provinces, states, and countries. You get to eat local food, learn local habits, and visit special areas. I guess it helps to like to travel.

Everything I learned in library school and throughout my various work experience was useful. For example, if I had not worked as a cataloger I would not have been able to handle difficult questions during our numerous presentations. On the other hand, I had to learn and to add other skills that were obviously not taught in library school. But with an open mind, the desire to learn more, and the willingness to go into unknown areas you will succeed.

I don't think my story is different from many others. Everybody needs and wants to work and sometimes the difference is small between someone who succeeds and someone who cannot obtain good opportunities. One fact remains though: Your attitude more than anything else will make you win jobs. After being in the job market during the past eight years, I quickly realized that most of the time people are hired not because they had the highest grades in school but because they look like positive individuals with a good attitude. Of course, after a certain number of years, your experience, what you have accomplished, and who you know all play in your favor. If you are a future librarian, keep that in mind.

I have been very flexible in my career, ready to move, and willing to try different types of jobs. Of course, it is always easier to be flexible when you do not have a spouse who also has a job, when you do not have a house, kids, and dogs. You might, however, want to consider such flexibility seriously when you start your new career; it can potentially offer you excellent opportunities.

If I had only one piece of advice to give today, I would recommend to everyone not to go into librarianship with the idea of doing just one specific job. You should rather try to be as versatile as possible. Remember, I ended up working as a cataloger, while in library school I never really wished to do that type of work.

Now, in the middle of 1995, I have left DRA Information and have started my own company, Textel-D.B. in Chambley, Quebec. I am the authorized dealer in Canada for Chadwick-Healey which publishes CD-ROM, magnetic tape, and microform materials. Another important step in my career.

46.

Argus Associates: Information Systems Design

By Louis B. Rosenfeld

Let me first tell you that I never expected to be employed as a traditional librarian, and, to date, I really haven't been. In fact, I was one of those folks who started showing up in library schools during the late 1980s who wasn't quite sold on librarianship. Now in my role as an information systems design consultant, I truly understand the value of our profession. I credit the success of my company, Argus Associates, to the librarianship skills of our staff; these skills enable us to stand out in a very crowded field of World Wide Web design firms.

I'm too young to pretend I can offer you wisdom. But I do have sufficient experience to share this message with you: Our field is not dying; in fact, it's growing by leaps and bounds, becoming more recognized and more important all the time. This is, of course, happening outside libraries for the most part, as this book surely demonstrates. But isn't our field about information wherever and however it exists, rather than about managing books and journals housed in the physical structures we call libraries? Ah, but that's another topic and I digress. Jobs that are fulfilling, or well paying, or even both, are out there, but they're not waiting for you; you need to look in all sorts of places you may have not considered before. But, if you are already a librarian, that shouldn't be too hard. Consider the information searching skills that distinguish you from the folks who come to you at the reference desk; those same skills can be applied to hunting for, and even creating, your dream job outside a library. You probably rely on asking individuals for help answering a query, as well as searching databases and catalogs. So of course you should be willing to network and ask people in the field for help identifying that job.

Now that I've told you the moral, let me tell you the story. After obtaining a B.A. in U.S. history from the University of Michigan in 1987, I was perfectly trained and groomed to do what I did next: panic. Not that anything is wrong with a history degree, but the subsequent career path isn't too wide or too obvious. So I tried many different jobs, ranging from selling used sofas to delivering phone books to wiping kids' noses at a daycare center. Through the process of elimination, I learned that what I liked to do was come up with information systems for just about every place I worked. So, for example, the idea of selling sofas didn't appeal much to me, but, boy, wouldn't life be easier if the boss let me build an inventory system so we knew what actually we had to sell?

Finally knowing something about my own career interests, I resolved to return to college for a master's degree in an information-oriented profession. Computer science was interesting, but I didn't think I'd look good with a pocket protector. Similarly, an M.B.A. in computer information systems was appealing, but it was hard to imagine taking required courses in accounting. So I compromised by choosing library science, and why not—how different could managing databases of books be from managing furniture inventories?

Let's step back for a moment. My assumption was wrong, and that it is a common mistake. The rest of the world believes that databases and textbases are the same animal, but you and I know that it's *much* easier for a system to answer the query "How many naugahyde sofas do we have in stock?" than "I'd like some information on the economic and social status of women in South Africa." Information retrieval is trickier than data retrieval, and it's the sort of thing that makes librarians so valuable. Ultimately it's up to you to let folks know the difference, especially in such situations as a job interview. Believe me, they'll be impressed at what you take for granted.

Back to our story. The School of Information and Library Studies at the University of Michigan has been and remains in a technology-induced state of flux. In this respect it's unremarkable among library schools. This type of "up-in-the-air" situation can be frustrating, and if you're currently enrolled in such a program, you'll know exactly what I mean. But such situations also present quite a few new opportunities. Back in the late 1980s, many of us "techies" were able to work on new projects that were outside our school's traditional curriculum. In many cases, we served as the impetus for our own projects—setting up and working on field placements in systems offices and hi-tech companies, using desktop publishing programs to create school newsletters, producing orientation videotapes, and teaching e-mail workshops are just a few examples. These experiences not only allowed us to become experts in those technologies, but also gave us a sense of accomplishment and confidence. We *could* independently apply new information technologies to solve real problems. We didn't have to be programmers or Ph.D. students, and we didn't need faculty supervision. We could take on new, nontraditional projects and the people we helped really appreciated our work, regardless of whether this work took place in a library or somewhere else. Through taking such chances, we learned that we had valued, marketable skills the general public didn't necessarily associate with the term "librarian."

Besides giving us experience and confidence, taking on new projects provided many of us with higher visibility both within our program and around campus. When I was finishing up my M.I.L.S., our dean was approached by the dean of the University of Michigan's College of Engineering, who was looking for what he described as a "new-age librarian." Our dean passed my name to his counterpart, and almost immediately I had a job. I didn't actively lobby for the position, nor did I make the effort to network with either dean, but I did enough to be visible, so when the time came my name came up. Certainly I was fortunate, but luck probably plays a role in any good thing that happens to anyone; you still need to work hard and take chances in order to get noticed.

That first position out of library school was as a researcher in the field of information filtering, and required me to work with programmers and cognitive psychologists. It was followed by two concurrent half-time positions—one as the technology manager for the library school where I set up hardware, software, and networks; the other as an assistant librarian at the University of Michigan Library, where I taught Internet workshops and helped manage our Gopher server. Eventually, I was back in school as an instructor and Ph.D. student.

All of these positions required me to work with many different types of people, and to deal with both the theoretical and the practical. And all of them involved in one way or another this new thing called the Internet. Of course, adapting to all these new situations, technologies, and coworkers was a piece of cake.

I only wish it had been so easy! Instead, every job was a new struggle. At every point I questioned my capabilities and my knowledge, but each time I took on something new, it got easier. As you strip away the fear and frustration of new situations, you find that what remains are interesting and entertaining opportunities. I also was quite fortunate that the good people around me were willing to help me out; but once again, I had to be visible for eventual mentors like Maurita Holland and Joe Janes to take note and get involved.

Somewhere back there, Joe Janes and I started Argus Associates, Inc., as a sideline operation. Increasingly, interesting projects came our way, and like the profession, Argus went through many changes to keep up with the opportunities. We began with the intent to sell some software we'd designed, then started doing database work for nonprofits, followed by Internet training workshops. Now Argus is a regular business, with full-time employees and enough exciting opportunities to pull me away from pursuing my Ph.D. in information and library studies.

Argus's primary work involves consulting on the design of large-scale World Wide Web sites. This is a new niche in a new industry, and, as you might expect, there aren't a lot of textbooks or accounts of others' experiences that we can easily draw on for guidance in our line of work. But we seem to be succeeding for the following reasons:

- We have drawn directly on our own experiences in designing Internet-based information systems (primarily using the Gopher software) while working at the University of Michigan's library and library schools (not many folks in our business can say they've been designing such systems for years).
- We have applied librarianship to every aspect of our work. In an industry dominated by computer programmers and marketing types, knowing the difference between text retrieval and data retrieval, or understanding a thing or two about cataloging comes in quite handy when designing a large Web-based information system.
- We realize that we must continue to adapt. Anyone directly involved in information technology must be willing to envision doing something radically different in 6 or 12 months (you would be horrified to see how many business plans Argus has been through!).

As you can see, each of these reasons directly derives from risks taken, and from skills, experiences, and outlook obtained in (and out of) classes in library school or on the job in a library. The need for individuals with such skills will only continue to increase. After all, who will help us select from the 500 cable TV channels we've been told to expect? Who will help us figure out a way to filter the hundreds of e-mail messages we might receive in a day? Who will help the world's scientific community get its arms around the massive volume of studies that it produces every day? Librarians, of course, but librarians who are willing to take some risks and roll with a few punches.

PART V

Association Work and Work in the Academic World

47.

Association Management: ALA

by Cathleen Bourdon

Associations play an enormous role in American society. With over 22,000 associations in the United States, these nonprofit groups offer both social and economic benefits to individuals and the country. Associations provide education for their members and the public, set professional standards, stimulate and organize volunteerism, inform the public, develop and disseminate information, and establish forums for the exchange of information. Seven out of ten Americans belong to at least one association.

Associations employ over 8.6 million people and represent an excellent alternative for librarians. The skills learned in library school are those needed in association management. Good problem-solving, analysis, communications, and organization skills are key abilities for association managers.

Why I Went to Library School

I did not grow up planning to be an association manager or a librarian. My goal instead was to be a journalist. That's what I pursued in college and perhaps I would have followed that road if a stint in the

Peace Corps hadn't diverted me. I spent three years in Ethiopia teaching English to secondary school students.

While in the Peace Corps, something happened to lead me to library school. The secondary school where I taught was fairly isolated in the countryside. For the first year I was there, the school had few books and no library. Then with funding from the World Bank, the school received not only textbooks but books for a school library. I'll never forget the total euphoria I felt when that shipment of books arrived. The students were even more excited at the prospect of practicing their new English reading skills. Their excitement led to disappointment however when they realized that there was little available for them on their reading level. In the shipment of books, however, there was a copy of *Tom Sawyer* and, with apologies to Mark Twain, I prepared simplified installments for my students. In a small village in southwest Ethiopia, a group of young boys and girls learned to read with Tom, Huck, and Becky.

Another class I taught was called home economics but it was really health and sanitation. After one of my students died of dysentery, we spent a good portion of each term reviewing basic sanitation principles. Information really provided life-and-death power for these students. These experiences led me to library school. Although I realized that librarianship in the United States wouldn't be quite as exciting, the basic principles of information and knowledge transfer were intriguing to me.

Life After Library School

When I graduated from library school in the mid-1970s, I had the good fortune to be able to choose between two job offers. I chose a position in the cataloging department of a private women's college in the Midwest. After a couple of years I advanced to be head of the department, and then in a few more years to be director of the library.

The college was a pioneer in outcomes or competency-based education. Such competencies as analysis, problem solving, and social interaction were explicitly taught using the context of the subject matter. Students would actively demonstrate mastery of these skills in assessment center situations.

This emphasis on competency-based education was integral to the programs and services the library offered. We developed an active library instruction program, stressing the research process. Our goal was to help students develop skills to become independent, lifelong learners.

Transfer to Association Management

Seeking a change from the college environment in the mid-1980s, I again had the advantage of choosing between two job offers. The one I selected brought me to association management, but with a direct link to librarianship. I became the deputy executive director of the Association of College and Research Libraries (ACRL), a division of the American Library Association (ALA). My colleagues at my old job thought the title was amusing and presented me with a deputy sheriff's badge at my going away party.

My first days on the job were somewhat of a shock. After almost ten years as a college librarian, I had come to define myself in relation to faculty, students, and the learning process. My clients now were other librarians, not students and faculty. The period of adjustment lasted some time, but once it concluded, I was hooked. I enjoyed association management so much that after a number of years with ACRL, I left to become the executive director of two other divisions of the American Library Association—the Association of Specialized and Cooperative Library Agencies and the Reference and Adult Services Division.

Working for the American Library Association has proven to be both challenging and exciting. No two days are ever the same and change is the only constant. In order for an association to remain true to its mission, it must constantly assess member needs and adapt the products and services to meet those needs. The educational program or book that was useful last year may be completely inadequate today. As Peter Drucker advises in *Managing the Nonprofit Organization*, you must organize yourself for systematic innovation and build the search for opportunities into the organization.[1]

What I Do

Successful management of a nonprofit organization is not measured by profits. It is measured by the benefits to members and the accomplishment of the mission. But nonprofit does not mean that the association can be unprofitable. One of my key responsibilities is fiscal management. Although the goal is not profit driven, each proposed program or service must be fully evaluated to determine its costs and benefits.

As the executive director of two divisions with a combined membership of over 6,500 members, another one of my responsibilities is responding to member requests for assistance. Whether it is questions on current research and statistics or how to submit a manuscript for publication, the days are full of phone calls, e-mail messages, and letters from all over the country. The work of the divisions is organized into over 100 committees and it is the responsibility of the staff to provide advice and assistance to all of them.

The divisions have an active publishing program, so staff must develop publishing expertise. The divisions also provide many continuing education opportunities, and staff provide support in all the logistical arrangements. Negotiating hotel and catering contracts, organizing and processing registrations, and working with audiovisual technicians are not things you learn in library school. What you do learn in library school is how to plan and organize. These skills can be applied to almost any situation.

Association staff work closely with the elected leadership. Each of the divisions I work with has a board of directors. It is their responsibility to set the policy for the association and it is the staff's responsibility to carry it out. Staff work closely with the board on developing and evaluating long- and short-range plans, identifying new program opportunities and assessing progress toward the mission.

To continue to be successful, an association needs to attract new members, as well as retain current members. Staff work with member committees in preparing annual recruitment and retention plans. These plans identify the numerical goals for both recruitment and retention and spell out the specific campaigns to meet the goals.

Two things I learned in library school directly prepared me for association management—a commitment to service and good social interaction skills. A commitment to service is essential to succeed both in librarianship and in association management. If we fail to provide excellent service to our members, they will soon cease to be our members. Good social interaction skills are also essential in both arenas.

Advice to Job Seekers

Associations are one of the fastest growing industries in the United States and the job outlook is good. As in any job search, it is always wise to learn as much as possible about the association. A good place to start is Gale's *Encyclopedia of Associations*.[2] You'll want to identify associations in your area of interest and then write to them for information.

You may also want to join an organization for association executives. The national association is the American Society for Association Executives and many areas also have a regional chapter.[3] These organizations provide continuing education, networking, and job placement services for their members.

Associations have many positions that are natural for persons with a library background. Membership director, publications officer, program planner, communications officer, and executive director are all excellent positions for someone with a library science education.

In applying for an association position, you need to be careful not to be pigeonholed into the category marked "library." Although many larger associations have an information center or library, you need to stress that your abilities go beyond the library's walls. Demonstrating your ability to plan, organize, and solve problems will go a long way. During the interview process you have an excellent opportunity to demonstrate your effective social interaction skills.

Association management is an excellent career alternative for library school graduates. It is an opportunity to apply what you've learned in a different environment. It is also an opportunity to work for a cause you love.

Notes

1. Peter F. Drucker, *Managing the Nonprofit Organization: Principles and Practices* (New York: HarperCollins, 1990), 12.
2. *Encyclopedia of Associations* (Detroit, Mich.: Gale Research).
3. Contact ASAE at 1575 I St., NW, Washington, DC 20005 (202) 626-2723.

48.

Association Management: ALISE

by Ilse Moon

One of the things you can do with a library degree is manage a library association—or become part of the management team for one.

Antioch College had given me a good basic liberal arts education. I then worked for several years as a statistician and general assistant in a university experimental psychology laboratory. After this I worked in a one-person special library devoted to marine sciences, doing a bit of everything before I got my M.L.S. After library school at Columbia, I was a cataloger and then a reference librarian in two different academic libraries. From there I moved to a variety of positions at the Montclair Public Library, a wonderful institution that encouraged its staff to attend conferences and continue their education. Service on several committees of the New Jersey Library Association led to my being invited to be Director of Professional Development at what was then the Rutgers Graduate School of Library Service.

When my husband retired we moved to Florida, where I found myself looking around for some way to use my talents and experience in a part-time job. All this time, I kept up with the professional literature, including checking the job ads in *Library Journal, American Libraries*, and the *Chronicle of Higher Education*. After a few years of writing pieces for *Current Biography* and doing a bit of indexing, I saw an announcement for an opening as Executive Secretary for the Association for Library and Information Science Education (ALISE). I applied, made the initial cuts, was interviewed at the ALA midwinter meeting, and won one of the most interesting jobs of my professional career.

What helped in securing the job? My variety of library experience, including the teaching and administration of continuing education courses that I had done at Rutgers, helped convince the search committee that I would understand the concerns of the ALISE membership. The fact that I had met many of them in the course of attending ALA meetings and serving on education-related ALA committees, and that I had letters of recommendation from respected ALISE members didn't hurt, either.

ALISE is essentially the service organization for the schools with ALA-accredited master's degree programs in library and information studies, for some programs in other countries that are comparable to our graduate programs, and for a few programs in the United States that are not ALA-accredited. The membership consists of these schools, those of their faculty and doctoral students who choose to join as personal members, and a few at-large members who are interested in library and information science education. In 1992, my last year as its executive, there were 72 institutional members from the United States and Canada (59 with accredited programs) and 11 international affiliate institutions. Personal membership was approximately 2,000.

ALISE was looking for a half-time director who could work from home. A computer with word processing, spreadsheet, and database programs was essential, as was an answering machine. A copy machine and modem proved to be necessary in a short time.

Running a small professional association is a bit like running a special library. I was responsible for a great variety of tasks, and most of what I had done during my library career proved useful. Most useful of all was probably the understanding I had gained, over years of watching and working with ALA and various state library associations, of the delicate balance between an association's policy-making board and its management.

For ALISE I helped the board develop a budget and worked to live within it. I managed the association's finances; gathered data for and prepared an annual directory of the association; arranged for the publication of the scholarly quarterly *Journal of Education for Library and Information Science* and an annual *Statistical Report* (including negotiating the publishing and printing contracts); handled the logistics of the annual meeting (including contracting for the site as well as gathering, editing, and producing its program and abstracts document); kept membership files up to date and prepared mailing labels as needed; worked with doctoral students in their search for teaching jobs; answered basic telephone and mail questions about library education and referred questioners to member specialists; and, most important of all, kept in regular contact with members and the board.

Apart from understanding the profession, interest in the members and their concerns was essential for success in this work. An ability to manage a budget and keep close track of finances was also an important aspect of the job. Never undertake a job like this unless you can balance your checkbook regularly without thinking it a dreadful chore! Another important aspect of the work is understanding the role of the executive as one who carries out policy but who does not make policy. This is a narrow line to tread with a changing elected board, a membership with full-time professional duties, and an executive who becomes perforce the "corporate memory." Diplomacy and sensitivity to the needs and problems of members is essential.

For me, the best parts of managing the association were

- meeting new colleagues and becoming part of the family of library and information science educators
- being in the center of library activities through contact with our members and through representing the association at meetings with managers of other library associations
- helping the association gain a sound financial footing
- producing a useful reference tool, the annual directory
- feeling that I helped doctoral students and new library educators along their career paths
- learning such new skills as use of the computer in database management, bookkeeping, word processing, and electronic communication
- enhancing and broadening such skills as conference management
- having the opportunity to work at home with more or less flexible hours

There were also some less-than-wonderful parts of managing the association.

- As a small association, ALISE was always strapped for funds and did not feel it could afford to expand its activities nor provide a full-time salary and health benefits. The space requirements also became substantial—back issues of journals took over my garage and my guest room disappeared. Although the board encouraged me to hire part-time clerical help, this was impractical in a small one-room office.
- The pressure of dunning members for late renewals, conference presenters and program chairs for last-minute abstracts, and schools for late survey forms was constant.
- As a one-person operation, the "half-time" job grew to fill most of every day, including evening hours.
- Despite the fact that I could set my own hours, there were so many telephone queries, such volume of mail, and so many

things that had deadlines that traveling (one of the joys of semiretirement) was severely restricted.

- Working with some presidents and boards was not so easy as with others.

When I retired from ALISE, primarily to gain more freedom to travel, I recommended to the board that it consider hiring a management company instead of a lone person working from a home office. This would give the association the benefit of a group of managers with specialized skills in conference management, accounting, and publication. It would require, if the management firm had little library experience, a great deal more work on the part of the board and committee chairs in handling the library and information professional aspects of the association's work. In retrospect, I think the association may have lost as much as it gained from following this recommendation.

For someone contemplating a job managing a small professional association, I can only recommend what I would do if considering it, knowing what I know now. I would certainly be more honest with myself about my time-management skills. Setting and keeping realistic hours—without being *too* rigid about it—will prevent burnout and allow for a more reasonable private life. Insist on an appropriate title. Calling the manager Executive Secretary did not prevent the executive from assuming functions the board might have preferred to keep to itself, but it did restrict the effectiveness of the executive in dealing with outside agencies. The executive who followed me was called Executive Director, a more appropriate designation.

49.

Academic Career Services for Information Professionals

by Barbara Ward Welsh

As placement director at the College of Information Science and Technology, Drexel University, I provide career services to information professionals. In this position, I combine my professional experience, master's degree in library and information science, and personal strengths. How did I develop my career path from a library degree and library experience to an alternative career in the field?

Typical of many librarians, I had worked in libraries before earning my master's degree. I had volunteered in my children's school library while I considered my career choices for reentering the job market. I saw the wisdom of earning a professional master's degree to help me retool for a new career. The experience as a library volunteer had been extremely positive, and I was fortunate enough to have an accredited library and information program nearby. Another encouraging factor to enroll at Drexel was the presence of a placement office and full-time placement director as part of the program at the then-named School of Library and Information Science.

As I progressed toward the completion of my master's degree, I followed Placement Director Jane Spivack's advice to gain preprofessional work experience and I worked in a local public library to practice the library theory that I was learning in the classroom. This practical experience helped me obtain a professional job after graduation in June 1982, with the help of Drexel's placement office which provided a printed published job list, counseling, and job search workshops.

My professional library work experience consisted of managing one-person information centers in two corporations—TRW Electronic Components Group and Ametek Inc.—from 1982 through 1986. I gained useful administrative experience in the management of a small library. I learned to manage processes, such as the acquisitions-cataloging-accounting process. I learned to fit into an organization, publicize the information center and its services, and to campaign for what the center needed. I also put to work the information-gathering and problem-solving skills that I had learned at Drexel. My ability to solve information needs, especially through searching commercial databases, was valued highly by the organization. I also continued to build my professional network of special librarians within the area, and I attended meetings of the local Special Libraries chapter.

Besides the information-gathering and management skills that I learned during that period, I also learned career-building skills. TRW downsized its North American electronics operations in 1985, and I was laid off after three years. In truth, I was "half-sized" because so many engineers had been laid off from the Philadelphia facility that the librarian was reduced to part-time. I chose a layoff and looked for a job. This was a more valuable experience than I realized at the time.

My next employment experience would be shorter than I expected. I was reemployed within a week as the researcher for a start-up information brokerage, which was owned by two partners. I gained first-hand experience observing them build their business, which is much the work of an information broker. The business didn't come in fast enough, however, so I was laid off after three months, while the partners built the business in the hopes of being able to afford additional paid staff in the future.

I now found myself unemployed for the second time in three months, which was not an enviable position. Within a few more weeks, I took a part-time, temporary reference position at a local college. This is the same strategy I have suggested to unemployed information professionals. Part-time work is helpful to maintain professional contacts and maintain a good organization in your daily life, and it allows enough free time to look for a new permanent position. My colleagues in my part-time job became an important part of my network as they suggested I apply to jobs they had heard about or had seen advertised. They also kept my spirits up, which is an important issue in the job search of an unemployed librarian. One of the important things I learned from being unemployed is the need to be aware of vacancies and to keep current about what is going on in the job market.

The Drexel placement office was always an important part of my job search during this time. The postings of available library positions were invaluable in my job search. Because Drexel has an active placement office, library and information employers post jobs in this central facility. Alums and new graduates in the area always check the Drexel placement office first when looking for a job. Here is an example of the service that Drexel's placement office provides: I called the placement office the day I was notified by the information broker that I was being laid off. By the end of the same day I was referred to a job posting; I called the employer and had an appointment scheduled for the very next day!

My next job after temporary reference work was the one I currently hold. I learned a great deal from my job-hunting experience in 1986, and when I heard that the placement director position at Drexel would be available I applied for it. My past experiences working in school, special, public, and academic libraries would be useful in this job. My biggest reservation about interviewing for the directorship was my uncertainty about the future career path for such a position.

Once I interviewed for the placement director position, I knew that this was a job that would combine my interests, past experience, and strengths. Besides my varied experience working in libraries, I could offer my strong interpersonal skills. I like working with people and helping them. What better way to help people than to help them grow in their careers? Helping people see their strengths and positive points is a very important part of career counseling. I also like to "teach" people. As I learned about the career planning process, I learned how to pass this knowledge along to others to help them understand how to plan and build their careers.

I was excited to meet the challenge of learning this new field of career counseling. I would pursue an alternative career using everything I knew about libraries and the delivery of information, but I would be using it in a new way, and I would have the opportunity to learn a great deal.

How Did I Prepare Myself for My New Career?

To prepare for my new career, I used the same principles (with the exception of earning an additional degree) that I used to learn the information industry. I joined the professional association of academic career professionals, which is now called the National Association of Colleges and Employers, and its regional affiliate, the Middle Atlantic Association of Colleges and Employers (MAACE). MAACE's annual regional meeting offered workshops on legal and ethical issues and how-to sessions in career services. The monthly newsletter and quarterly journal presented articles on interpretations of the latest court decisions and legislation, state-of-the-art technology, success stories in career services, and research in the field. The most important asset of MAACE membership and involvement was being part of the career services network and being able to get advice and suggestions from these more experienced career services professionals. In particular, I sought help from Dina Lindquist, the director of Drexel's Career Services Center.

What Does a Career Professional Do?

The College of Information Science and Technology's placement office supports its students when they seek preprofessional work experience, when they graduate and get their first professional job, and throughout their careers. I provide workshops for students on job searching, interviewing skills, and résumé-writing. I am available for job counseling appointments at any time for students and alumni. My office maintains a telephone jobline of new local professional jobs and posts the same in hard copy.

I maintain statistics and data on placement of College of Information Science and Technology alumni, undergraduates, and master's and doctoral students in the library and information science program and the information systems program. I collect survey data (including job title, name of employer, skills, salary, and length of job search) from questionnaires that are sent to all graduates. Data from master of science in library and information science graduates is submitted to *Library Journal* for publication each October in the annual report of graduates from all ALA-accredited programs.

Another skill that I have acquired since becoming placement director is that of making presentations. I had to overcome my fear of making presentations and I now rather enjoy the opportunity to stand before a group to make a presentation. I make presentations to students in my career workshops; I make a short presentation on résumé writing in a course that most of our students take; I make a short presentation on the placement office as part of the orientation of all new master's students; and I have made numerous presentations to professional groups, groups of students in other programs, and outside groups.

Trends in Library and Information Employment

The Drexel Placement Office holds a unique position in the information science job market in the greater Philadelphia area. The office posts positions for local employers and works with most of Drexel's students and graduates. Employment trends that I observe in the mid-1990s include a tight job market for professionals and very competitive job searches. In particular, new graduates have a longer and more difficult job search than they would have had in the past. Employers are looking for three to five years of previous experience for many entry-level jobs and they want extensive automation, information systems, database, and Internet experience. Salaries for entry-level positions continue to improve, with employed Drexel 1994 master of science graduates earning a mean salary of $32,500 and a median salary of $28,300. Of the 1994 Drexel library and information science graduates who are placed in jobs, 22 percent worked in public libraries, 31 percent worked in academic libraries, 9 percent worked in school libraries, and 38 percent worked in special libraries.

Combining my information science background with a new career as a career services professional in academia has been a very rewarding move for me. I enjoy the ability to use my information science background in this nontraditional way.

50.

Back in the Classroom Again

by Judith J. Field

How Did I End Up in the Classroom Again?

This is a question I am often asked by my friends, and by colleagues who worked with me or knew me when I worked in various libraries or who served with me on various association committees over a period of 25 years. I certainly did not start out to teach library science courses and I certainly did not intend to do it full time. It was just the next opportunity in the information field that presented itself in my professional career, at a time that I could afford to take advantage of it.

Background

While still a sophomore in college, I decided that I wanted to be a librarian—not just a librarian but a library director. Thus I did what seemed obvious to me and switched my major to business administration. I had already noted that, while collections appeared to be handled well, libraries in general were not well managed. I then earned my master's degree and went off to the corporate world where my first challenge was setting up a technical library for two engineering divisions. It was exciting and I enjoyed working with the engineers, but after three years most of the challenges had been met. The time had come to move on.

My next assignment was an academic library in a subject field for which I had minimal knowledge. This lack of knowledge was not to be a big problem, because the unit head knew the field and was happy to let me reorganize, and develop policies and procedures and staff training, so that she could concentrate on providing reference services. In about seven months the reorganization was completed and I moved on to join the staff of the business administration library.

This next position also included reorganization responsibilities and the position of associate director, in my major field of interest. I thought I had found my permanent career track and took time to earn an M.B.A. to strengthen my subject specialization. Then the Institute of International Commerce was formed as a separately funded unit of the school, and after a couple of years it was determined they needed an international trade library to serve the needs of their researchers and the local businesspeople who wanted to conduct business overseas. I agreed to develop a library and to participate in their seminars for the businesspeople, showing them where they could locate appropriate information, developing brochures and conducting requested research. After four years, the institute was informed that its funding was to be cut and the collection transferred to the business library, which would eliminate my position.

I started to apply for various special library positions when a colleague asked me to apply for a position in a public library as the head of reference. While I was not interested in working in a public library, I finally agreed to do the interview as a courtesy. I went to the interview and detailed my concerns about not being the right person for their job. I was offered the job at a very lucrative salary, but the deciding factor was that I would supervise 24 FTEs. I decided this would look good on my résumé as I continued to work toward achieving my dream of becoming a library director, and I took the position. It was a fantastic job with many challenges.

After 13 years I left and accepted a position as director of a legislative reference library, acquiring greater insight into a still different corporate culture. After completing another reorganization of library services, I decided to go into consulting and to do some writing. I was debating at this time whether to become a full-time consultant in management issues or to go back into the corporate world.

During this time I had been very active in three professional associations, had served on a variety of committees, and had held office. It was the interaction from these committee activities and the time spent with other librarians that I recognized the need for quality continuing education courses. The end result was that I ended up serving on several professional development committees and was asked to teach several continuing education courses.

While I was still doing consulting work, I was invited to become an adjunct faculty member of a nearby library science program to teach a general reference course. Teaching a course to library science students rather than practitioners sounded interesting and I knew that several of my colleagues had found it a worthwhile and revitalizing experience. A year later I was teaching full time and made a lecturer, initially teaching the core courses but then teaching in my specialties.

Now four years later I am a senior lecturer, still teaching reference as a core course but also teaching business reference, government documents, and special libraries. I find myself fully involved as a faculty member serving on committees, doing presentations, and writing.

So What Does This Mean?

Many practicing librarians with subject specialties or technical expertise are sought out by library schools to be guest lecturers for a particular class or to teach a specialized course. As guest lecturers the practitioners bring to the classroom relevant information to highlight the instructor's information, in most instances providing practical applications for the theory. If they are asked to teach a complete course, they usually receive the designation of adjunct faculty. Adjunct faculty do not have the added responsibility of advising students, nor do they have to meet the research and publication requirements of full-time faculty.

Adjuncts bring to the classroom their views of the real world of librarianship, providing practical applications from their own experiences. Students appreciate this since in just a few months they will be looking for positions in libraries and information centers. The limitations of having adjuncts teach core courses is that adjuncts often do not know the theoretical framework of library practice. I know that in the four years I have taught, my initially totally pragmatic lectures have evolved to include information theory concepts. It has taken me this long to realize the importance of these concepts to provide an appropriate structure for the students' continual professional growth. In my specialty courses, however, I still teach the pragmatic "this is how you really do it" or "this is how you should do it if you want to be successful" in the real world. Achieving the proper blend of practical experience with the appropriate amount of theory is a continuing battle in a field that is so strongly influenced by technology and stringent new business practices.

What, No Ph.D.?!

I do not have a Ph.D., and with my other professional activities and the fact that I carry a full teaching load, I have neither the time, nor the interest to pursue that degree. What does the lack of a Ph.D.

mean to me, the school, and the students? At my institution it means that I cannot be on the tenure track. Am I losing sleep over this? To be honest, no. I do not have to write grants, and I do not have to develop a research agenda or constantly be submitting articles for publication. The faculty have accepted this lack of a terminal degree and recognize the value that I bring to the program: 25 years of experience in several different types of libraries, that I have held important positions in two major library associations (including being made a fellow in the Special Libraries Association), and that I have given presentations and published several articles and books. This experience gives me credibility as a member of the faculty. The advantage of having me as a lecturer is that I can carry a full teaching load each semester, providing the opportunity for other faculty members to apply for released time to work on their research projects. Also my appointment means that I can assume more administrative tasks, again freeing faculty to do their research. In this case it is a win-win proposition since I get to teach and they get more time to do their research. ALA-accredited programs cannot, however, rely strictly on lecturers to fulfill their teaching mission while their tenure-track faculty just do research. (I am well aware of this fact since I currently serve on the ALA Committee on Accreditation.)

The fact that I lack a Ph.D. matters little to the other members of the faculty, and students are often surprised that I do not have one, but they continue to take the advance classes from me. The primary concerns of the administration, the faculty, and the students are that I am a good instructor.

In various universities there will be some committees limited to those faculty who are tenured or on a tenure-track. Salaries will usually be lower for adjuncts and lecturers too, and there may be time limitations to an appointment. If these limitations are a problem for you, then do not plan a long-term teaching career without the Ph.D. degree.

Not having taken the Ph.D.-level courses that study the theories of information-seeking behaviors—not being familiar with the work that adds richness to the core courses—is the biggest disadvantage. If you are only going to teach a specialized course, this background is often not as important. When you decide to accept a full-time teaching assignment, you need to address these gaps in your knowledge of the information field.

Advantages and Disadvantages

For me the biggest advantage of teaching is what I learn from my students. Teaching keeps you alert; there is no opportunity to rest on your laurels and speak authoritatively. In today's rapidly evolving technological world, it is hard just to keep only one step behind the latest improvement. Yet when they graduate, students need that expertise for their new jobs. Today's environment also provides more opportunity to experiment and assignments permit students to deal with the current realities of working in libraries. My position provides the opportunity to place students in their first professional positions and to watch them mature and gain competence.

The disadvantage of teaching is that your end customers are your students and you do not have a chance to observe firsthand how they implement what they learned in the classroom. Also I find it disconcerting that students leave my classes with greater expertise in searching or manipulating particular products than I have (since I do not work with most of the new tools on a day-to-day basis). Finally, as a former practitioner, I miss the satisfaction of using my knowledge to satisfy a client.

Some Final Thoughts

From my vantage point of having completed four years of teaching and my second year on the ALA Committee on Accreditation, I feel that adjuncts and lecturers help to provide a reality check for library schools. The increasing pressure to do research and to publish in refereed journals makes it harder for faculty members to maintain relationships with practitioners and to be active in professional associations. Lecturers and adjuncts can help provide that connection for faculty and students.

The position of lecturer would not be a normal career path for most people because of the limits in salary and promotional opportunities. If you are considering moving into library education, however, then a year or two as a lecturer would allow you to decide if this is the career you want. If you have had an extensive career and want to share your expertise, becoming a full-time lecturer would give you that opportunity. It is hard work, but the rewards of turning students on to the world of information science makes it a worthwhile venture.

51.

Prospect Research

By Charlotte Carl-Mitchell and Ann Webb

Charlotte's Story

"Ferret out the unknown, unearth the arcane, expose the obscure." That's how one employment advertisement colorfully described what we do to find prospective donors for our university. Other aspects of the job were characterized by a fellow researcher in a playful list he called the "Top Ten Wonderful Things About Being a Prospect Researcher." My favorite was "the chance to read articles detailing the exploits of those who cleared more this year than most people will in a lifetime." If you have an inquiring mind, enjoy discovering little-known facts about people, and want to work in one of the few fields that grow when resources are tight, you should consider prospect research.

When the first edition of this book was published in 1980, prospect research as a profession did not exist. Fund-raising efforts at educational and other nonprofit institutions have increased rapidly since then as a result of the financial pressure brought on by changing demographics, an economic downturn during the 1980s, and reduced government support. Most nonprofits have had to strengthen and enlarge their development efforts in order to survive. The American Prospect Research Association[1] (APRA) began in 1988 to promote educational and professional opportunities in the area of fund-raising research. I became aware of the field when I applied for my present job in late 1993. What I have learned in the past year and a half is that it is an appealing and interesting alternative to traditional librarianship. I earned an M.L.S. in 1974 from the University of Texas at Austin. My bachelor's degree was in Latin and English, and I had planned to be a teacher. But student teaching changed my mind, and like many who are the products of a liberal arts education, I looked to library school as a viable vocational choice that could lead to a job.

After graduation I worked as a library assistant at the LBJ School of Public Affairs Library at the University of Texas. I stayed there for a year and then accepted a position at UT's Humanities Research Center. HRC is an internationally known collection of rare books, manuscripts, photographs, film, and theater material. It houses a Gutenberg Bible, the world's first photograph, and one of the most important collections of nineteenth- and twentieth-century British and American books and manuscripts in the world. Though I started as a paraprofessional working in the reading room, ephemera, and special collections, I was promoted to a professional position as manuscripts cataloger. I subsequently worked in the theater collection and on special projects. In my 11 years at HRC, I worked in six different departments, establishing a new record and gaining many skills.

By the mid-1980s I decided to leave the profession to follow a personal interest in services for older adults. I spent six years working in nonprofit social services, and, because of the constant challenge of finding funding, all of my jobs involved fund-raising as well as administration and programming. In fact, I had decided my library career was over until I saw an ad for a program director for prospect research at St. Edward's University in Austin. The job required experience in fund-raising and research, both of which I had. After I applied, I discovered that the person who would become my boss, the director of records and research, was delighted that I had an M.L.S., and I was hired.

Mission Possible

It intrigued me that this job entailed gathering and analyzing biographical and financial information on prospective donors (individuals, corporations, and foundations) and preparing comprehensive dossiers for the university fund-raising department. This would be done by accessing and gathering data from various information sources including in-house records, published directories, online databases, and informant review sessions; reviewing local, national, professional, and financial publications for prospect information, interest, and activities; and analyzing and synthesizing accumulated information to assess prospects' financial assets, interests, and connections to the university.

A bachelor's degree, some knowledge of research, and computer experience were preferred. The computer experience included online database searching, word processing and data entry. Other qualifications were knowledge of research methods, library resources, and public records; skill in analyzing and organizing information; the ability to communicate effectively, analyze, plan, and execute projects to meet deadlines; and demonstrated organizational and interpersonal skills, curiosity, and attention to detail.

Even though the job sounded straightforward, it took me several months to understand the type of information each development director needed. Our department is considered a "small shop" with two researchers supporting the directors of major gifts, corporate foundation government relations, planned giving (trusts and bequests), alumni relations, and public relations publications under the vice president for university relations. We also respond to non-prospect-related research requests from the president's office and other offices on campus. Our primary responsibility, however, is to compile the information necessary for our directors to ask the right individual for the right amount for the right project at the right time.

Where the Jobs Are

Prospect researchers work primarily for private and public educational institutions and hospitals, but members of APRA represent a wide variety of nonprofit organizations, including museums, symphonies, zoos, associations, public television, and such community organizations as the Boy Scouts, Humane Society, League of Women Voters, Planned Parenthood, Recording for the Blind, United Negro College Fund, and many others.

All nonprofits must raise money to support their programs. This money may come from government grants or constituencies (such as alumni, parents, trustees, and friends in the case of a university), but in these days of reduced government funding, most organizations, including ours, are looking further afield for support—which means cultivating and educating individuals, corporations, and foundations that may be sympathetic to a particular cause. That is where prospect researchers start to work. Has one of our alumni recently made a fortune in the stock market or real estate? Researchers scan stacks of publications in order to find that out. Or is there a prominent local person who does not have a connection with our university but who is known to support the kind of minority education programs that we offer? We bring such people to the attention of our directors—it may be the right time to solicit a donation. Has someone associated with our university reached an age to be considering estate planning? That person should know about the benefits of planned giving. Researchers help their organizations make the right connections.

Ann's Story

As a recent library school graduate with an interest in electronic information sources and research in general, I take on technical projects at St. Edward's such as developing online search strategies, organizing prospecting projects, working with new vendors and tools, and trying to keep a handle on internal data management. The opportunity to work in these areas and my interest in business information and market research drew me to prospect research at St. Edward's.

Although rapid growth is changing the job environment here, for many years most professional school graduates who wanted to stay in Austin were forced to develop alternative approaches. The bad news used to be that there were too many lawyers in Austin; the good news was they did great yardwork. The same could be said for librarians, except that they tended to work in state government or for the university system and pretty well overloaded the professional ranks. While in graduate school, I offered document delivery services in Austin on contract for the national company Information on Demand (now called Article Express). I found I loved working independently and I enjoyed doing research whenever I had a chance. I had been considering offering private research services. I wanted to specialize in an area that suited my personal tastes, something in the public interest or consumer research. I think I may still move in that direction, and working as a prospect researcher has allowed me to continue to develop research and analytical skills that support this path. I have also recently enrolled in St. Edward's M.B.A. program, which I think raises the level of analysis I am able to provide.

Prospect Research and Traditional Librarianship

Skills we use as fund-raising researchers are common to other kinds of library work, but one of the main differences, and for me one of the main draws, of doing research is the focus on projects with concrete results rather than a focus on providing day-to-day services. I have a sense that our work is critically important both to the immediate and long-term success of our fundraising campaigns, whether we are working to endow a scholarship program or raising funds to construct a building. I also appreciate the overview of the organization that we have and the sense that we are out in front. We are usually among the first to know about and respond to critical planning issues. We are not cloistered because the work we do affects the whole organization. Initiative and creativity are welcome and rewarded in this kind of environment, as we work on developing approaches to our constituency and beyond.

One advantage of working in prospect research is that prospect researchers may have more opportunity than traditional librarians to use online services for obtaining up-to-date business, financial, and government information. Our tools help us bring in money, and it isn't hard to justify research that will bring in more money than it costs. This setting provides us with an excellent way not only to keep up technically, but to stay on top of the marketplace. It also gives us a chance to work with vendors not traditionally found in libraries, such as local public records providers.

A Prospector's Tools

We look at a broad range of sources for biographical and financial information. When considering a company as a potential corporate donor, we might look at the people involved, the organizational structure, the history of community involvement, and the size or market share of the company. We might use company information from Dun & Bradstreet and Standard and Poor's, and from such sources as Dow Jones News/Retrieval, ABI/Inform, *Business Periodical Index*, the *Directory of Corporate Affiliations*, or industrial expansion newsletters. If it is a public company we may also consult Moody's manuals, or retrieve full-text proxies and annual and quarterly reports via EDGAR on the Internet. We also consult Disclosure (SEC Online), Mergers and Acquisitions, and other services through companies such as LEXIS/NEXIS and DIALOG.

If we are tracking gifts or potential gifts of stock, for example, we might examine investment information, such as an individual's holdings or the stock's current price, available through different commercial vendors and brokers, through direct SEC filings on the Internet, or in value-added products such as Investnet's Insider Trading Monitor.

Many types of public records are available online through LEXIS/NEXIS, TRW, Dataquick, Information America, Prentice Hall Online, local real estate data vendors, our Secretary of State's office, and even our local county courthouse. These kinds of records along with traditional public sources of vital records can be used to locate our older or "lost" alumni. We also use traditional biographical sources, in print and online, to learn more about our prominent constituents: BioBase (*Biography and Geneology Master Index*), Marquis Who's Who directories, Standard and Poor's products, Bowker Biographical Directory, and specialized directories for attorneys, doctors, and other occupations.

Foundation support accounts for a large part of our income, and we consult a growing body of commercial sources to locate and describe foundations. We also refer to the federal and state documents that foundations must file so that we can keep up with giving trends and personnel changes within foundations. Federal program details are available on the Internet and in value-added formats through commercial sources. Newsletters can also provide up-to-date information, alerting a prospector to new grant opportunities. Major vendors have a presence on DIALOG and NewsNet, and one major vendor has started an entire series of CDs that details corporate and foundation information.

There are also a number of businesses, known as screening companies, that collect and organize information used to identify and quantify the wealth of individuals. The information in their databanks is often run against the constituent lists of nonprofits and used to identify potential donors. Such a service may be offered in the context of a general consultancy, or simply as an information service. The role of the prospect researcher is usually to follow up and verify the results of the automated service.

Because of the large numbers of prospective donors, my job also involves a significant amount of internal data management. We have thousands of constituents, and the data we work with may involve such attributes as measures of affluence and models of interpersonal and organizational relationships. To complicate matters, our "data" (some of it more than 100 years old) resides not only in files, archives, PCs, and mainframes, but also in people's memories. I enjoy the challenge of envisioning ways to model and retrieve the information that we need because each constituent or potential donor represents such an important relationship for the university.

Prospects for the Future

According to Jon Thorson, president of APRA, a growing number of organizations are introducing research functions in their organizations. This means the field is growing, but not in the same way as in the past. The major difference is that the core research function is less centralized. Development officers and other "front line" people who have not previously done research are now diving in, sometimes using a professional researcher for guidance. The prospect researcher may now spend less time doing research and take on additional responsibilities such as information systems management, stewardship, or grant writing. Another strong trend is that more freelancers are assisting the smaller nonprofits which are less likely to have the resources to dedicate a permanent position to research. The wide availability of online resources has made freelancing an increasingly popular way to provide research services. For APRA members, salaries seem to be steady or increasing, and the results of a 1994 APRA salary survey suggested that most prospect researchers earn between $25,000 and $45,000 a year.

Some of our work is analytical; some is investigative. If you enjoy investigative work that is anchored to a very strong ethical premise—appreciation and respect for the donor—you should feel comfortable in the field of prospect research. We have an excellent professional network, with regular state and national meetings, and a very active and energetic exchange on our Internet group.

Prospect research helps organizations find resources to support their programs, which means it is a field that can flourish when resources become limited. For those in the field, this can mean job security and the satisfaction of doing an important job.

Note

1. American Prospect Research Association has since changed its name to the Association of Professional Researchers for Advancement.

52.

A Zigzag Route to Fund-Raising

by Dick Luxner

Major Owens said, in the first edition of this book, that generalists are persons who have mastered the encyclopedic approach to problem solving. Of all the generalists, he said, librarians are probably the best organized and possess the broadest scope.

That generalist approach along with a natural curiosity has propelled me in many directions ever since I was little. My father gave me a jigsaw and taught me to work with my hands. My mother read to me and gave me my lifelong devotion to books and reading. She also gave me a flute and fostered my love for music. Someone started me on stamp collecting, and another on the game of chess. In basic training at Fort Dix someone suggested weather forecasting school and I became a meteorologist during World War II. Back at college I learned to fly and earned a private pilot's license, got my bachelor's degree in English, and went to work as the shipping and traffic manager for a jam, jelly, and preserve factory. Later I joined my father selling auto parts and imported Sheffield cutlery. When he died I carried on the importing business for awhile until someone suggested library school.

I enrolled at Rutgers part time and went to work at the Brooklyn Public Library as a trainee. After each semester and summer session at Rutgers I got a raise at BPL, and when I graduated with an M.L.S.

my salary climbed to all of $6,000, working full time. I gave up the importing business and married my boss, the assistant chief of BPL's science and industry division, who was immediately transferred to the business library since they did not approve of spouses working together.

I am telling you all this to explain the idea of a generalist—one who is curious and knows a little about a lot of things, and one who just wallowed in courses in bibliography, indexing, abstracting, reference, database searching, thesaurus development, and information theory. The two most memorable courses for me at Rutgers were Ralph Shaw's Information Theory and Charles Bernier's Indexing and Abstracting. I'll never forget Shaw's insights into the future of information retrieval, precision, and recall at a time when computers consisted of such monsters as Big Blue's mainframes. And I'll always remember Bernier's lessons on the right ways to create index terms, still a challenging art which, even today, cannot be fully computerized.

After serving my apprentice year at the Brooklyn Public Library, I went to IBM's T. J. Watson Research Center Library. There the challenge was to help scientific and technical geniuses find information in fields with which they were not familiar. The atmosphere was heady with physics, organic chemistry, nuclear radiation, and lots of secrecy about computers, future systems not yet invented, IBM's internal technical information retrieval center, KWIC indexes to the report literature, DIALOG, and chess games at lunchtime. I worked with many scientists in several fields and sat down with them to construct search profiles made up of relevant terms in Boolean format for their literature searches. These were run weekly in batch mode on both internal and DIALOG databases of indexes and abstracts to the scientific literature. (No one at that time was using full text). The results were printed on continuous three-by-five cards for the scientists, and I was called in to hear their complaints when profiles had to be narrowed or expanded, or otherwise modified. One of our gaffes concerned a search for venetian blinds which turned up references to blind Venetians! Oh well, "garbage in, garbage out!"

What has all this to do with fund-raising? Have you ever heard of prospect research? The Association of Professional Researchers for Advancement, New England Development Research Association and other local groups around the country, many of which are chapters of APRA have a combined membership of over 2,000, very few of whom are graduate librarians. Prospect researchers are the ones who find and organize the few major prospects among our nonprofit constituencies who are capable of giving the largest gifts to a capital campaign. Since about 95 percent of the total gifts will come from only about 5 percent of the donors, it pays off handsomely to hire people who can do the necessary research. Not only do we search internal records and external public databases for biographical, business, professional, and community backgrounds, but we also manage our computer software to help solicitors and volunteers keep the cultivation process on track. We fill the gaps in our knowledge of our prospects' wealth, financial holdings, income, obligations, net worth, and giving to others. We conduct biweekly tracking and strategy meetings where all concerned arrive at a consensus on the right personnel, timing, and strategy for each solicitation of a major prospect.

The research office is the pivotal center of the development office, just as the library is the pivotal center of the campus, research lab, teaching hospital or law firm. Some nonprofit organizations are huge. Large universities, for example, have several hundred thousand alumni, all of whom must be screened for the major prospects among them. This sometimes takes a staff of a dozen or more researchers. But a small college, museum, hospital, community orchestra might only be able to afford one research officer who may also be the systems manager as well as the director of the annual fund. This is the perfect environment for a librarian generalist who has mastered the encyclopedic approach to problem solving.

How did I discover such a perfect niche for myself? I had been a branch librarian at one of City University of New York's four-year colleges in Brooklyn when a job announcement appeared in the *Chronicle of Higher Education* for a sci-tech librarian at Stevens Institute of Technology in New Jersey. I was then commuting to Brooklyn from our New Jersey home and my wife was the director of a public library in New Jersey. I wanted to work nearer home. The interview at Stevens seemed encouraging but the job went to someone else. When I opened up the next *Chronicle of Higher Education* I spotted the Stevens logo and an ad which said its vice president for development needed someone to start a research office to identify and profile major prospects for a coming capital campaign. I knew instantly that I could do that and phoned the Stevens librarian. He said, "Sure you could," and referred me to the VP. Within two weeks I had the job and my new office was *in* the library.

That was 12 years ago. Since then I have not only started a second research office in another college, but I have also worked as a senior researcher in a very large university. Now I am consulting and help colleges and other nonprofits inaugurate or upgrade their research offices with state-of-the-art resources, procedures, and systems. It is all very stimulating and satisfying, since I can pass along my experience and knowledge to beginners in a research office. I train them to search any library's print and electronic resources to find all the information they need to help the fund-raising process.

Researchers today can begin earning in the mid-$20s with a bachelor's degree and no library degree. However, with a modern M.L.S. that includes training in computer systems, database and online information retrieval theory and practice, as well as indexing, abstracting, and cataloging, one can earn ten times what I earned at the Brooklyn Public Library almost 30 years ago. And the potential for much higher income is right there in the development office. Successful major gift solicitors, directors of development, planned-giving specialists, corporate and foundation grant officers, and vice presidents of advancement and public relations all can earn up to $100,000, depending on the size of the organization.

But money is not the only reward. My most satisfying challenge was to convince people of the importance of the research office. It took time, but eventually everyone from presidents and deans to faculty and volunteers came to rely on research for timely and often crucial information. This, of course, is the kind of gratification one needs to make it fun.

I'll never forget the case of an alumnus whose name showed up in a clipping from a Caribbean newspaper. The article was caught by our clipping service because he was identified as a Stevens graduate. When I looked him up in our database I was shocked to see that mail had been returned from his last known address many years ago—he was "lost." The article said his factory in Puerto Rico had earned its first million dollars supplying lithographic plates to most of the publishers and printers in Latin America. When I looked up his master's dissertation and phoned his academic advisor, the professor said he had been a guest at five of the alumnus's weddings and that they were still in touch. Lesson for today: Keep in touch with your own faculty.

If you want to know more about research in fund-raising you can subscribe to our forum on the Internet. Send an e-mail message to: listserv@uci.edu. In the body of your message type SUBSCRIBE and your first name and last name (e.g., SUBSCRIBE DICK LUXNER). Here you will find some 20 to 30 messages a day on many topics ranging from a (non-librarian) beginner's query on where to find a basic list of tools for a new research office to an extended posting of a letter to U.S. Securities and Exchange Commission Chairman Levitt on why the EDGAR project of free public access to the SEC database should remain free and not be privatized. (This letter, by the way, was instrumental in helping to convince the chairman to keep the database of securities filings by companies and insiders free and open to the taxpaying public which had already paid millions of dollars to fund the system.)

You may wish to contact the Association of Professional Researchers for Advancement[1] for membership information. APRA publishes a quarterly newsletter with job postings and an annual directory of members, and holds an annual convention in August. A recent convention was held jointly with the New England Development Research Association.[2] NEDRA publishes a membership directory and an excellent quarterly newsletter with job openings, articles for beginners, software reviews, and news of meetings for all levels of research people. It also convenes an annual meeting featuring well-known and experienced speakers. Throughout the year NEDRA also presents numerous workshops and roundtables all over New England for beginners and practitioners.

To find job openings around the country look at the ads in the

Chronicle of Philanthropy, published every other week. Not only will you find ads, but you will also find articles about the entire area of nonprofit fund-raising. It is your single most valuable source of timely information on grants, capital campaigns, major gifts, surveys, statistics, profiles, government and tax developments, and ethical issues.

Yes, there are ethical issues concerning privacy and demographic pinpointing at the household level, for example. In fact, APRA has a lengthy code of ethics which includes sections on relevance, honesty, confidentiality, accuracy, and the collection, recording, and use of information, all to the end of maintaining a prospect's right to privacy.

I am fascinated with the fact that most of the best researchers I have known over the years have been history majors, either with or without library degrees. I suspect that anyone who majors in history would have to be curious, would be concerned with detailed facts, and would be able to write a narrative history of a person or family, or company or foundation. So, if you are a generalist, have mastered the encyclopedic approach to problem solving, write well, and are looking for a rewarding career—and especially if you are accurate, thorough, patient, and have a sense of humor—try fund-raising research.

Notes

1. Association of Professional Researchers for Advancement
   414 Plaza Dr., Suite 209
   Westmont, IL 60559
   (708) 655-0177
   Fax: (708) 655-0391
   apra@adminsys.com
2. New England Development Research Association
   1770 Massachusetts Ave., Suite 288
   Cambridge, MA 02140
   (508) 934-2213
   (membership chair Robin Good, good@rgang.uml.edu)

PART VI

Librarians Employed in the Corporate World

53.

The Challenges of Cataloging Images

by Elizabeth Bellas, Katherine DeBruler,
and Mary Forster

An archive of images rather than printed materials presents cataloging challenges for the information processing (IP) department of Corbis Corporation where we work. IP attaches text records to the digital images in the archive. These images are used in CD-ROM products produced by Corbis, and they are licensed to other users of images, including multimedia companies, advertisers, book publishers, and so on. Several members of the IP department have graduate degrees in library science. Although we are working in a high-tech, nontraditional environment cataloging visual images rather than text, the "media catalogers" and "media cataloger leads" (supervisors) have the same basic mission as traditional librarians: to provide content, context, and access to information.

Working for a young company like Corbis has both advantages and disadvantages. We are not bound by existing cataloging systems, so we have been able to create a cataloging system that is more tailored to image retrieval than MARC or AACR2. Unfortunately, we have few endusers at this point so we have to make assumptions based on the feedback of internal searchers, research, trial and error, and intuition.

The cataloging system is based on dozens of value tags that are stored in a relational database. The value tags are analogous to database fields, but they allow catalogers to enter multiple values for a particular tag, without having to assign a priority to a value as a main or added entry. A combination of controlled vocabulary and free-text tags are used, in order to balance and maximize precision and recall when searching.

A hierarchically arranged thesaurus created in-house provides the authorized terms for all controlled tags. A controlled vocabulary development (CVD) team is creating this thesaurus from a top-down as well as a bottom-up approach. The CVD develops broad hierarchies of terms, such as "Animals," and creates the structure into which each animal term will be placed. At this point, many terms are added to the thesaurus by the CVD; in addition, catalogers suggest terms as they come across them. For example, the CVD may add the broad term "Birds" and several narrow terms. The catalogers then suggest the specific types of birds, such as "Roseate spoonbills," as they catalog images of them.

A variety of information is included in a cataloging record. Such facts as photographer, artist, date photographed, date created, and so on are recorded. In addition descriptive, conceptual, and contextual information is captured. Catalogers describe what is depicted in an image: for example, a dog, a tree, soldiers, a holiday party. Subject terms are attached to the record to capture the main concept(s) of the image—what the image is about. Prose captions, titles, and other tags allow the cataloger to put the image in a context. For example, one photograph in the archive depicts a barn and a telephone pole near a wooded area. Visually the image is simple, but the concept and context tags allow the enduser to learn that the barn is really a camouflaged radar station in Oregon that was operated during World War II.

Day-to-Day Operations

Our cataloging team consists of both generalists, who catalog a variety of subjects, and specialists, who focus on a particular area such as art history. Catalogers handle each individual image, creating text records to allow for retrieval. Catalogers attempt to verify information obtained from image providers, using both print and electronic reference sources. In addition, they add contextual and conceptual information to the records, to provide the most complete access possible.

Supervisors in information processing (some have M.L.S. degrees, and another holds a Ph.D. in Art History) oversee the day-to-day cataloging of images and manage each collection of images as it flows through the department. They perform a variety of functions including training, supervising, and evaluating catalogers to ensure consistent, high-quality cataloging; creating cataloging plans for each collection of images; seeking out information about images; and reviewing and refining cataloging procedures.

Recruiting catalogers is a team endeavor. Several members of the department review résumés and interview candidates to ensure a strong team of catalogers. Initial training is intensive, and biweekly department meetings provide ongoing instruction. Supervisors ("leads") conduct formal biannual reviews of catalogers, random catalog records are reviewed for quality, and informal feedback is given nearly every day.

Each collection of images is assigned to a supervisor. In order to maintain both high production rates and high quality, they must come up with the most efficient method for cataloging a collection. A variety of software applications may be used for cataloging. This allows supervisors to determine the most efficient application to use for a collection. Also, different levels of cataloging are possible, depending on the subject matter of a collection. For example, a collection of landscapes is contextually more simple than World War II photographs. A lower level of cataloging using fewer tags (and taking less time) may be sufficient for the landscapes; the WWII photos may need a wider variety of tags for adequate retrieval and will therefore be cataloged to a higher level.

Another factor that affects the cataloging plan is the extent and format of information obtained by the image provider. Whenever possible, supervisors obtain electronic information from sources, to reduce time spent on data entry. Electronic information is often manipulated by supervisors, in order to further reduce the time catalogers must spend with each individual image record. For example, information may come in as a word processing document. The project supervisor might convert this to a spreadsheet or database and make various formatting text changes to make the data easy for catalogers to edit.

Leads seek out information about the images so catalogers can be thorough and accurate. This process requires dealing with photographers and museums to obtain caption information. Leads also work to develop a reference collection of both print and electronic sources to help catalogers put the images in a context, as well as to verify photographers' captions.

Guidelines for each value tag must be clearly defined. A committee composed of the department manager, leads, and others analyzes and refines each tag definition, trying to eliminate the "gray areas" of cataloging. We base our tag analysis on various factors, including ease of cataloging, ease of searching, and consistency throughout the cataloging system. Guidelines we have established for one value tag should parallel guidelines for other value tags. This lessens the learning curve for both the cataloger and the enduser, thereby leading to consistent cataloging and successful searching.

Searchers

Currently, client service representatives (CSRs) are the primary searchers of the database. The CSRs are those people who talk to clients and try to fill requests for images. The information processing department works closely with the CSRs. Leads train them on our cataloging methods so they can effectively use the tag system, controlled vocabulary, and free-text search techniques when searching the database.

We, in turn, receive feedback from CSRs in terms of how clients ask for images. We analyze client requests to see whether our cataloging methods are effective for fulfilling these requests. Among other things, we are looking at whether clients ask for general categories of items or specific items, and how complex each request is. By working with CSRs and analyzing requests, we will continue to refine and improve our cataloging system to meet the needs of our clients.

How an M.L.S. Helps

The librarians at Corbis come from a variety of backgrounds. We hold M.L.S. degrees from such schools as the University of California at Berkeley, the University of Washington, and the University of Michigan. Our undergraduate degrees are different, our training in library school is varied, and we held various traditional library positions before coming to Corbis. The general principles learned in library school, however, are very applicable to what we are doing now. In particular, database skills, cataloging skills, thesaurus construction skills, a general tendency toward organization, an ability to analyze topics from a variety of angles, and reference skills are all invaluable in our work. We use databases and cataloging and thesaurus principles in our work every day, and even though we are not reference librarians, reference skills are valuable because we must attempt to think from an enduser's point of view.

We would advise current M.L.S. students to become comfortable with computers. Learn to use a variety of software and hardware to the point that you can be intuitive when faced with a new application. You don't necessarily need to have programming skills, but you need to be a good enduser.

Also, students in library school should be flexible. Look at change as something good, not something bad. Learn to apply skills in different ways. Keep up a broad knowledge base, keep an open mind, and enjoy learning new things.

54.

Opportunities in Imaging

by Kenneth Cory

If you like being well paid for managing information, consider a career in electronic image management. Imaging, as it is popularly known, involves converting information from print, microform, photographic, video, or voice formats to digital format (that is, to computer-readable ones and zeros) for the purposes of preservation, manipulation, and transmission.

Most imaging happens in offices. A document is received in the mail. With a paper-based manual filing system, a clerk files it under a single index term. Additional terms may necessitate photocopying. The document is filed. When needed for processing, the clerk spends two or three minutes searching for it and then, perhaps, several employees sequentially act on it. Between actions, the document is in "information float," its whereabouts often unknown. Afterward, the document is refiled.

In an image-enabled office, the document is fed into a scanner, which digitizes the text and any graphics. Immediately, its likeness appears on the computer's monitor. Indexing fields are requested. These may appear with the image on a split screen. Indexing terms, as many as required, are assigned. The document resides on the computer's hard disk, but only temporarily. Hard disks are susceptible to crashes. Moreover, scanned images voraciously consume storage space. Therefore, the ones and zeros representing the image are "written" to a storage medium, normally a WORM (Write Once, Read Many times) optical disk.

Keyword searching returns the document to the monitor where it can be read, printed, and/or faxed. Cost savings accrue from eliminating extraneous clerks, file cabinets, refiling, recalls to inquiring customers, and misplaced documents. Because digitizing creates a common file "cabinet," staff members may process documents simultaneously. Information float is reduced; productivity is increased.

Getting to Know the Imaging Industry

For many decades, microfilm was the sole alternative to paper. Microfilm storage is long lasting and inexpensive. Retrieval time is slow, however, and the resolution of magnified illustrations is poor. These shortcomings were overcome by digitized imaging, which began in the early 1980s when scanning and optical disk technologies were coupled with the computer. The first major vendor was FileNet Corp. Others, including AT&T, Bell & Howell, Hewlett-Packard, IBM, Eastman Kodak, Minolta, Unisys, and Wang, joined soon afterward. There are hundreds of "systems integrators" who construct systems with selected components from a variety of suppliers.

Projections

Imaging is poised for takeoff. Currently, imaging revenues are about $3.5 billion. Based on a Deloitte & Touche study, the Association for Information and Image Management predicts "revenues to increase at a compound rate of 11 percent resulting in a $7.61 billion industry by 1998."[1] Growth, which translates into jobs, is inevitable. Now, when the rule is "automate, innovate, or evaporate," competitive organizations that spurn imaging will not survive. And, 95 percent of the nation's information still resides on paper.

Imaging and the M.L.S. Degree

Originally, micrographic personnel migrated to imaging. The new industry also recruited personnel with technical knowledge. Now, as the tasks described below will indicate, information management expertise—the kind learned in M.L.S. programs—is required. Readers are invited to match their experiences, interests, and abilities to these tasks. And remember that "any large body of data requiring fast, accurate, detailed multiple access can benefit from a librarian's skills."[2]

Classification and Indexing

Every day, one billion paper documents are generated in the United States, nearly all in need of classification and indexing. As imaging technology permeates offices, millions of existing databases are expanded and new ones are created. Imaging applications are database intensive. Each database must be organized according to accepted principles of vocabulary control, which includes choosing the primary term, standardizing terms, maintaining consistency in term selection, and cross-referencing related terms.

Anyone who has analyzed the futile attempts of office clerks to index text and/or picture files knows that most office managers are unprepared to create efficient, multiple-term databases. Because many pictures almost defy classification, the problem will be more acute as picture databases become common. Even where industrywide thesauri are available, specialists need to tailor a general thesaurus to a particular application.

Unschooled in vocabulary control, vendors and customers are slowly becoming aware of how vexing indexing can be. As Locke points out, "Rather than a task that can be handed off to low-cost temporary help, indexing . . . requires knowledge engineering skills." And, of course, only one professional program produces the requisite expertise: "The American Library Association and Special Library [sic] Association are good sources for locating such people."[3]

Analyzing Workflow

Originally, imaging's rationale was the provision of secure, space-saving storage in electronic format, and rapid document retrieval. That proved insufficient, however. One vendor was overheard saying, "We were selling million-dollar filing cabinets." A basic management precept prevailed: a new technology will not replace an existing one until the return on investment (ROI) reaches 10:1.

As long as information was in paper format, office automation failed to achieve an acceptable ROI. Imaging makes business process reengineering (BPR), and a 10:1 ROI, possible. Prior to BPR, the workflow is analyzed. Workflow is the "movement of all objects (data, documents, electronic forms, text, voice, etc.), and processing and monitoring activities carried out on these objects during each step of the life cycles of the process to perform a value added function."[4] Note the dynamic terms: movement, processing, monitoring.

Librarians need a dynamic mindset to apply their information management training to business process reengineering. Normally they acquire, classify, retrieve, route, and preserve information that is essentially static. They seek information residing in printed books or periodicals, or in digital format on CD-ROM, hard disks, or magnetic tape. They move information from place to place, but, except when they repackage information (still uncommon), it remains unchanged.

Analyzing workflow, however, requires dealing with information in motion. As information moves through an image-enabled organization, it changes formats. Normally entering as print, it will be converted to digital format. Often it is reconverted to print. It may be preserved on microfilm. Completely new documents may be assembled from several media types. Information may be added to or subtracted from an incoming document. Most important for productivity, several users may process a document simultaneously. To permit these changes, imaging professionals choose from a bewildering assortment of computer hardware and software. Finally, they perform a systems analysis in which current and proposed procedures are charted and compared with the benefits of the latter affecting a 10:1 ROI.

Business process reengineering substantially contributes to efficiency and profitability. What librarians learn about information management lends itself to workflow analysis as applied to imaging. Those who achieve BPR proficiency will be in an excellent position to gain a financial reward commensurate with the effort expended in earning an M.L.S.

Sales

Students with good social skills should consider sales work. Selling is associated with some common misperceptions. Does the profession's service orientation exclude commercial activities? Not at all! To sell an imaging solution is to render a valuable service. Must selling be equated with sleazy tactics? Not when selling "big-ticket" items. Finally, contrary to popular belief, sales representatives are not born. Selling is a learned behavior—and it's easier than earning an M.L.S.

Selling in the imaging environment is similar to justifying library automation. Representatives analyze customer needs and propose solutions. They must react instantly to customer inquiries (as in a reference interview). As imaging customers are not always right, selling usually requires protracted customer education. One caveat: rejections must not be taken personally. Closing a major sale is a source of great personal satisfaction. The commission is nice too.

Conversion Projects

An image-enabled organization must decide whether to digitize only documents received "from this day forward," or also to convert backfiles. Backfile conversion, from print or microfilm, is another growing business.

An information specialist with an M.L.S. degree makes a logical project manager. Decisions must be made about indexing schemes, which usually require thesaurus construction for vocabulary control, as well as file management software and hardware. Is a heavy-duty scanner necessary? What storage medium is suitable? Records management principles come into play. What records should be retained, and for how long? Fragile documents must be handled carefully. For off-site conversions, provision must be made for careful and quick file transportation. Errors being intolerable, reliable personnel must be carefully hired, trained, and constantly inspired.

Info-Mapping

Info-mapping consists of uncovering all information held in any format by an organization. It can also include information the organization could profitably access, such as online sources. Locating "unknown" information, digitizing it, and indexing it with cross-references increases the sum of an organization's knowledge. Info-mapping is often performed in conjunction with imaging because an organization needs to know if it possesses information deserving electronic preservation.

Consulting

Consulting involves doing some or all of the above tasks, with the advantage of self-employment. Organizations often hire a consultant before contacting a vendor, or afterward for a second opinion. Consultants listen carefully, then plan appropriately. Because imaging applications are tantamount to creating electronic libraries, consulting is a natural, if not immediate, career path for an M.L.S. graduate.

Imaging for Libraries and Archives

Converting whole libraries is cost prohibitive. Special collections can be digitized. When copyright is not a barrier, conversion costs may be recovered by putting a collection on a compact disc and selling it. Imaging offers several advantages. Digitization converts an archive to a library so that fragile and/or rare materials can be printed and circulated. That provides access to multiple patrons while reducing conservation and security concerns. Enhancement software is available to make faded documents look better than new. Even barely visible text can be made easy to read. Would-be librarians and archivists who know imaging will have an edge when job hunting.

Employment Opportunities for Minorities

Perhaps because imaging is a relatively new industry, it has no exclusionary network. At the risk of offering a personal observation for which no statistical data are available, imaging is a career option in which anyone with expertise can do very well. Attendees of Association for Information and Image Management (AIIM) conferences and imaging business seminars will find women and minorities in status positions in almost the same ratio as found at library conferences.

Securing Employment

As most jobs result from personal contact, arrange to meet imaging professionals. Join AIIM. Volunteer for committee work. Attend local imaging conferences—many are free. Request contact names at every opportunity. Tell prospective employers what librarians can do. Then prove it by doing a gratis study on an organization's information practices. That creates a valuable learning experience and an impressive résumé item. Seek intern opportunities with imaging firms. Incidentally, if "librarian" generates negative images, change it to "information manager/specialist."

Educational Requirements

Obviously, you should become knowledgeable about information technology. Take all courses offered in indexing, and in cataloging and classification. Remember that educational preparation or work experiences in pharmaceutical, government, military, health care, insurance, banking, manufacturing, and so forth are résumé items of interest for imaging firms penetrating those markets. Finally, practice at home! Anyone with a PC and a printer can create a desktop imaging system for only $600 by attaching a single-page scanner that both converts and indexes papers, and by adding a drive using Bernoulli disks to allow off-site storage.

Working Conditions

Systems integrators, being small, tend to be structured according to emerging organizational concepts. Hierarchical structure and career ladders are out. Professional staff work with minimal supervision, often from their homes. Employees are not internally focused as in large bureaucracies. In sum, these firms offer attractive monetary rewards, excitement, novel career paths, and independence.

Notes

1. *Imaging World* 43 (August 24, 1994): 1.
2. Sulinda Cole, in *What Else You Can Do with a Library Degree*, by Betty-Carol Sellen (Syracuse, NY: Gaylord Professional Publications, 1980), 149.
3. Christopher Locke, quoted in Kenneth A. Cory, "The Imaging Industry Wants Us," *Cataloging and Classification Quarterly* 15 (April, 1991): 10.
4. Ray Abi, *Image Processing: Workflow Automation; the New Competitive Edge, Tools, Techniques, and Software* (Stamford, Conn.: Unitech International Corp., 1992), 6.

55.

Risk Management Research

by Anne McDonald

My job is not quite what I first envisioned as a librarian's job. Five years ago, I had thoughts of being a public librarian. When I decided on librarianship as a career I had reached a crossroads in my life—I had been a high school French teacher for years, and I was contemplating whether I wanted to continue or consider other options.

While working as a high school teacher and considering other career options, quite unexpectedly I had an opportunity to take a position as a media center librarian at the school. This proved to be the first step to my conversion. I was able to maintain my contact with the students, and in turn, as the librarian, I became for them a trusted source and guide.

A year later, my journey continued on to a public library reference librarian position. By then I started a master's program which included general reference and business reference courses. My job as a reference librarian involved working the reference desk, collection development of nonfiction books, and selection of all audiovisual materials. I consider myself very fortunate to have had the opportunity to work as a reference librarian even though I had not yet received my professional degree. In one year I learned more about librarianship than any course or future course I would take! Daily I worked with all types of reference sources, from our nonelectronic card catalog to our vast selection of encyclopedias, dictionaries, atlases, and whatever else the reference staff decided to designate as "reference." I loved my work but I decided it was time to take the plunge and pursue my master's degree full-time.

I started my program at Rosary College and decided to follow a technical services route, with the thinking that I could make use of my foreign language skills. I plowed through cataloging and AACR2 and other courses that I felt would provide me with a well-rounded program. Many of the beginning or core courses provided for me a good base for understanding the "philosophy" of the organization of information. As most master's programs required courses of this type, they were laborious and boring, but nevertheless useful. The required reference courses were the most time-consuming, but provided the most hands-on experience. I remember spending long hours with classmates sharing the library's reference books, all of us trying to finish our weekly assignments.

As an elective, I took what turned out to be the class that would change my career destiny—a course on the world of online searching. I was amazed at the speed at which I could obtain materials, and the vast amount of subject coverage all available at my finger tips. I was hooked. The electronic retrieval world was where I wanted to live. My master's program took a turn right into the lightning-quick world of online database searching. The online searching course required very little reading. We were all thrown into a real-world situation where information is needed and needed fast. No books, no indexes, no ready-reference sources—information was all available through database sources. As with our reference courses, we were assigned questions that had to be answered by using online searching. The goal of our task was to go online to retrieve the information and get off as quickly as possible, because time is money. As most of the class was new to online searching, many of us were scared and some of us were quite panicked. How does one choose from over 300 databases and be sure that the information retrieved is correct without spending a small fortune doing it? My fascination grew, and soon my anxiety over online searching subsided. I started to look forward to the chance to test my Boolean skills. I spent my free time online time in trying out new databases and commands. By the end of the semester, I had become quite proficient and I knew that I wanted to be an online searcher. I was excited at the thought of working for a large firm in a fast-paced information center.

Online searching turned out to be the most important class of my master's program. Additional courses that proved valuable were indexing and abstracting, business reference sources, reference sources in the sciences. Of these courses, indexing and abstracting taught me how to analyze and extract the most important information from a document. I learned how to write in brief and concise language, and how to use and construct a thesaurus. I learned how a database is constructed which helped me understand the makeup of an online database. Unfortunately, however, the master's program provided me with a minimum of real-world information or skills. Once graduated, it was up to me to make the career of my dreams.

My first job out of library school was a job advertised in a local newspaper for a library clerk in a food testing laboratory. I convinced my future boss that they needed someone (like me) who could perform online scientific and business searches, provide document delivery, and organize their resource materials. The company provided food testing services to food companies and housed a full research staff in each of its 12 locations across the country. My job was to provide information support to the research staff as well as for the marketing department. Within the span of two years, I organized an information center. I cataloged their resource materials, set up the information center's online services, and implemented document delivery, interlibrary loan, and resource material loan procedures for the staff. I provided scientific database searches to our research staff, as well as business-related information to the company's marketing department. I learned a lot about foodborne bacteria, microbiology, and chemistry, but I also felt that I was in some small way helping the world eat food that was a little safer. This job turned out to be the most rewarding job of my career, but I was still interested in finding a job in a corporate situation with a large firm.

After a brief period setting up another library for a high-profile national nonprofit association in Chicago, I finally landed my dream job. I consider this my dream job because I am an online searcher and my world exists in front of a computer screen. I now work for a worldwide service organization as a nontraditional information professional, a risk management researcher. I am a kind of online detective or private eye who is looking for dirt. Before the firm takes on a new client, our group of seven researchers —all degreed librarians —makes sure that this potential new client is reputable. Each new client is "checked out" by a researcher. We search databases for negative press coverage such as negative character issues, financial problems, or problems with the law. We check litigation databases for any negative litigation and public records for any judgments, liens, or bankruptcies. All of this information is checked through online services. We use no reference materials, no books. Gathering the data is the easy part and I suspect most information professionals routinely perform this function for their corporate clients. The distinction for our group is that we add value to the raw data by summarizing our findings in a written report after the databases are fully searched. Each investigation takes between eight and ten hours from the database searches to the final written report. We are an investigative group that provides a risk assessment like no other for the firm and our work is highly valued and respected. What we do essentially breaks us out of the traditional mold of librarians; we are thought of as highly skilled risk management consultants. Aside from the love of online searching, this job requires a natural curiosity and a keen eye for detail. I routinely read up to 200 news citations that may or may not be relevant to my investigation. Though I have no legal experience I am sometimes required to read long cases that may turn out to be of a routine or negative nature. Our group has learned to understand public records and the obligatory legal jargon of lawsuits. Our work is detailed and intense, we work at minimum a ten-hour day. In the long run, our intense investigation and analysis prevent our firm from taking on risky clients and thus they avoid unnecessary litigation. My reward for this work is the value placed on my skills as an online searcher.

56.

Director of Research in a Venture Capital Company

by Claudia Chidester

What was I? Shy, afraid to fail, afraid to succeed, unable to compose a sentence, and perpetually consumed with what everyone else thought of me. I vividly remember my Dad reprimanding me on how I shook hands. I would swing my hand out and keep my forehead parallel to the floor. He used to say, "If you can't look at their eyes, then look at their forehead." And you know, to this day people are always asking me if something is wrong with their hair.

So is it any wonder I became a librarian? True, I'm a different sort of librarian—sort of a combination marketing master and research recluse. Since there is no cure, I've had to curb or control my shyness. So now I just let the adrenaline, cold sweats, and shakes have their 30 seconds of torture and then I go on.

Currently I am the director of research for a venture capital company. One of my functions is to find growing companies in the state, using all the usual business sources, and to import data on them to a database. The trick is to make the data work and to find out more than what's public by calling the companies. I speak to the president and generally request further information. Every once in a while I'll get lucky when the president is immediately interested, knows us well, and offers to send a business plan.

The other part of the job, the research part, is what I really like. Nothing pleases me more than to sit quietly and think hard about a strategy and, every once in a while, get a creative solution that works. I then dazzle my clients, which quickly solves that need-for-approval thing.

I am put to work almost as soon as a partner receives a business plan. I verify the market with other sources and look for any gaps. It's a terrific challenge. In a given week I may research such diverse subjects as security alarm monitoring, online resources for classified advertising, software for printer output, and prospects for acquisitions by one of our companies. I also make customer checks—to ask customers for their honest assessment of a company, executive, or product before we invest in a company. The fact that I can see the results of my work in a final investment memorandum offers more satisfaction than I'd ever felt working in a traditional library setting.

In addition to all those rewards they've also handed me the glory of executing our marketing program which entails negotiating advertising rates in local publications, sending out our press releases, and basically keeping track of our decisions. There are benefits to working in a small company. There are always more opportunities for job titles than people to fill the position—one can't help but learn new skills.

My first mentor was a wonderful Scottish librarian. I was at Smith College as a reference assistant, a job I landed after paying my dues on the night shift at the reserve desk for nine months, and Jean was with us on a librarian exchange program from the University of Edinburgh. She was someone you couldn't help but learn from, every minute you spent with her. The experience of working with someone so positive led me to take advantage of every tool around me. I began to use the computing resources on campus—the VAX to build a database to catalog a collection of art prints, bibliographic software created by one of our professors, the OCLC system. What I learned became a critical set of skills that opened doors for me in later job applications.

Finally, the time came to make a decision about my future. Reference assistants cannot advance far without an M.L.S. degree. I needed to go to graduate school, but that fear of failure paralyzed me, until a fateful evening in a bar. I was sitting in a gentrified all-wood, highly lacquered setting, talking to the bartender, who had a Ph.D. in linguistics (as in most college towns, maids and carpenters had at least one degree and were working on another). He was very clever, and I was trying to figure out my life, which can be easier than you think after your fourth Beck's. So I asked him, "Tell me *why* I should go to graduate school." As any good doctor of philosophy would answer, he said "Why *not?*" I had no retort for him and in six months I was in Austin at the University of Texas.

Graduate school was fine, since I knew almost everything from having done it for six years. I spent most of my energy experiencing 6th Street, a younger version of Bourbon Street in New Orleans, and discovering the southwest culture of "having fun till you drop," so contrary to New England's "work harder till you drop." All that fun did a lot for my morale and optimism. Then I encountered the second influential mentor in my life, Kate. Kate was a New Yorker with an uncanny business and math sense and an ability to draw people out of their shells. She was in graduate school with me, but unlike me, she hadn't a clue about running a library. So we struck up a synergistic relationship, which started with me tutoring her in mnemonics for remembering the LC classifications and with her tutoring me in Pascal programming.

Kate insisted I apply for an internship at the IBM library, explaining that the experience would make all the difference in getting better salaries later. She was absolutely right. And all that silly work on the VAX at Smith College, as well as reference work, made the difference, even though I knew about as much about IBM's technology as I did about dressing in a business suit. (I had to buy a suit the day before the IBM interview, and to this day I have a superstition that every interview requires a new suit—every new suit has landed me a job). Fortunately there were multiple openings and both Kate and I landed a job.

The next big push also came from Kate. After graduation I left IBM and got married. About six weeks after the birth of my son, I received a call from Kate suggesting that I go to work for Texas Instruments. She was about to leave the library she had started there, for a marketing job in their international division. In this case the experience at IBM and my knowledge of how to market information made the difference. I spent the next five years doing all I could to sell the library at Texas Instruments, by making presentations at department meetings, writing a monthly column in the company newspaper, bringing in lots of new technology, being one of the first to use the Internet, managing the database of prospects for the sales force, and serving Friday morning croissants and coffee. But in the month before getting my five-year pin, TI sold the division I supported to Hewlett-Packard. Soon both Kate and I were looking for work and unknowingly we applied for the same position at Austin Ventures. She was offered the job since she had much more business analysis experience. I stayed on at TI as a freelance online researcher, or cyberlibrarian, without a library or much clientele.

Fortunately for me, however, Kate soon found an even more challenging job in New York, and left me with the extraordinary challenges of serving venture capitalists, at Austin Ventures. My experience managing TI's prospect databases and my understanding of technology research—and this time two new suits—got me my new job.

The irony is that, in a sense, I am still a freelance researcher/cyberlibrarian and my clientele is reduced from 800 to 6, but the pay is better. Recently Austin Ventures has expanded my market by including the executives of the companies in which we invest. I rarely see them face-to-face—almost everything is by phone or by e-mail—

but the questions are always nontrivial and the questioners are always extremely grateful. I love getting flowers, tickets to restaurants, requests to make presentations at other companies and having endless praise sent to my bosses. I overlook the fact that my company has actually turned my position into a sales tool. Now we not only give money and obtain ownership in other companies, but we also support them with boundless information resources. Access to information is an asset that the business community is willing to pay for.

The next step is to go beyond being the gatherer and provider of information to becoming the producer of information. That's going to be a challenge, and I'll probably start it on the Net, now that I've pushed aside shyness, fear of failure, and writing blocks. All that's left is fear of success!

PART VII

Some Librarians Who Have Traveled Farther Afield

57.

Private Investigator

by Karen Alderson

... I just wanted to tell you I've spoken to Jean. She called our mother. She's spoken to our other sister and it's been wonderful. Jean is just beside herself over this. She's so happy and grateful to me and of course we're all grateful to you and it's just a real happy ending so I just wanted you to know that ...

This message was left on my telephone answering machine by an investigative client whose older half-sister I had located. All we knew at the beginning of the search was the information on Jean's 1926 birth certificate. It took me about ten hours over a ten-day period to locate Jean. How does a small-town Iowa girl evolve from introverted bookworm who's good at math to private investigator with clients all over the country? By taking advantage of opportunities, even when they are disguised as roadblocks.

The Dull Chronology

B.A. degree, summa cum laude, Upper Iowa University, Fayette, Iowa, with majors in mathematics and library science and teacher certification, 1968; librarian, North Linn High School, Coggon, Iowa, 1968–1979; M.A. degree, University of Denver Graduate School of Librarianship and Information Management, 1979; cataloger/acquisitions librarian, College of St. Mary, Omaha, Nebraska, 1982; technical services/information librarian, Mason City (Iowa) Public Library, 1982–1986; freelance librarian, Cedar Rapids, Iowa area, 1986 to date and licensed private investigator since 1990.

Freelance Librarian

My first freelance project came from a set of circumstances over which I had no real control: my library position was eliminated for budget reasons. I was living in Mason City, Iowa, at the time but later in the year moved to Marion, Iowa, part of the Cedar Rapids metropolitan area.

By late summer 1986 I was doing freelance work full time. I purchased business cards and professional stationery, joined the Cedar Rapids Area Chamber of Commerce, and started marketing my services. That's the tough part—not doing the work, but getting the work. It was and still is an education process. People were not used to having a freelance librarian available and did not know what one can do for them and their business.

I have done and continue to do things normally thought of as done by a librarian: research, document retrieval, literature searches, indexing, consulting on information management, organizing and cataloging special libraries, genealogical research. Accuracy and completeness in the work I do, and presentation (packaging) of the information I provide are important. To obtain referrals and repeat business, an information professional must provide first-class services at a reasonable rate.

Some of my more unusual freelance assignments and the skills required include: serving as the local coordinator of a parade sponsored by Hills Brothers Coffee (communication, customer service, and organizational skills); conducting telephone surveys of clients of a human service organization to gauge the effectiveness of one of its services (communication skills); appointment setting with one city's "movers and shakers" for a consultant needing to interview them (communication and organizational skills), and local program coordinator for National Seminars Group, one of the country's largest training companies (customer service, organizational, and money-handling skills). One of the most fascinating types of research I do makes up approximately 25 percent of my current work: private investigations.

Private Investigator

In May 1989 a woman from Oregon called. Marcia told me she was doing genealogical research and needed information on a family that lived in Cedar Rapids in the late 1940s and early 1950s but she had lost track of them after 1952. She said she had checked the Cedar

Rapids telephone book at her local public library but couldn't find the family listed in it. "Yes," I said, "I could check city directories," her original request. I took all the information, we agreed on a fee, and I thought the conversation was over. Then Marcia said, "Would it help you if I told you the real reason I want to locate this family?" Well, as every librarian knows, the more we know, the more we may be able to help.

Marcia was a 41–year-old adoptee born in California. The Cedar Rapids woman was her birth mother. Marcia told me she was consumed by the need to find her birth mother. It was vitally important to her.

With this additional information I told Marcia I could do more than check the city directories. I did fewer than three hours of research at the library and the courthouse and found information about the family. Four phone calls later Marcia was joyfully talking with her birth mother who has not lived in Iowa for many years. We were careful to protect the privacy of the birth mother, so that no one knew why we were trying to locate her. The birth mother's response when asked by Marcia if she ever thought about her: "Every day of my life."

After doing this, I discovered it was illegal for me to charge or accept a fee for "researching" the whereabouts of persons. According to Iowa law anyone "making, for hire or reward, an investigation for the purpose of obtaining information on . . . the habits, conduct, movements, whereabouts, associations, transactions, reputations, or character of a person"[1] must have private investigator licensing. Other investigations also require private investigator licensing, but "whereabouts of a person" is enough to catch me. There are categories of persons exempt from this licensing (government employees while working, peace officers, attorneys, credit bureau personnel, insurance investigators, and some others) but not freelance librarians. Anyone who gets paid for finding people is supposed to have this licensing. This is true for a majority of states.

Finding Marcia's mother was so easy. I did it by using basic research skills I already had, mainly things learned from genealogy and a lifelong love of reading mysteries. Could I do more of this specialized "research"? Was there a market for it? Could I get the necessary licensing? It was time to do serious research on my own project.

First things first. Could I qualify for Iowa licensing as a private investigator? One must be at least 18 years old; never have been convicted of a felony or aggravated misdemeanor; not be an abuser of alcohol or a controlled substance; not have a history of repeated acts of violence; be of good moral character and not have been judged guilty of a crime involving moral turpitude; complete an application to the Iowa Department of Public Safety which requests, among other things, "a brief summary of your training or experience, if any, related to the private investigative" business; be fingerprinted; provide two photographs; provide a surety bond; provide proof of financial responsibility; pay a fee; get a sales tax permit; have a registered business name; and, last but not least, take a test based on the criminal code of the state of Iowa and the statutes regulating private investigative agencies. Once a license is issued, the proof of financial responsibility must be renewed annually and the license itself renewed every two years. Except under certain circumstances, a PI license is valid only in the state in which it is issued. Luckily for me, Iowa does not require a law enforcement background or a period of internship with an existing agency; some states do. If I could pass the test, I could get the licensing!

Next question: Was there a market for this type of research? I wrote to every adoption search organization I could identity in the *Encyclopedia of Associations*,[2] briefly describing my background and asking if the recipient of the letter thought there was a market for another person in this field. Some of the responses were positive and some negative. Because I was already "hooked" on the idea I didn't let the negative ones deter me.

Final question: Could I successfully conduct missing persons investigations? I had found Marcia's birth mother. In 1988 and 1989 I had located "missing" women for the American Association of University Women. AAUW, celebrating 100 years of its and its predecessor organizations' support of higher education for women, had lost track of approximately 2,000 of the women to whom it had provided financial aid over the years. It sponsored a "Find a Fellow" contest for its members to locate these women. Having always loved mysteries and believing a librarian could do well in something like this, I decided to give it a try. With the support of my local branch of AAUW, I started searching standard biographical reference books and directories. Many of the recipients of AAUW awards received professional degrees or a Ph.D. and are or were prominent in their academic fields. By the end of the 1988 contest, I had located over 75 "missing" AAUW fellows, enough to win. The original contest was so popular that the next year the AAUW repeated the campaign. I didn't have as much time to spend on it in 1989, but I didn't want to lose by default. I entered and found enough women to win the second year too.

Conclusions: I could get the necessary licensing, there was enough of a market for this specialized type of research that it should more than pay for itself, and, yes, I could conduct successful missing person investigations. On January 23, 1990, I received my private investigator licensing from the state of Iowa and started on my first case. Marcia had been calling me since the previous summer, wanting me to find her birth father—six weeks later, success.

And that's how it began. I have had some fascinating investigative cases. I strictly limit the type of cases I take to public records research and missing persons. I have no experience in finding people who are missing because of foul play or because they want to be missing. I specialize in finding people who are missing because they don't know anyone is looking for them: long-lost friends and relatives, lost loves, military friends, classmates, birth family members of adult adoptees, subjects of quiet title searches, people owed money. My success rate is unbelievably high. During the first year of my licensing I joined the Iowa Association of Private Investigators. I was cordially welcomed. A majority of the members have law enforcement backgrounds and do many different types of investigations. The association conducts two educational seminars each year. I attend as many of these as my schedule allows and I learn something each time, sometimes during the seminar itself and at other times during the networking before and after the formal sessions. In 1994 I was honored by the association when it asked me to present a seminar session on missing persons. I have had calls from other investigators asking my advice on their missing person cases while some investigators simply refer all their calls of that type to me.

Can Librarians Do Investigative Work?

Many of our research, interviewing, communications, and people skills transfer directly to investigative work. Attention to detail is extremely important. So are patience and persistence. Do I recommend investigative work to everyone wanting to leave the library? Not necessarily. If you want to accept employment in an established agency, check it out first. Consider it as you would any prospective employment.

Is Self-Employment for You?

Before anyone seriously considers self-employment or starting his or her own information business or investigative agency, it is vital that the pros and cons be seriously studied. Read, read, read. Research running a small business, whether the self-employment, home office type or one with rented office space and employees.

Success or failure in an entrepreneurial business isn't only determined by expertise in your chosen specialty; it is often determined by your skills as a business person.

My Future

I have approximately 20 more years before retirement. Will I continue doing for those 20 years what I am now doing? I honestly don't know. It all depends on what opportunities present themselves. If I work hard enough and build a national reputation as "the best people finder," I may decide to expand the investigative side of my business and conduct only "missing persons" searches. I would love to work in a special library at some point. I wouldn't even mind going back to the right junior high or high school library, public library, or academic library. Or maybe something totally different that I haven't yet considered will come along. All jobs have their own advantages and disadvantages, their own stresses and rewards. For me, one of the rewards of my current work is receiving messages like this one, left on my telephone answering machine by a librarian acquaintance after I had located the 40-year-old son of a friend of hers. This son had been relinquished for adoption by the then 16-year-old mother:

. . . Thank you. Thank you. Thank you for helping Nancy. I told Nancy when I gave her your name, "Nancy, if anyone can find your son it is a librarian." And you of course have proven my words to be true. . . . The outcome, the letter he wrote, that her son wrote, is magnificent. . . .You've done the profession proud. All that training really helps, doesn't it, in some very life-affirming ways. It's really a nice thing to be able to do.

Notes

1. Iowa Code § 80A.1.
2. *Encyclopedia of Associations*, (Detroit, Mich., Gale Research).

58.

Art Dealer

by Jim Linderman

I have been employed as a librarian for 20 years, but have seldom been called one on a job description. I also rarely describe myself as one, though I could, by virtue of my degree from the Western Michigan University M.L.S. program. Some of my job titles have been "information science specialist" at a large pharmaceutical research facility, "senior researcher" at a large advertising agency, and "serials librarian" at a network news broadcasting operation. At the latter job I spent more time researching stories for broadcast than I did on the more mundane periodical chores. It is not these jobs I wish to discuss, however; it is how I use skills and techniques learned in library school and on the job to support my chosen vocation as a private dealer of twentieth-century American folk art.

I have found it possible to apply librarianship training in a business outside of the nine-to-five world. I believe use of these skills allows me to compete with other, more established dealers who preceded me in the field by many years. Making use of published sources, archives, computer databases, and libraries has made it possible for me to make informed purchases and avoid mistakes that a novice collector and dealer might make without these skills. Staying on top of the literature, both specialized art publications and the general press, has helped me locate new artists and established artists and to track down art objects to purchase.

Twentieth-century American folk art, more recently labeled "outsider art," "self-taught art," and "visionary art," is a recent development in the art world as a field for collection, discussion, research, and marketing. In fact, even the first significant collections of the more familiar eighteenth- and nineteenth-century folk art collections in the United States were put together as recently as the 1920s. The first public museum showings of self-taught painters and sculptors took place in the 1930s. Despite the ancient crackled veneer and rusted surfaces of the woodcarvings and weathervanes that come to almost every mind when thinking "folk art," even these were not treated as art objects until relatively recently.

It may still be possible to locate significant folk art objects from the nineteenth century on back roads today, though it is much harder and most dealers have given up trying. Folk art and artists of the twentieth century have, however, become big business and the focus of a growing number of collectors and others. (We are not speaking here of the faux folk or "country" look, or ethnic community traditions.)

In the early 1970s, a small group of pioneers set out to prove that folk art, art by the people, was still being created in this century. Among these pioneers was Herbert Wade Hemphill, Jr., a New York collector and early curator at the Museum of American Folk Art. When he started, Hemphill did not have a large body of published literature to aid in his search for these contemporary self-taught outsider artists. Thus his advice to would-be collectors in this field had much to do with the personal search. He advised visiting small towns, looking in the windows of country stores and shops, and asking questions of the local newspaper editor or church minister.

This searching was necessary because twentieth-century folk, self-taught, or outsider art was and is frequently created in isolation—geographical, institutional, or personal. The artists may be "marginalized" by physical disability, by mental problems, by age, by poverty, by race. They also may be ordinary, successful and popular members of their communities who work at their art without bringing attention to it. Many of the twentieth-century American folk artists, living and dead, did not and do not describe themselves as artists. Others, knew that what they were making was art, but they were nevertheless too isolated to get the attention of the "official" art world. (Often they still can't—the result of "attitude" toward the untrained.) Thus, because the folk artist is absent from the mainstream art world and its resources, the skilled searcher for folk artists has a great advantage over those dealers who are not as skilled.

The field of twentieth-century folk art is highly competitive. Dealers and gallery owners delight in being the single source for the work of a particular artist. Because many believe that these untrained artists do their best and most important work early in their creative years, dealers are always on the lookout for unknown bodies of work, perhaps in the hands of family, friends, or neighbors. It is every dealer's dream to find one of these collections. Ferreting out these obscure and hidden artists and their work is an area where library skills are useful.

Newspapers and their indexes are a good source known to librarians and one seldom known or used with ease by others in the folk art field. Virtually every sizable newspaper is available online today through such commercial services as DIALOG, Datatimes, and NEXIS. Art periodicals are also available through a variety of databases. By scanning these sources on a regular basis it is possible to keep informed of folk art discoveries at the local level or in distant places.

Librarians are trained to be aware of the subtleties in finding information and may recognize a lead when others don't. Often there are "local color" or local interest stories that are not especially focused on folk art. A good example of how the local press can reveal the existence of a folk artist is the case of "Artist Chuckie" Williams, a wonderful, naive and expressionist painter from northern Louisiana. He had created hundreds of wonderful paintings of his heroes, drawn from popular culture—particularly television—over many years. His work was not known until a fire next door threatened the house he shares with his mother. As he evacuated his house, Chuckie moved dozens of his vibrant paintings to the front yard where they were spotted by a reporter for the *Shreveport Times*. This resulted in an article "Chuckie Keeps Right on Drawing" which got attention from those in the folk art world who follow newspapers as a potential source for such information. Today there is a good market for Artist Chuckie's paintings and he has been included in museum shows and auctions. Regular scanning of the popular press can keep one informed of exhibitions and shows that might provide leads to artists. The dealer who does this is well ahead of those who do not.

In addition to Herbert Hemphill's advice to check country stores and shops for folk artists, I can add a most valuable source: the local public library. Librarians operating on a local level are valuable sources of information. Librarians in small towns often fill the role of local historian and local information source. They frequently exhibit the work of local artists in the library itself. I first discovered the visionary drawings of Max Romain in a public library exhibition. Noted Chicago woodcarver William Dawson had his first show in a neighborhood branch of the Chicago Public Library. In one small North Carolina town, the local librarian referred me to a lawyer who knew a great deal about an artist I was researching, the lawyer having represented the artist in a case involving his neighbors.

The librarians' awareness of the many formats and sources in which information may be found is of great importance to me as a dealer in folk art. In addition to computer-based sources and human and institutional sources, there is the librarians' knowledge that the literature of any given field is important. Because of this training I keep aware of the literature of folk art. Being familiar with the literature has led to valuable finds for me. For example at a recent and very crowded antiques show, I spotted a small wooden carving of a dog which I had seen pictured in an exhibition catalog and in a book featuring animals as subjects in the work of folk artists. I purchased the article for a small sum, sure in my knowledge, because of keeping up with the literature, that this well-documented piece was worth more.

Many contemporary self-taught artists leave good-sized bodies of work at the time of their deaths, some of which are known and some yet to be discovered. It is in locating these artists and their art works that my librarianship skills become useful to my vocation as a dealer of twentieth-century American folk art.

59.

Be an Archivist!

by Carol Jacobs

Once while I was driving on a freeway near Cleveland to a graduate library school class at Kent State University, a black, round object suddenly appeared out of nowhere. I realized it was a huge truck tire. Directly in front of my car, it seemed to be flying through the air and it just missed crashing through my windshield. Having no idea where that tire came from or what to do about it, I felt as though I had narrowly missed disaster. The road to obtaining a master's of library science degree was fraught with other perils, but none quite as mystifying.

Plenty of roadblocks existed for a 41-year-old woman who hadn't attended graduate school classes in 17 years. Included among the deterrents were three children ages 6, 10, and 13, plus a husband who traveled; a large home over an hour away from the closest library school; an eight-year-old station wagon with brakes that failed on the freeway; winter storms; and middle-aged eyes that did not respond to fine-print books filled with cataloging rules. Fortunately, funding did not pose a serious problem due to a small inheritance from a grandmother.

With an average amount of persistence and hard work, obstacles were overcome and the M.L.S. begun in January 1988 was completed December 1989. The thought of driving one more winter from a suburb west of Cleveland to Kent State University, located 40 miles to the southeast, provided a strong motivator to complete the degree.

While driving home from my last class I began to realize my uncertainty about returning to work in a library. Before entering library school I had worked, for 15 years (mostly part time), as a paraprofessional librarian in a large suburban public library. The dead-end aspect of that job and the subtle class distinctions between professionals and paraprofessionals convinced me I needed that piece of paper known as the M.L.S.. Once I had that paper, however, I could see broader horizons. A class in archival administration, taught by a practicing archivist, rekindled an earlier interest in history. (In the late 1960s and early 1970s I had received my B.A. in history, and completed two year of graduate study with an emphasis on modern German history.)

Archival administration, I discovered, was an alternative to becoming a librarian or a teacher that would enable me to utilize skills and knowledge from both the fields of library science and history. What a relief. I finally knew what I really wanted to do—become a archivist. The only problem was finding a job. Since library jobs seemed more plentiful, I dutifully sent out letters and résumés to a wide circle of Cleveland-area libraries. Nothing happened. To avoid sinking into post-graduate-school depression, I acted on an impulse and drove to the small town of Oberlin, about 40 miles to the southwest. I reasoned that Oberlin College, with its academic excellence and distinguished history, must not only have a fine library, but also a rich archival collection. That turned out to be true.

After seeing samples of my writing, and learning that I had just completed a class in archival administration taught by one of his colleagues, the Oberlin College archivist offered me the opportunity to work in the archives, first as a post-graduate intern, then as an archival assistant. For a total of six months I had the priceless experience of working in one of the profession's most respected archives. I engaged in a wide variety of archival activities in the areas of reference, processing collections, donor relations, and creating exhibits.

During the spring of 1990 an opening occurred in the archives of the Musical Arts Association. I missed the posting, but, in a brilliant piece of networking, the dean of my library school sent me the advertisement from the local newspaper. Uncertain as to what the Musical Arts Association was, I called anyway. When a voice answered "Severance Hall," my suspicions were confirmed—I was applying for a position as archivist for the Cleveland Orchestra! To say the least, although I felt unready for a position of this type, I applied anyway, since archival positions did not come along every day. I told myself that the application process would be a valuable experience.

To my surprise I was offered the job. Having been raised in a musical family, and having had the obligatory music and dance lessons, I had adequate background knowledge of the subject matter of this position. During my interview I concentrated on job-related experiences and academic background. Finally my interviewer asked, "But do you have any cultural arts background?" I was not accustomed to discussing my avocations and interests during a job interview, but in this case it was relevant.

Managing the historical records of the Cleveland Orchestra, the Musical Arts Association (the orchestra's operating organization), Severance Hall (the orchestra's home since 1931), and Blossom Music Center (the orchestra's summer home since 1968) turned out to be a monumental and multifaceted task. As is typical of most solo archives and library positions, the archivist is responsible for both the activities and the administration of the archives. Except for an occasional intern or volunteer, there is no one to whom to delegate anything. Therefore, time management and the ordering of priorities attain critical importance.

People often mistakenly assume that since I'm the archivist of the Cleveland Orchestra, I must spend a lot of time cataloging music. Nothing could be further from the truth. The orchestra employs three music librarians who carry out all activities related to the orchestra's music. The archivist, on the other hand, is responsible for the organization, preservation, and promotion of the orchestra's historical records.

The term "records" refers to all items of information in all formats. Most archives collections contain more than simply textual documents, and the orchestra archives is no exception, In addition to the usual correspondence, minutes, contracts, reports, and financial statements the orchestra archives also holds such media as posters, programs, blueprints, sound recordings, photographs, slides, films, videotapes, art objects, computer disks, and artifacts. What all these records have in common is that each one tells something about how the organization functioned, and about the people, places, events, and ideas with which the organization dealt.

In general, both libraries and archives deal with information. A library, however, holds mostly published or secondary information, while an archives collection holds unpublished or primary source materials. In a library, materials are treated as discrete entities and are organized by subject. In archives, individual items are treated as part of a larger whole and are organized according to the archival principal of provenance (whereby items are arranged by office or person of origin).

At the Severance Hall archives, for example, all the information generated by the executive director is arranged and kept together in a "record group." All the information created by the public relations department is kept together in another record group. Both departments may treat the same subject matter, but from different perspectives. Thus the manner in which items are arranged in an institution's archives reflects the organizational chart of the institution.

In a sense an institution's archivist is the chronicler of that institution. Ideally, the institutional archivist becomes more than a passive receiver of records, and assumes a proactive role in the entire life cycle of records in the organization. Ultimately, the archivist becomes a promoter of that institution's historical tradition, by demonstrating its relevance to current and future trends and activities. At its best, the archives functions as a working resource center wherever the past helps to shape the future.

An institutional archives collection bears many similarities to an institutional special library. The staffing of each is often a solo situation. Both, unlike public libraries, require that service be based not on democratic principles, but on the needs of the organization. Like a special library, the archives' first duty is to serve the institution of which it is a part. In-house reference requests take precedence over external queries, and requests from top management take precedence over everything else. Even with those guidelines, it is often difficult to order tasks in the archives, due to the labor-intensive nature of archival work. Typically, special librarians and institutional archivists must both deal with the allocation of resources by administrators who do not place a high priority on the special library or the archives.

How do the skills and education of librarianship contribute to a related field such as archival administration? First of all, since master's degree programs in archival administration are uncommon, most archival jobs require either an M.L.S. or an M.A. in history, or both. My résumé includes an M.L.S., and 45 hours of course work in European history. In recent years, archival education programs have increased, and a complete listing may be obtained by contacting the Society of American Archivists in Chicago.

Many aspects of graduate library education find practical applications in an archival setting. For example, although cataloging rules do not transfer directly to archival work, the organizational skills gained certainly do. In establishing a ready reference file in the Cleveland Orchestra archives, I used my knowledge of library cataloging and classification to produce consistent and logical subject headings.

The reference skills utilized in librarianship transfer quite well to the field of archival administration. An institutional archivist performs two primary functions—managing the historical and semicurrent records of the organization, and disseminating information. In my particular position, the latter function involves a significant amount of reference and research activities, as well as other outreach activities such as conducting tours of Severance Hall, mounting exhibits, and giving speeches. The many years of interaction with people in a public library setting and the skills gained in conducting countless reference interviews proved extremely helpful in an archival setting.

In comparison to public library users, institutional archives users constitute a far more specialized audience whose questions concern a much narrower subject field. Internal queries from the staff of the institution can come from all levels—from executive to custodian. External queries can also come from many different sources. At Severance Hall, reference questions involving varying degrees of research have come from journalists, genealogists, scholars, music critics, other arts institutions, and all levels of students—from elementary school pupils to Ph.D. candidates. In addition, when one works for an organization that is considered one of the best in the world, there is the added component of dealing with prominent people, such as conductors, community leaders, authors, and of course musicians.

The heavy load of research and writing typical of most library schools serves as effective preparation for archival work. Many of the special projects undertaken by an institution have a historical element, requiring investigation by the archivist. A thorough researcher and skilled writer can often turn the results of such investigations into arresting stories that serve as promotional tools for the organization. Bringing the past to life becomes especially important at the time of an anniversary or significant milestone in the life of the institution.

Some of the methodology of historical research employed in library school has had direct usefulness in my work as archivist for the Cleveland Orchestra. In producing my master's research paper, which analyzed the early directors of a large suburban public library, I had utilized the research tool of oral history. As a complement to other forms of documentation, oral history interviews can illuminate relationships, describe what went on behind the scenes, clarify how and why decisions were made, and in general flesh out the official record with human and emotional content. Little did I know that a few years after writing my master's paper I would embark on a project to record the firsthand recollections of those who had significant, longer or early associations with the Cleveland Orchestra. Included among this group of people have been orchestra musicians, conductors, staff members, trustees, subscribers, and even a recording engineer.

The technological aspects of library and information science most definitely transfer to an archival setting. Like many smaller archives staffed by a single person the Cleveland Orchestra archives is not particularly advanced technologically. Even so, it has come a long way in five years. For example, when I first arrived at Severance Hall, I was fortunate to have a computer terminal and a telephone in my office. Soon came a printer and an answering machine. In the past two years Severance Hall has installed a new telephone system (enabling each telephone in the hall to have voice mail) and has updated the entire management information system.

In addition, all staff members are able to access the Internet. This has made it possible for me to subscribe to the Archive ListServe, an electronic discussion forum that keeps one informed of current issues in the profession. Internet access is crucial for the solo archivist, not only for keeping abreast of current professional issues, but for communicating with fellow archivists.

Specific requirements for obtaining an archival position include a graduate degree in library science or archival administration and/or a graduate degree in history (in this country, public history or American history are usually the most desired). The highest level of jobs usually go to those with a Ph.D. or at least two master's degrees. Computer facility is essential, and knowledge of one or two foreign languages is often helpful. Practical experience, in the form of a practicum or internship or even volunteer work, has become almost requisite in recent years. Since archival jobs are not plentiful, mobility can be helpful—especially in obtaining that first job. Except for a few top positions, archival jobs do not tip the high end of the remuneration scale. The level of job satisfaction, however, is usually above average.

Like librarians, archivists have a profusion of professional organizations that provide an avenue for professional involvement and activism and also serve as a source for services, support, and information. On the national level, the counterpart to the American Library Association is the Society of American Archivists. Both organizations are headquartered in Chicago. Other professional organizations exist on the regional, state, and local levels.

When I graduated from library school, if someone had told me that I would become archivist for the Cleveland Orchestra, I never would have believed it. I wasn't even sure, at that point, if I was going into library or archival work. The point is, when making career decisions, be prepared for "flying tires" or unexpected events and be ready to turn them into opportunities. Learn to recognize which opportunities are the most appropriate for your situation, and then capitalize on them. Learn how to market yourself and make the most of all elements in your background.

60.

A Computer Workshop

by Dee Baily

The doors of Creative Computer Workshop opened in 1994. We offer in-shop computer rental of high-end Macintosh and Pentium workstations for the computer graphics market, and teach classes in graphics programs. We offer free use of audio tapes, CD-ROMs, and books on computer graphics programs which people can use while renting computer time, for self-paced learning. We have many color and black-and-white printing options, and a full range of peripheral equipment, so people can do their own scanning, video capture, or optical character recognition work. It has been very exciting for me to combine the love of teaching and helping people that I brought from my academic library background with the satisfaction of owning and developing this business.

The idea for Creative Computer Workshop arose from my interests as an amateur photographer. When a friend showed me *Adobe Photoshop*, I was enthralled and wanted to learn it. I found out that there were not many places where people could go and learn computer graphics unless they invested a lot of money in equipment and software for their own personal use. The main business of places that did exist was in large-scale copying, and they did not cater to graphic artists. Other than college courses, which don't always fit into busy schedules, there seemed to be no one place where people could go to get hands-on training and laboratory time to practice their skills.

I've always loved to teach and work with people. Offering a place where people could get training and practice in using the software, as well as rent state-of-the-art products and print copies at reasonable prices, seemed like a good idea.

Until starting this company, I was in the academic world almost exclusively, working on college and university levels as a public services librarian, manager, and instructor. In New York City I was a tenured associate professor at Brooklyn College, City University of New York, managing the music library. The only exception was some time as an information specialist at DIALOG Information Services, helping people do online searching. I studied to be a music librarian, combining my background and interest in music and my love of learning and books. I successfully managed several independent library divisions, including a music library and a media center. I had a lot of experience buying and maintaining audio and computer equipment as a result. These divisions were a microcosm of the whole library, because we did everything that the main library did—we ordered and maintained a wide range of media, equipment, and supplies; ran circulation; provided reference—and we maintained a separate facility. I was able to learn about many different aspects of management including employee supervision and dealing with vendors, service people, and maintenance workers as well as students, administrators, and faculty.

Not long after I became a librarian, bibliographic instruction resurfaced as an important service in academic libraries. I had a background as a singer and actress, so "performing" in front of a group of students was not intimidating to me. I had originally thought of teaching music history as a career, so I was enthusiastic about being involved in library instruction. When I relocated to the San Francisco Bay area, I taught in the library schools at both the University of California at Berkeley and San Jose State University.

When I first considered becoming an entrepreneur, the idea seemed exotic but also challenging. I would be able to use my past experience and training as a librarian, and skills I developed from working in librarianship, to both analyze whether it was a realistic step for me to take, and to make the transition from the academic to the business world. There were many books on how to write a business plan (this is, in my opinion, an essential first step); what qualities, skills, and temperament might be important to be successful in business; and even books on what it was like to be a woman entrepreneur. When I compiled lists of my skills and interests with those common to the entrepreneurial spirit, it was very liberating. I discovered that by making the career switch, I'd be able to create a job that contained a lot of what I most enjoyed (teaching and reference work), get help to do the things I did not know how to do well (such as accounting), and eliminate a lot of what I didn't like. Of course, I knew that I'd have to put in longer hours, and I wouldn't have paid vacations for quite a while, but there are always tradeoffs.

I believe librarians often don't recognize their skills in public relations, teaching, creating budgets, short- and long-range planning, management, and bookkeeping. Applying those same skills to create a profitable business does have its differences, however. To understand the differences, it helps to use common sense as well as one's considerable experience as a consumer. Also one needs to seek mentors and business colleagues with whom one can discuss problems and solutions.

I was pretty lucky in finding one of my mentors: I married an entrepreneur! Jon Heiner, my husband, started his own business in electronic industrial controls 17 years ago. He has given me valuable advice, not the least of which has been a sense of how intense the work can be, which anyone should know before making the commitment to start a business. He is also fond of saying that people are not in the business of making widgets (or teaching or renting computer time): they are in the business of *selling* widgets. If the idea of selling your services or products does not appeal to you, then you should reconsider starting a business. Before letting the idea of selling intimidate you, consider this: If you've been able to get library patrons to use the *Library of Congress Subject Headings* of their own free will, you may be able to sell just about anything (no offense intended to LC, which created this valuable tool).

In the business world, it's amazing what having a good concept of service, second-nature to librarians, can do for you. Unfortunately, few businesses put a high value on good service. People appreciate good service, and they are willing to pay for it. Service is the librarian's stock in trade.

Librarians have experience in hiring and training people who work well with the public, a useful skill in business. The health of my business depends on service as well as knowledge of computers. In computer graphics there are plenty of people who know the software and hardware we use, but there are far fewer who are able to work well with customers and who enjoy doing so. I believe librarians have experience in recognizing these attributes in people and consequently are able to hire and train a good staff. Also, librarians are often good at staff development.

I am also responsible for Creative Computer Workshop's long-range planning. This one aspect of my new job is more satisfying than previously, because I have to deal with a lot less red tape than in an academic institution. As the owner, I can decide what to buy or do, within the confines of my financial and personnel resources, rather than having to rely on the often shaky fiscal underpinnings of a state-supported institution.

Librarians know how to network with other people to solve problems or answer questions at a busy reference desk. It is equally important in business to get feedback from others (including one's customers). I was initially advised to share my business plan with as many people as possible, because I would gain experience in explaining it to people with many backgrounds (something one has to do constantly when the store is open), would get a sense of how feasible it sounded, and would get some really good business ideas.

I very much enjoy what I am doing. It seems quite similar to my academic work. I am now an information resource person for computers and software, instead of for reference facts, books, and media. I deal with day-to-day management of a busy resource center, just as I did before. And I learn from my customers every day, just as I did from my patrons and colleagues in academia. Through my customers' software and hardware questions, and their knowledge of areas outside my expertise, I have learned a great deal.

Many software and hardware companies have recognized the uniqueness of our service and have been very supportive. They felt that by making their products available to people on a rental basis, and providing training, that we would generate publicity and sales for them. Fractal Design Corporation donated their wonderful *Painter* program and helped us to promote our classes, taught by the noted digital portrait artist Jeremy Sutton. We are currently working with *Ray Dream* to develop classes in using their 3D Designer; they not only donated their software, but also their instructor Reuben Loya to help us with the course. Wacom has donated tablets and styluses (many folks use them for the very first time in our store, and immediately want one of their own). Fauve Software is sponsoring a lecture/demonstration of some of their products at our store. *Adobe* and *Specular* have generously helped us upgrade our software, so that we have the latest and best those companies have to offer.

One great idea received from Kent Manske, one of my computer graphics instructors, was to have a digital art gallery. I now have 14 artists exhibiting, and seven others who have shown their work on our walls. We are the only gallery in the San Francisco peninsula devoted to digital art, and we are listed in ten publications. The exhibits have broadened people's awareness of what artists can do with the computer; many are stunned to learn that what they see has been created and printed with the use of computers. The gallery has also generated much more publicity than perhaps the more mundane concept of having rental computers. Our artists include: John Lund, Helen Golden, Corinne Okada, Jeremy Sutton, and Marius Johnston. The art gallery has been featured in *Publish Magazine* (April, 1995) and *MicroPublishing News* (October, 1994) as well as in many articles in the local press. The gallery also demonstrates the many types of digital printing that exist: from fine art Iris prints from Digital Pond to color photocopying techniques, dye sublimation, and Fiery prints.

We became profitable after only seven months of operation. Why have we been successful so far? Because people want to have access to computer graphics at a reasonable price and they also appreciate prompt, friendly service. We try to help our customers in many ways: familiarize them with our setup, help them get the best print results, and answer their software and hardware questions within our knowledge and time limitations. We have taught many people how to scan, digitize video, and use digital tablets and pens. We offer a tutorial rate if they want one-on-one instruction for longer periods of time.

We are also successful renting the tools in this new computer technology, simply because the technology changes so quickly. For instance, an individual consumer or business who buys a 24-bit flatbed scanner, is often not willing or able to upgrade to another model for quite some time. We, on the other hand, can acquire a new scanner that captures 30 bits and the customer has access to this superior technology when needed, at a reasonable price. Most people can afford a home laser printer (or even a color printer, these days), but few could justify acquiring a dye sublimation printer or 800 dpi oversize tabloid laser printer, such as we have. But they can get their files printed at our shop for a very good price.

People are fascinated by the new technology. For example, there has been an explosion of activity within businesses to build home pages for the World Wide Web on the Internet. Many people who have never been involved in computer graphics before are interested in establishing a Web site. When they hear about us, they come to use our services. Also, people love photography, and *Adobe Photoshop* has such a high profile that everyone wants to learn it. As a result, my Photoshop classes have been especially popular. We also have courses in *Fractal Painter*, *Ray Dream Designer*, and an introduction to scanning.

I am very optimistic about the future for the company. It generally takes about five years of operation to predict whether a business will ultimately be successful, but we are off to a good start. Since computer graphics technology is changing so fast, the one thing we can safely predict is that we'll do our best to change with the times, and offer what our customers want.

61.

An Alternative Business: Natural Language Translations

by Betty Welker

Getting my library degree 25 years ago was a smart career decision, and I have never regretted it. After working 20 or more years as a librarian I decided to start my own business. I left a corporate library to develop a business that would offer two services to clients: natural language translations and information services. In this article I will concentrate on the translation component of my work, on the relationship between translation and a library science background.

How did I acquire foreign language skills to the degree required to become a translator, a knowledge beyond the speaking or working knowledge of another language? My knowledge was primarily acquired and inspired because of my job in a library as well as through continuing education classes and intensive study. Before starting my own business I worked for a company engaged in international business. This was my first exposure to Spanish other than in high school. This company had a contract to develop markets for products made in Spain and to encourage U.S. companies to invest in Spain through joint ventures and technology transfer. I was in charge of the information center, which I was hired to set up and manage. Early on I realized that we needed to acquire reference sources in Spanish as well as in English. Driven by this need and the desire to communicate with the clients of the company, I learned Spanish.

When my job ended through downsizing of the company, I figured it was a good time to reevaluate my career goals, and the idea that most appealed to me was having my own business. I remembered that one of my former career advisers, a woman for whom I have a great deal of respect, once told me that one must build a career on one's strengths. My strengths were knowing how to find information and language skills. I decided to find out how I could further develop my skills and use them to start a business.

Translation seemed to be part of the answer and one of the services I could offer in a new business. (I am only referring to translations of written text, not interpretation or oral translation, which is a related skill and not part of my business.) I enrolled in the translation program at New York University. I sought out situations where I could fine-tune my language and writing skills. My first surprise was that one does not become a translator overnight just because you know how to read and write in two languages. It takes time and practice along with an exposure to as wide a variety of materials as possible, such as those documents a professional translator would find in the marketplace and be expected to be able to translate. One must be a good and grammatically correct writer. Fortunately in New York City it is not difficult to find help, and I learned an incredible amount about translation from the instructors at the university.

How does a library science background aid a translator? A good translation, especially in technical fields, relies heavily on research, and a background in research is extremely helpful to a translator. A translator takes the text of a document and renders it from one language into another language with the goal of staying as true to the original as possible, while at the same time ensuring that the reader or client finds the resulting product intelligible. A further objective is to have a final version that does not sound translated but like natural language. One needs to have a thorough knowledge of both languages—what we refer to as the source language, or the language in which the original text is written, and the target language, or the language into which the text will be translated.

In addition to a thorough knowledge of the source and target languages, a translator needs to know the terminology of the particular field or discipline in which the text is written. Every profession, whether law, accounting, finance, medicine, or whatever has a common language that other professionals of that group understand. A translator has not only to know languages but also have some knowledge of the subject area in which he or she is working. One simply cannot translate word for word (that is, literally) because the resulting text will be unintelligible to the reader.

I worked as a reference librarian for many years, and the value of what I have learned in that capacity is apparent whenever I do a translation. The body of knowledge a librarian accumulates—exposure to many different subject areas, knowing how to find information and how to do it quickly, having an awareness of the reference tools that exist, how information is organized, and how you access it—is useful and practical and gives me an advantage over many translators. Moreover, just as a reference librarian never knows what a library user will ask, translators never know what subject will pop up in the next translation.

One of my first experiences as a new translator in which I used my research skills extensively was with the translation of a book on animals. The original text was written in Spanish, and the U.S. publisher wanted an English translation. The book was an illustrated book of 32 different animals viewed from the inside, a discussion of the characteristics of a selection of animals and what makes them unique. Each inside look at an animal had drawings depicting body parts with an explanation of how they function.

In order to understand and translate the text, I had to become an instant expert on 32 animals. Words become problematic when they have multiple meanings or if one language has more precision than another. For example, I did a great deal of research on feet and paws since the source text used the same word to describe both. In English, an animal may have feet, paws, or limbs. I had to research which animals are commonly described as having feet and which have paws. Let's look at another example. We have choices in English to describe the outer layer of an object, the shell of an egg, the peel of an orange, the bark of a tree, but another language may not have this precision. It would sound funny, however, if I used the wrong word in English and said, for example, that trees have shells.

Words therefore must be, if possible, verified against a source text written in English. A librarian knows how to do this task with ease, and since he or she is familiar with basic reference tools, the task is simplified. Encyclopedias, dictionaries, handbooks, manuals, and online services are second nature to someone with a library background. During the process of translating the book on animals, whenever the meaning of a word, group of words, or process was unclear from the source text, I had to research and verify my translation. Multiply that by 32 animals and it's not hard to imagine the research effort required.

As many other entrepreneurs have discovered, everything takes a lot longer than you think it will. During these first two years I have learned how to set up a new business, how to become a professional translator, and also how to become an information broker. I took as many seminars, lectures, and courses and did as much networking as possible in these areas. I read widely and joined many professional associations.

What do you need to combine the two services in your business? One must learn to deal with two distinct markets; it would be easier if I could sell both services to the same clients, but translation services and information services are rarely needed in the same place. This means a lot of work and more marketing. Conversely, it also means a larger market.

As an entrepreneur, you must plan to meet people who are going to give you business. You must be active in professional organizations not only of your profession but also of your target market. Beyond membership, one must be active in order to meet people and gain credibility and exposure.

You must be willing to invest in yourself, and you will need financial support from a nest egg or a working spouse until your business is up and running. Marketing takes tremendous effort and time. Allow for this with a long lead time and work at a paid position as long as you can before you open the business. Beyond that

- Do your homework first, talk to other professionals who are doing what you want to do.
- Join groups.
- Identify your niche as early as possible.
- Research how to set up a business.
- Learn as much as you can about marketing techniques.
- Don't give up.

After two years I am not sure I have all the answers, and I have a way to go toward profitability. I do have these rewards: independence from a corporate structure, the ability to make my own day-to-day decisions and decide on what direction I want my business to go, and the challenge of doing things I have never done before.

62.

Children's Books in a Museum Setting

by Roslyn Beitler

When the British scientist James Smithson bequeathed his fortune to the United States "for the increase and diffusion of knowledge," Congress debated for seven years how best to carry out his mission. The Smithsonian Institution was established in 1846 and today is the world's largest complex of museums and art galleries. There are 13 museums located in Washington, D.C., ranging from the National Museum of African Art to the National Zoo.

The Smithsonian's commitment to children was evident early on, and in 1901 the Children's Room was established in the Smithsonian Castle. As a former children's librarian with a master's degree in librarianship from the University of Chicago, and the current program manager for children's and family activities with the private, continuing education arm of the Smithsonian, I am keeping this tradition alive and incorporating children's books in the process. Each month I plan a variety of activities that complement the exhibitions of all the Smithsonian museums; children's books are an important resource in programming these activities. Individual workshops, multisession courses, study tours on and off the Mall, performances, films, and lectures provide young people and families with a wealth of educational opportunities in an informal setting.

Participation in a continuing education activity with the Smithsonian Resident Associate Program (RAP) is often a young person's first introduction to the Smithsonian and can pave the way for increased participation for the young person as well as the accompanying adult. RAP was created in 1965 to bring the Smithsonian to life for the residents of the Washington metropolitan area. It is the largest membership association affiliated with a museum and has over 60,000 members—8,000 of whom are family members.

The largest public outreach activity that RAP sponsors is the Smithsonian Kite Festival, which comes under the Young Associates Department. The Kite Festival is a wonderful, intergenerational family activity and on a good day it can attract 10,000 spectators. The festival actually begins the weekend before at a kite display, film, and discussion followed by a kite-making workshop with kite professionals. The highlight of the festival is a competition for handmade kites made by small children as well as kite professionals. Our Kite Festival symbolizes the educational activity offered by RAP, which combines education with entertainment in the best sense of that word. It is a good jumping-off point for a number of educational activities, as handmade kites depend on mathematics, art, and science in order to fly for one minute. There are books on kite making, poems and stories that feature kites, and films and filmstrips. I believe in the process approach to education and the more senses that can be involved in an educational experience, the more knowledge can be reinforced and retained.

On the flip side of this huge event are the small, hands-on learning experiences that are a specialty of Young Associates. Many of these smaller programs utilize children's books as their raison d'être or have children's books on display in the classroom. Most programs are limited to 15 children, but some are for adults and children. Adult-child programs are an intriguing way for adults (older siblings, neighbors, grandparents) to see a child's creative process at work. The activities usually require them to work as teams and are wonderful for reinforcement after the activity has ended.

These small workshops, which are one-time events or classes that last for four to six weeks, are offered for children from the ages of 4 to 15, usually in two-year increments. Workshops range from creating portable volcanoes to creating portrait partners in clay. Whenever possible, I tie into a Smithsonian exhibit and use Smithsonian staff, but the bottom line is that the exhibit and the instructor be accessible to children.

For older children, I offer a behind-the-scenes program with a Smithsonian curator for career awareness. A recent program featured an overview of shark teeth and shark-bitten bones with the fossil vertebrate collections manager at the National Museum of Natural History. This type of program adds an insider's glance, such as described in Peggy Thomson's *Auks, Rocks, and the Odd Dinosaur: Inside Stories from the Smithsonian's Museum of Natural History*, to the workings of a museum.

I also am able to have RAP children and families participate in prototype testing of new galleries and exhibits, such as Beyond the Limits gallery at the National Air and Space Museum. I try to collaborate
with the Smithsonian museums whenever possible in order to produce innovative programming that shares ideas, staff, and finances.
Because I am active in the American Library Association and maintain
contacts with publishers, I am also able to bring notable children's
book authors and illustrators to the Smithsonian. For RAP's twenty-
fifth anniversary, we presented Tomie dePaola to our younger audience and David Macaulay to our older audience. Following Macaulay's
appearance, *Smithsonian* magazine ran a feature article on him in its
May 1992 issue.

Many of our children's book programs take place in the intimate
Discovery Theater in the Arts and Industries Building. We follow the
presentation with a minireception and a book signing. Some of the recent children's authors to appear have been Marc Brown, Jan Brett,
Joanna Cole and Bruce Degan, and Michael Hague. This year our
Valentine's Day treat was local Newbery heroine Phyllis Reynolds
Naylor.

Whenever Discovery Theater is in season, I plan a workshop to enhance the live performance by having the participants interact with
the performer after the show. David Wisniewski, the brilliant puppeteer of Clarion Shadow Theatre, will present a puppet show in Discovery Theater based on his book *Rain Player*. Following the performance, Young Associates will have an introduction to the art of
shadow puppetry as they construct their own shadow puppets based
on characters in the story.

In addition to planning programs based on children's books and
recommending children's books to instructors whom I hire, another
way I use my library background is in being aware of theme months
and festivals. For Black History Month in February we offered a special tour and workshop at the National Museum of American Art to
highlight the exhibition "Homecoming: William H. Johnson and Afro-
America, 1938–1946." The workshop featured the book *Lil' Sis and
Uncle Willie*, based on the exhibition and written by Gwen Everett and
illustrated by William H. Johnson. We have celebrated Hispanic Heritage Month in September with a workshop led by Lulu Delacre and
based on her book *Arroz Con Leche: Popular Songs and Rhymes from
Latin America*. Lulu Delacre shared her love for her native Puerto Rico
as she taught the participants bilingual songs and dances and ended
the workshop with a festival piñata and dessert.

In November 1995 we will celebrate American Indian Heritage
Month with the Smithsonian's first exhibition based on a children's
book. I worked with Philomel and the International Gallery to arrange
a display of Thomas Locker's original art for *The First Thanksgiving* by
Jean Craighead George. We will fete Locker and George at a special
program during Children's Book Week.

Being situated in Washington, D.C., with all of the embassies can create an international festival. I try to collaborate with embassies to celebrate International Children's Day, which was established in 1953 by UNICEF to honor children every day of the year. The countries that participate choose a month in which to honor children. I offer a program just for RAP members to introduce them to a new culture at an embassy with the children of the embassy staff. There is usually some type of interactive activity involving music, storytelling, dancing, or games. This program ends with light refreshments so that everyone can intermingle. With some embassies we have observed a country's national day, and with others we have celebrated International Children's Day.

Mathematics and science are our forte. Get Into Shapes, an adult-child mathematics class, utilizes many children's books for activities as well as resources in the classroom. One of our newest science workshops is a collaboration with the American Chemical Society and the American Institute of Physics using activities from their joint magazine, *WonderScience: Fun Physical Science Activities for Children and Adults to Do Together.* Research scientists and engineers were trained to work with children, and the children in RAP were prototypes for the nation. The program, called "Science with a Scientist," allows scientists to instruct and to play games one-on-one with children before conducting a workshop of their own. We are now offering Holiday Science Camps with the scientists during Christmas, spring, and summer school breaks.

In my summer course term, Smithsonian Summer Camp, I offer a collaboration by pairing teachers of different disciplines to work with children. One of our most popular summer camps is Super Sleuths, where a scientist is paired with a writer. The children learn about lifting fingerprints and other crime lab analysis, visit exhibits such as the spy satellite exhibit at the National Air and Space Museum, hear guest speakers such as a forensic paleontologist from the Smithsonian and a police artist, and then produce a mystery play. Children's books are a vital ingredient of this program.

Last summer we offered a pan-Smithsonian venture based on the Seeds of Change quincentenary exhibit at the National Museum of Natural History and utilizing Smithsonian horticulture to maintain a garden bed for our campers. Each week the children planted and harvested in their old-world, new-world garden. A cooking teacher was paired with a science teacher and an art teacher. The children made a book of recipes embellished with their various art or science projects.

It pleases me that all of our classes, including Summer Camp, have spaces reserved for scholarship students from the D.C. public schools. RAP commissions original art to be reproduced and sold to help underwrite this outreach effort, and Tomie dePaola's poster for RAP's twenty-fifth anniversary is one of several art works that benefit scholarship students. My favorite collaboration is with families. Even babes in arms are introduced to the Smithsonian through the Young Associates department at our Evening Picnic at the Zoo and at our

Family Halloween Party that moves to a different museum each year. The Evening Picnic at the Zoo features musical entertainment and late animal feedings with a brief overview by the keepers (a la *Keepers and Creatures at the National Zoo* by Peggy Thomson and photographer Paul S. Conklin). Our Family Halloween Party introduces children to exhibits in a playful manner via a Treasure Hunt and entertainment. Everyone, adults included, wears costumes or masks, and characters based on children's books are very popular.

My career goal had been, from the beginning, to work with children as a children's librarian. I was, in fact, a children's librarian at the Annapolis, Maryland, public library for six years. As a public librarian, I planned programs for children and families. I got my job at the Smithsonian by answering an advertisement in the *Washington Post*. My predecessor was also a children's librarian. My work and experience as a librarian contributed directly to my ability to do the work at the Smithsonian.

Appendix:

Organizations for Independent Information Professionals

Association for Independent Information Professionals (AIIP)

AIIP was founded in 1987 by 26 information professionals. They recognized that their success as individuals would be enhanced by an organization that brought together the experience and ideas of independent information professionals such as consultants, researchers, brokers, writers, publishers, document providers, and freelance librarians. The goals of the organization are to provide a forum for a discussion of issues and concerns shared by independent information professionals; to promote professional and ethical standards among members; and to advance knowledge and understanding of the information profession in general and independent information professionals in particular. AIIP now has more than 600 members. A quarterly newsletter, *AIIP Connections*, is published.

For additional information write to

AIIP Membership Information
245 Fifth Ave., Suite 2103
New York, NY 10016

American Library Association/Independent Librarians Exchange Round Table (ILERT)

ILERT was founded in 1985 and is a group within the structure of the American Library Association. The purposes of ILERT are to provide a network for librarians working outside traditional library settings; to foster understanding of the services provided by individuals who have chosen alternative careers within the profession; and to provide programs, publications, and related activities addressing the needs of the members. The members of ILERT represent a wide range of interests including publishing, writing, indexing, information brokering, and systems design. The round table presents programs at annual ALA conferences and schedules regular time for the exchange of information. ILERT publishes a biannual newsletter, *ILERT ALERT.*

For membership information contact

American Library Association
50 East Huron St.
Chicago, IL 60611

Special Libraries Association/The Professional Librarians in Alternative Non-Traditional Careers Caucus

Caucuses are informal groups within the Special Libraries Association that provide a means of interaction for members who share a common interest that may not be covered elsewhere in the association. The purpose of this caucus is to provide a forum for the concerns and issues of professional librarians whose present work role is not as a librarian or library manager. Caucus members also provide a networking resource for association members who want to learn more about alternative career paths.

For information about membership contact the Special Libraries Association or the current caucus convener. (At the time of this writing, the convener is Ray Niro, Knight-Ridder Information, Inc., 3 Cambridge Center, 2nd fl., Cambridge, MA 02142.)

Contributors

Karen Alderson is a licensed private investigator headquartered in Marion, Iowa. She has been responsible for several joyful reunions among people separated by circumstances for many years. In addition to her work as an investigator, Alderson is a freelance librarian and information broker. She has an undergraduate degree in mathematics from Upper Iowa University and a master's degree in library science from the University of Denver.

Rao Aluri founded Parkway Publishers in 1992 in Boone, North Carolina. He has had experience as a corporate librarian, as a reference librarian in an academic library, and in the research department at OCLC, and was a member of the faculty at Pima Community College in Tucson and Emory University in Atlanta. Aluri received his Ph.D. from the State University of New York at Buffalo in 1981. He has an M.L.S. degree, 1972, from the University of Western Ontario, London, Ontario, and an M.Sc. in physics from the same institution. He has been active in many professional associations and has an extensive publishing record.

Dee Baily is president of Creative Computer Workshop, Inc., a self-service computer graphics center in Palo Alto, California. The Workshop offers in-shop computer rental as well as classes and tutoring in computer graphics programs. Baily's other experience has included being head of the music library at Brooklyn College of the City University of New York; being an information specialist at DIALOG Information Services; and teaching in the library schools at the University of California at Berkeley and San Jose State University.

Reva Basch is president of Aubergine Information Services, an online research and consulting firm in Berkeley, California. Prior to starting her own company in 1986, she was vice president and director of research at Information on Demand. She has designed front-end search software for Mead Data Central, has written and consulted on technical, marketing, and educational issues for online services and database producers, and has published extensively in information industry journals. Basch received her master's in library science from UC Berkeley in 1971, began her career as a corporate librarian, and has been an online searcher since the mid-1970s. She is an active participant in The Well and on The River, two thriving virtual communities. She hosts several conferences on those systems, and is an interested and enthusiastic observer and explorer of cyberspace in its various manifestations.

Caroline Feller Bauer has traveled to 62 countries and 50 states with her message that "there is absolutely no excuse for a child not to read." Bauer, who lives in Miami Beach, Florida, says she always travels with a supply of books because, "You never know when you'll be held up by a flood, flat tire, or a revolution, and it's nice to have something to read." Born in Washington, D.C, and raised in New York City, where her father was General Counsel to the United Nations, Bauer has received awards for her work and has written many children's and professional books. Bauer has a bachelor's degree from Sarah Lawrence College, a master's in library science from Columbia University, and a doctorate in speech from the University of Oregon.

Roslyn Beitler graduated from the University of Chicago library school in 1976. She planned to work as a children's librarian and this she did for six years at the Annapolis Public Library. Beitler was program manager for Young Associates and Families with the Smithsonian Resident Associates Program at the time of writing her article. Her program, "Science with a Scientist," won a Creative Programming Award from the National University Continuing Education Association. Beitler left the Smithsonian because they cut back on children's programs, and is now an elementary school librarian in Arlington, Virginia, and "loves it."

Elizabeth Bellas is senior media cataloger lead at Corbis Corporation in Bellevue, Washington. She graduated from the M.I.L.S. program at the University of Michigan after receiving her B.A. in history and sociology, also from that institution. She worked as a reference librarian in Toledo, Ohio, and as an information consultant for New Bulgarian University in Sofia, Bulgaria, before joining Corbis.

Carol Ann Berger is the founder and president of C. Berger and Company, a library personnel and information management services firm headquartered in Carol Stream, Illinois. Berger directs 15 office staff members and over 100 temporary workers in several states. She founded CBC after over 15 years of professional experience in non-profit and business libraries and information centers. She is active in a number of professional organizations and has served in leadership roles. In addition she is widely published and is a frequent speaker to local and national professional and student groups on library and business related topics.

Katherine Bertolucci is president of Isis Information Services in Oakland, California. As a consultant, she specializes in the development of corporate and subject-based libraries. Katherine received her M.A. in library science from the University of Chicago in 1977 and began organizing collections shortly thereafter. Her clients include many types of businesses with a wide variety of subjects and materials.

Raymond Bial has been creating nonfiction photo-essays for children for many years and is a full-time library director at Parkland College in Champaign, Illinois. About his love of photography he says, "Just as when I was a child, I still love to be outside, absolutely free, making photographs. With every photograph I try to recapture that heightened sense of feeling for people, places, and things which meant so much to me as a child."

Susanne Bjørner, principal and senior information specialist of Bjørner & Associates, provides research, editorial, training, and consulting services under contract in the areas of new and emerging technologies, market research, technical education, and information science. Her most recent assignment was as consultant at the Technical Knowledge Center & Library of Denmark (DTV-Danmarks Tekniske Videncenter), where she worked on projects related to fee-based services to business and digital libraries, and pricing models for document delivery through the World Wide Web.

Daniel Boivin has an undergraduate degree in geology and a master's degree in library science from the University of Montreal. He recently left DRA/MultiLIS, where he had been account manager since 1990, and started his own company, Textel-D.B., in Chambley, Quebec. He has had many interesting and varied work situations which are described in his article.

Cathleen Bourdon is the executive director of the Association of Specialized and Cooperative Library Agencies and the Reference and User Services Association, both divisions of the American Library Association. She once served as a Peace Corps volunteer in Ethiopia. After receiving her M.A. in library science from the University of Wisconsin, she held a number of positions, including director, at the Alverno College Library, Milwaukee, Wisconsin. She also served as the deputy executive director for ten years at the Association of College and Research Libraries.

Phil Bradley has a degree in librarianship from the Polytechnic of North London. He worked for the British Council for six years and then went to SilverPlatter where he eventually became their "global training director." He now works for them part-time, spending the rest of his time offering general CD-ROM courses and Internet courses to librarians in the United Kingdom, as well as providing a consulting service to companies considering the Internet.

Deborah Bowerman Brennan received her B.A. from Wellesley College in 1963 and her M.L.S. from the University of Rhode Island Graduate Library School in 1974. She had ten years of experience as a public librarian before entering the world of freelance librarianship as a consulting grantwriter and project director for a variety of humanities program series.

Charlotte Carl-Mitchell is assistant director for prospect research at St. Edward's University in Austin, Texas. She earned her M.L.S. from the Graduate School of Library and Information Science at the University of Texas at Austin. She has worked in the LBJ School of Public Affairs Library and the Humanities Research Center at UT, as well as in services for older adults.

Joni L. Cassidy is the president and founder of Cassidy Cataloguing Services, Inc., and has an M.L.S. degree from Long Island University, Palmer Graduate Library School. Prior to self-employment with her husband, she set up a federally funded job information center and a small nursing library for a branch campus, worked as a young adult services and audiovisual librarian, a public services librarian, and an adjunct reference librarian for three campuses of a community college.

Claudia F. Chidester was born in Frankfurt, Germany, the daughter of abstract painter Paul E. Fontaine. At the age of 12 she moved to Guadalajara, Mexico. She graduated from Wellesley College, in 1978, with a degree in art history. She obtained her M.L.I.S. from University of Texas Graduate School of Library and Information Science in 1986. Chidester was librarian and research analyst at Texas Instruments, Austin, from 1987 to 1992. Since 1992 she has been director of research, Austin Ventures.

John Cohn has been director of the Sherman H. Masten Learning Resource Center at Community College of Morris, New Jersey, since 1978. He previously held positions at the City University of New York, Pratt Institute, and Hofstra University. He has served since 1981 as a member of evaluation teams for the Middle States Association of Colleges and Schools and has been a presenter on automation and planning at programs and conferences in New Jersey and elsewhere. He holds a master's degree in library science from Pratt Institute, New York, and a Ph.D in political science from New York University. He is active in several library associations.

Kenneth A. Cory is an assistant professor in the library and information program at Wayne State University in Detroit, Michigan. After 14 years as director of the library at Western Montana College, he earned his doctorate in information studies from the University of Michigan in 1990. His experience includes being an information specialist for

Kirsch Technologies, a pioneering imaging firm. He remains involved in imaging as a consultant and as a member of the executive board of the Michigan chapter of AIIM.

Katherine DeBruler, media cataloger, holds an M.L.S. degree from the University of Washington and a bachelor's degree in English from Gonzaga University. Before joining Corbis Corporation, she worked in historical and audio archives.

Gloria Dinerman is founder and president of The Library Co-Op, Inc., a 14-year-old consulting corporation specializing in library development, management, and automation. She received her master's degree in library science from Rutgers University and her undergraduate degree from Brown University. Her prior experience includes five years as the director of training at a major stockbrokerage company, six years as an investment advisor, and two years as a contract personnel consultant.

Lynne Martin Erickson and Kathryn Leide are cofounders of Bi-Folkal Productions, Inc., a 501 (c)(3) nonprofit corporation in Madison, Wisconsin. Erickson does most of the words (writing scripts and letters and making phone calls), Leide does the pictures (design, graphics, and photography), and together they manage the corporation. They are both graduates of the University of Wisconsin-Madison library school.

Monica Ertel is director of knowledge systems at Apple Computer, Inc. She was hired by Apple in 1981 to establish their corporate library, and while doing so she also founded the Apple Library Users Group, which has over 10,000 members from around the world. She is actively involved in several international information organizations and was the founding chairperson for the Silicon Valley Information Center Advisory Board. Ertel has a bachelor of arts in social science, a master of arts in library science from San Jose State University, and a master's in business administration from the University of Santa Clara in California.

Mary K. Feldman returned to college at the age of 42 to complete her college career and then went on to get her library science degree. Her experience includes being head of technical services at a small college in Washington, D.C., and providing cataloging and reference service for the U S. Department of Transportation. Feldman then went to work at the National Center for Family Studies. After the center was dissolved, she started her own business.

Judith J. Field is currently senior lecturer in the library and information program at Wayne State University. She does some consulting, but not as much as she did prior to teaching. Field has worked in academic, government, corporate, and public libraries and has worked with subject collections in engineering and telecommunications, and business; with general reference and legislative material;

and with depository collections of local, state, and federal documents. In addition, she has been very active in professional associations.

Mary Forster, media cataloger lead and reference specialist, earned an M.L.S. from the University of Washington and a B.A. in French from Whitman College. She worked as a reference librarian before joining the Corbis Corporation full time.

Denise K. Fourie has an M.L.S. from the University of Southern California and has worked in public and academic libraries in New Jersey and California. She is sole owner of Library Concepts, an information consulting service specializing in start-up and reorganization of libraries and resource centers. Based in San Luis Obispo, California, her clients include government agencies, schools and colleges, and private industry throughout the state. In addition, Fourie is an instructor of library technology at Cuesta Community College.

Andrew Garoogian and Rhoda Garoogian received their respective M.L.S. degrees from Pratt Institute in Brooklyn, New York. Andrew Garoogian retired from the reference division of the Brooklyn College Library as a full professor after 25 years of service. He attended library school while a trainee at the Brooklyn Public Library and then worked in the Social Science Division there before moving on to Brooklyn College. In addition to his M.L.S. degree, Mr. Garoogian has an M.A in political science. Rhoda Garoogian was dean of the Pratt Institute's Graduate School of Library and Information Science before she retired. Prior to her deanship she had been assistant dean at Pratt, a faculty member at C. W. Post's library school, and director of the Wilsonline Information System at the H.W. Wilson Company. She has written a number of articles and has had many speaking engagements. Ms. Garoogian has a post-master's certificate in Library and Information Science from Pratt and an M.A. in English from Brooklyn College. Andrew and Rhoda Garoogian are coauthors of the book *Careers in Other Fields for Librarians.*

Mary Jo Godwin is director of marketing services for Oryx Press in Phoenix, Arizona. Other professional positions have included editor-in-chief of *Wilson Library Bulletin* and director of the Edgecombe County Memorial Library in Tarboro, North Carolina. Godwin received a master of library science degree from East Carolina University. Her professional activities and contributions are numerous and she has received honors and awards in recognition of these, including the University of Illinois, Graduate School Of Library Science, Robert Downs Award for Intellectual Freedom in 1992.

Ruth I. Gordon is also known as "Dr. Ruth" and "Big Grandma" to those who follow messages on PUBYAC. She is proprietor of a freelance editing service and is an anthologist whose collections have garnered honors. A retired school librarian, she remains active in library organizations and is the fiction selector for *The Elementary School Library Collection* (Brodart Foundation). A graduate of Tufts

University (A.B.), Brown University (A.M.) and the University of California (Berkeley) (M.L.S., Ph.D.), she lives in wine country in the lovely County of Sonoma, California.

Fae K. Hamilton is dataloads analyst at the Research Libraries Group. After obtaining an M.L.S. degree from the University of Michigan in 1973, Hamilton worked in technical services in academic libraries. She then held a variety of positions at library automation companies, specializing in bibliographic data conversion. She worked at NELINET, a membership organization providing automation services to New England Libraries; at CLSI, a vendor of automated library systems; and at SilverPlatter Information, a publisher of databases on CD-ROM. Prior to joining the Research Libraries Group, Hamilton spent five years running her own business as a library automation freelancer.

Barbara Herzog has an M.L.S. degree and an M.B.A., the latter earned while working as a reference librarian at a state college. She was interested in finding the kind of job that would integrate the skills and knowledge acquired from each program of study, but she was not interested in library management. She eventually found her way to working for library vendors, which she likes very much. Herzog has worked for CLSI and now works for H. W. Wilson Company.

Sheila Hess attended Pratt Institute library school in Brooklyn where she earned her M.L.S. while working as a trainee at Queens Borough Public Library. She has had experience in special libraries and in public libraries. After leaving her position in Washington, D.C., as librarian for the National Organization for Women, she formed her own company, with Virginia Harris, called Harris-Hess Associates. Eventually leaving this venture, she worked for a family-owned business. Now she is manager of the contract services branch of the library division of TeleSec Staffing Services.

Carol Jacobs has worked at Severance Hall as archivist for the Cleveland Orchestra since 1990. Prior to that she worked for a short time at the Oberlin College archives and for 15 years as a librarian at Lakewood Public Library in Ohio. Jacobs has a B.A. in history from the University of Minnesota, an M.L.S. from Kent State University in Ohio, and graduate course work in history at Ohio State University.

David Jank has been described by colleagues as a "vendor representative" and "computer systems designer/trainer." He has an M.L.S. degree from Simmons College in Boston and currently works as a market researcher for FIND/SVP. Prior to that, he served as data processing manager at the New York Public Library, as a CD-ROM software designer for SilverPlatter Information, and as a computer systems designer and training manager at CLSI/GEAC.

Lorraine Knight has academic degrees from the University of Victoria, the University of Manitoba, and the University of Ottawa.

She has extensive experience as a teacher and teacher-librarian and has pursued training in a number of computer systems and information systems. Her present company specializes in on-site conversions of school libraries. She and her partner at Library Conversions Limited Company are, says Knight, "probably two of the first to pursue library careers under the North American Free Trade Agreement. We hope it is a trend and that the 'borders' between library worlds in Canada will fade as well they should."

Stephen T. Kochoff was a national sales coordinator for Readmore, Inc. His article includes interviews and information with other Readmore staff who have degrees in librarianship. Prior to his present job he spent ten years as national sales director for Turner Subscriptions. Before joining the vendor ranks, Kochoff had been director of public relations, adult programming, and fund-raising at the Providence (Rhode Island) Public Library. He began his professional career at the Chicago Public Library. He earned his M.S.L.S. from the University of Illinois and his D.L.S. from the School of Library Service at Columbia University.

Genevieve A. Krueger has been in the book-finding business for 18 years. A library science graduate of the College of St. Catherine in St. Paul, Minnesota, she spent many years in volunteer library work, and working with her local Friends of the Library, later beginning her own business as a way to stay into books and work from home. "It is exciting—every day some new combination of people and books."

Lauren K. Lee grew up in Memphis, Tennessee, and attended Southwestern at Memphis (now Rhodes College). After graduating in 1976, she went on to library school at Emory University. She stayed in Atlanta for 15 years, working for the Cobb County Public Library System, the Price Gilbert Memorial Library of the Georgia Institute of Technology, and the Atlanta-Fulton Public Library. In 1990 she joined the Books Division of the Brodart Company, moving to Williamsport, Pennsylvania, in the process. She has been active in professional associations, and her life away from work centers on dogs—including the adoption of retired racing greyhounds.

Kathryn Leide: see entry under Lynne Erickson.

Jim Linderman received his M.L.S. degree from Western Michigan University in 1977. He has been an information specialist for a pharmaceutical research facility, a researcher for an advertising agency, a serials librarian, and a researcher for a network news broadcasting operation. His employers have included the Upjohn Company, CBS News, Public Television, BBDO Worldwide, and other publishing and media organizations. He started collecting American folk art in the 1980s and has been a private dealer since 1990.

Anne Grodzins Lipow spent her entire library career "working at one of the finest libraries in the world, the University of California at Berkeley." Over a 30-year period she managed and developed many services and departments. In 1991 the University offered a retirement incentive to long-term employees that included a lump-sum payment that allowed Lipow to leave and start her own business, Library Solutions.

Nolan Lushington became interested in library buildings when working in some with problems. After leaving the Philadelphia Free Library, where he worked as a reference librarian, he arrived at the Greenwich (Connecticut) Public Library where the physical restraints of working in a poorly designed library became obvious. Thus was inspired his continuing study and work with library buildings. Lushington has now completed over 150 library consulting jobs.

Dick Luxner was director of prospect research at Marywood College until 1994, having established its first research office in 1990. Previously he was director of development research at Stevens Institute of Technology in Hoboken, New Jersey, for six years. Since 1994 he has worked as a senior development research associate at Boston University, and has been a consultant at other institutions. He has also created computerized tracking systems for major prospects, corporations and foundations, scholarships, and grants. He has an A.B. in English from Franklin and Marshall College and an M.L.S. in library service from Rutgers Graduate School of Library and Information Service. He is a charter member of the American Prospect Research Association, and a member of numerous other professional associations.

Josette Anne Lyders has a master of arts degree in liberal studies from Dartmouth, and both a master of science and a doctor of arts in library science from Simmons College. She has worked in libraries in Massachusetts, Connecticut, Wisconsin, Texas, and Vermont. She has been a professor of library science and an editor of state and national journals in the library field, and she wrote the book *Journal and Newsletter Editing*. Since 1967 she has been active in the American Library Association, with service on ALA Council, the Committee on Organization, the Chapter Relations Committee, the Newbery-Caldecott Awards Committee, the Standing Committee on Library Education, and the Publishing Committee. She now lives and works with her husband in Peacham, Vermont, sharing home and business with three literary cats.

Murray S. Martin has an M.A. degree from the University of New Zealand Library School. His work experience includes National Library Service of New Zealand, 1950–1963; University of Saskatchewan, 1963–1966; Pennsylvania State University, 1967–1981; Tufts University, 1981–1990. Martin has also taught at Penn State and Simmons College and has had editorial positions with *Bottom Line*, *Technicalities*, and *New Zealand Fiction List, 1960–63*. He has published four books and edited two more. His published articles number more than 30 on library science and ten on literature. His participation in professional associations has been extensive.

Judy Matz is Director of Sales in the Northeast U.S. and Canada for UMI's Academic and Public Library Division. She joined UMI in 1986 as an Account Executive, representing a broad spectrum of UMI products and services, including both traditional and electronic mediums. Prior to joining UMI, she held a sales position with an academic book jobber and has a broad background in assisting libraries with serials management issues, as well as the acquisition of periodicals, monographs and databases. Ms. Matz began her career in public libraries. She held public service and administrative positions at Wilmington Institute Library (DE) and at Cambridge Public Library (MA). Judy Matz earned her Bachelor of Arts degree from Rosary College, as a language major, and her MLS degree from Catholic University of America in Washington, DC. She resides in New York City.

Anne McDonald is a graduate of Indiana University with a degree in French and she received her master's degree in librarianship from Rosary College in 1992. She worked for Silliker Laboratories Group, Inc., in Homewood, Illinois, as a technical librarian from 1992 to 1994, and briefly for the National PTA in Chicago as the resource center librarian. Currently she works for Arthur Anderson & Company, in Chicago, as a risk management researcher.

Ilse Moon received a liberal arts education at Antioch and her M.L.S. degree at Columbia University. She has had a wide variety of library experience and has been very active in professional associations. After her husband's retirement and a move to Florida, she did some writing and indexing and then became executive secretary for the Association for Library and Information Science Education.

Camille A. Motta received a master of arts in Russian Languages and Literature from Wayne State University, and a master of science from Simmons College School of Library Science. She is currently a Ph.D. candidate at George Washington University, School of Business and Public Management. Her primary field is information and decision systems. She worked as a library professional for 20 years in university and special libraries in the Boston and Washington, D.C. areas. She is currently an independent information broker and consultant in the Washington, D.C., metropolitan area while pursuing her studies.

Sally Pore has her master's degree in librarianship from Simmons College and an M.Ed. from the department of communications disorders of Northeastern University in Boston. She has published several articles, is a member of professional associations, and has many years of experience as a speech/language pathologist. Pore has not been able to find a job in a library because, although she was encouraged while in graduate school, no library has been willing to hire her—probably because of her "disability." Recently she has been doing freelance research and writing.

Paula Lumpkin Presley is Associate Editor for the Thomas Jefferson University Press at Truman State University, Kirksville, Missouri. She earned her M.A. in history from that university, and the M.L.I.S. from the University of Iowa.

Ann M. Robertson received her M.L.S. from Texas Woman's University in 1969. She started her career as a corporate librarian for an engineering and construction company located in Houston, Texas. In early 1970 she was hired as an assistant science librarian at the University of Houston Libraries. Over the next ten years she worked in academic libraries and became head of a department in science and engineering reference and collection. Robertson's information management consulting career began when she moved to California and was recommended to Savage Information Services, where she worked for six years. In May 1986, while she and her cat sat in an empty house awaiting the furniture, her clothes, and her car to arrive, Ann received a call from Janice C. Anderson, president of Access Information Associates, asking to meet her about a job. Two weeks later Ann began working as a consultant for A.I.A. and she continues as vice president of the firm today.

Linda Robinson is currently the access services specialist at the OCLC Online Computer Library Center Information Center where she works with the Internet, the World Wide Web, and related automation. She received her M.L.S. from the University of Texas in Austin. Before coming to work at OCLC Robinson worked at William Paterson College Library in New Jersey; the Jones Library in Amherst, Massachusetts; and the Springfield (Massachusetts) City Library. She is active in the LITA division of the American Library Association.

Louis B. Rosenfeld is president of Argus Associates, Inc., an Ann Arbor, Michigan, company which provides consulting on the design of large-scale World Wide Web sites and other distributed information systems. He created and administers the Clearinghouse for Subject-Oriented Internet Resource Guides, a popular Internet reference resource cosponsored by Argus and the University of Michigan. Rosenfeld previously worked as a researcher, librarian, and instructor at the University of Michigan, where he cotaught some of academia's first Internet-related courses. He has written book chapters and articles, and is lead editor of the Internet Compendium series, published by Neal-Schuman. He obtained his M.I.L.S. in 1990 from the University of Michigan's School of Information and Library Studies.

Sue Rosenzweig has been an independent consultant since 1990. She served as director of information services of the Center for Early Adolescence, University of North Carolina at Chapel Hill, from 1982 to 1990. Prior to that she was a school librarian for seven years. She spent 1961 as a Fulbright scholar at Johns Hopkins University School of Advanced International Studies in Bologna, Italy. She has a B.A. in economics from Queens College (1960) and an M.L.S. from Drexel University (1975).

Rhea Joyce Rubin has been, since 1980, an independent library consultant specializing in extending public library services to people who cannot use them in traditional ways. Rubin has an extensive publishing record and is currently working on her tenth book. She has received many awards and honors, including three from the American Library Association: ASCLA Exceptional Service Award (1993), the RASD Margaret Monroe Award for Significant Contributions to Adult Services (1992), and the ALA Ralph Shaw Award for outstanding contribution to the literature of librarianship (1980).

Deborah C. Sawyer is president and founder of Information Plus, a firm of information brokers and consultants. Prior to starting the company, Sawyer worked for an association, editing two books for the education field. She holds a master's degree in library science and a B.A. in linguistics. She is a visiting lecturer at the library school at SUNY Buffalo where she is developing courses to train business information specialists. She writes extensively; in 1995 her first book, *Sawyer's Survival Guide for Information Brokers*, was published by Burwell Enterprises.

Ann Talley received her M.L.S. from the University of Alabama Graduate School of Library Service in 1981. Her experience has included jobs as a paraprofessional cataloger, circulation librarian, children's librarian, and system administrator. She worked for CLSI and is now the editor of *The Serials Directory: An International Reference Book* published by EBSCO Publishing. A native of Birmingham, Alabama, Talley "enjoys all things new, especially the role librarians can play in the information explosion in which we currently find ourselves."

Alice Sizer Warner has an undergraduate degree from Harvard/Radcliffe (1950). Her library degree is from Simmons Graduate School of Library and Information Science in Boston (1973). Currently, as the Information Guild, she is a teacher, writer, and consultant working out of the Warner home in Lexington, Massachusetts.

Kate Waters works for a publisher, Scholastic, Inc. She received her master's degree in librarianship from Simmons College in 1973. Although children's librarianship was not her original career goal she soon became interested in children's literature and worked for 11 years with children and young adults at the Boston Public Library. She then moved to New York City and accepted a job at Scholastic, Inc., in the children's magazine division. She has worked in several other divisions and is now a senior editor. Waters is also a writer of nonfiction for children.

Darlene E. Waterstreet is a graduate of the University of Wisconsin-Milwaukee School of Library Science. Since 1974 she has been president and sole proprietor of Badger Infosearch, which provides information services, including research, indexing, cataloging, and library and archives organization and management. Previously, Waterstreet worked in data processing for two business firms and for the University of Wisconsin. She has been an academic librarian and a librarian for an advertising agency.

Ann Webb is a prospect researcher at St. Edward's University in Austin, Texas. She received her master of library and information science degree from the University of Texas at Austin in 1993.

Betty Welker has been a librarian for 25 years. She received her M.L.S. degree from Case Western Reserve University in Cleveland, Ohio, and a bachelor's degree from Millersville University. She has done postgraduate work in translation and received a certificate in translation studies from New York University in 1995. She has held a variety of library positions including positions at Trans-National Trade Development Corporation, the New York and New Jersey Port Authority library, and the New York Public Library. Welker is presently an information broker and translator and she manages her own business which specializes in translation services and information services to business. She is a member of several professional associations for librarians and for translators.

Barbara Ward Welsh is placement director at the College of Information Science and Technology, Drexel University in Philadelphia, where she earned her master of science degree in 1982. Between earning her degree at Drexel and becoming placement director there in 1987, she worked as an information specialist at several companies, including TRW and Ametek, Inc. She also has experience working in school, public, and academic libraries.

Index

About the Author

Betty-Carol Sellen has a Master's Degree in librarianship from the University of Washington in Seattle and a Master's Degree in literature from New York University. At the time of her retirement, in 1990, she was the Associate Librarian for Public Services at Brooklyn College, City University of New York. Ms. Sellen has numerous publications to her credit, the most recent being *20th Century American Folk, Self Taught, and Outsider Art* (New York, Neal-Schuman Publishers). She is the proprietor of the Bywater Bed & Breakfast in New Orleans where librarians—traditional and non-traditional—are especially welcome.